DELICIOUS DEVELOPMENTS

Friends of Strong Memorial Hospital

Rochester, New York

ON THE COVER:

Leslie Wilson Wu, *illustrator*
Ron Wu, *photographer*
Kathy D'Amanda, *art director*

*This collaborative piece
started as a black-and-white
photograph that was then hand-colored
using oil paints and pastels.*

Copies of **Delicious Developments** may be obtained from:
Friends of Strong Memorial Hospital
601 Elmwood Avenue
Box 660
Rochester, NY 14642
Make checks payable to "Friends of Strong" for $19.95 plus $3.00 postage and handling.
New York State residents add sales tax.
For credit card orders, telephone (716) 275-2420.

Library of Congress Catalog Card Number: 94-61444
ISBN 0-9641841-0-9
First Printing 1994   20,000 copies

PRODUCTION CREDITS:

Cookbook Design:
Kathy D'Amanda / D'A Design

Printed in the USA by

WIMMER
The Wimmer Companies, Inc.
Memphis • Dallas

Published by University of Rochester — Friends of Strong Memorial Hospital

Strong Memorial Hospital
University of Rochester Medical Center

"We improve health through caring, discovery, teaching and learning."

Our mission statement says it clearly. Since our founding in 1926 as the teaching hospital of the University of Rochester, we have been committed to excellence in patient care, education and research.

Over the years, we have evolved into a nationally regarded, regional referral center, serving the residents of upstate New York with a full range of outstanding health care services. We take great pride in our holistic approach to patient care, recognizing the importance of providing for each patient's needs by employing all available medical, social and family resources. Together with the University of Rochester's School of Medicine and Dentistry, and School of Nursing, we contribute to the education of doctors, nurses and other professionals who are noted for their excellence in patient care and academic leadership.

This wonderful cookbook continues our tradition of excellence. Hundreds of volunteers have contributed literally thousands of hours to develop, test and refine these recipes to help ensure superb results. We are grateful to the Friends of Strong for the unflagging support of our mission, and are proud to be represented by *Delicious Developments*.

Friends of Strong Memorial Hospital

Friends of Strong is a unique organization of Strong Memorial Hospital which has successfully integrated the roles normally associated with a hospital's volunteer department and auxiliary.

Friends' 1,100 volunteers support the hospital's mission in a variety of ways. They contribute to quality patient care by providing valuable services to Strong's patients and their families. The Friends serve as Strong's ambassadors, representing the hospital throughout the community. In addition, all funds raised through their efforts are returned to the hospital in the form of much-needed capital items, educational opportunities for volunteers and staff, and the Friends of Strong Endowment Fund.

The proceeds of this cookbook will benefit the Trauma Center, which provides life-saving, comprehensive emergency and critical-care services to patients. It is the state-designated regional trauma center for the nine-county Finger Lakes Region.

Throughout its history,

the Genesee Valley and Finger Lakes area of upstate New York has always been one step ahead in industrial development. The land and climate seemed to sprout industrial visionaries as well as wheat and fruit. The Rochester area supplied basic necessities for the opening of the West, and supplied the nation and, in some cases, the world with quality products when they were most needed. As one need was met, another industry sprouted to fill the next, until today the region is considered the heart of the world's imaging and optical industries.

Hand-in-hand with Kodak cameras, Xerox copiers and Bausch and Lomb lenses came Genesee Flour, French's mustard and Jell-O as products of our region. In *Delicious Developments*, we have created a similar partnership. Photographs produced by some of our finest imagemakers from the past and present-day introduce each section of fine culinary accomplishments from our community. All of the more than 350 recipes are the dependable favorites of our contributors. Each has been carefully tested at least twice and rated outstanding. We hope that you will find our recipes to be the key to your own delicious developments.

Just a Few Notes...

All measurements for herbs are for dried herbs, unless "fresh" is stated. Fresh herbs can be substituted for dried by using 3 to 4 times the amount stated.

All recipes calling for eggs were tested using large eggs.

CONTENTS

APPETIZERS

area's success story can be credited to its natural resources. The Genesee River flows north from Pennsylvania, past the Finger Lakes, and empties into Lake Ontario near the city of Rochester. The river provides fertile soil deposits and energy from its many waterfalls. The Finger Lakes area tends to be dry and sunny, good for growing plants with deep roots, such as grapevines. Near Lake Ontario lies the region where cool air off the lake delays spring budding until the threat of frost is over. In the autumn, warm air from the lake extends the growing season. These conditions are ideal for growing vegetables and fruits.

Almost from the first glimpse of the area, travelers and soldiers gave the "Genesee Country" a larger-than-life reputation. There were descriptions of abundant wildlife, stories of grass growing ten feet tall, and new varieties of corn. It is no wonder then, that in 1798, there were reports of one hundred sleighs and wagons per week passing through the Finger Lakes area on their way to settle in "Genesee Country".

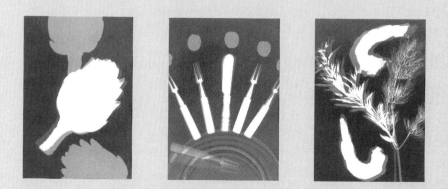

A P P E T I Z E R S

Whipped Fruit Dip

This recipe was contributed by photographer George Kamper.

12 ounces frozen whipped topping, thawed
8 ounces whipped cream cheese, room temperature
½ teaspoon vanilla extract

1 tablespoon berry jam
Fresh fruit (strawberries, apples, peaches, berries, etc.)

In large bowl, beat whipped topping and cream cheese. Add vanilla and jam, beating until fluffy. Transfer to serving bowl and serve immediately with strawberries, wedges of apples or peaches, or serve over fresh berries.

Makes 1½ cups

It's A Brie's Fruit Dip

Genesee (pronounced Jenna-see) is an Iroquois word meaning pleasant or beautiful valley.

Not all the land along the Genesee was pleasant. The land in the City of Rochester was originally a snake-infested swamp. Man-made improvements to the land began around 1809.

8 ounces ripened Brie, rind removed, room temperature
8 ounces cream cheese, room temperature
½ cup plain yogurt

¼ cup honey
⅛ teaspoon cinnamon
Fresh fruit (strawberries, pineapple, large grapes, etc.)

Combine all ingredients except fruit. Refrigerate. Before serving, arrange fruit in decorative pattern around bowl of dip. (Note: Additional yogurt may be added if dip is too thick.)

Makes 1½ cups

Crispy Snack Mix

2 egg whites, lightly beaten
4½ teaspoons Worcestershire sauce
1 teaspoon garlic powder
2 cups crispy corn or rice cereal squares
2 cups crispy wheat cereal squares

1 cup bite-sized whole wheat cereal biscuits
1 cup pretzels
1 cup peanuts
½ cup raisins (optional)

Preheat oven to 275°. Lightly coat a large shallow baking pan with cooking spray. In large bowl, combine egg whites, Worcestershire sauce and garlic powder. Add cereals, pretzels and peanuts, stirring to coat well. Spread mixture in prepared pan and bake for 50-60 minutes, stirring every 15 minutes. Add raisins (if using), toss gently, and let cool.

Makes 7 cups

Some believe that the Iroquois were the first to coat popcorn with maple syrup as a special treat.

Garlic Marinated Olives

¼ cup olive oil
¼ cup red wine vinegar
2 tablespoons fresh chives, chopped
1 teaspoon paprika

2 cloves garlic, minced
2 cans (16-ounce) pitted black olives, drained

In large bowl, mix together the first five ingredients. Place olives in mixture, cover and marinate in refrigerator for 2-3 days, stirring occasionally.

Serves 8

Caponata

1 small eggplant, unpeeled and finely
   chopped
1 medium onion, coarsely chopped
⅓ cup green pepper, chopped
4 ounces mushrooms, chopped
2 cloves garlic, minced
⅓ cup vegetable oil
1 teaspoon salt
½ teaspoon pepper
½ teaspoon oregano

1½ teaspoons sugar
6 ounces tomato paste
¼ cup water
2 tablespoons wine vinegar
3 tablespoons pine nuts or chopped
   almonds
¼ cup capers (optional)
⅓ cup green olives (without pimiento),
   halved (optional)

Combine first 6 ingredients in saucepan. Cover and simmer for 10 minutes. Add
remaining ingredients, mixing well. Cover and simmer for another 25 minutes,
until eggplant is tender. Chill overnight to allow flavor to develop. To serve,
bring to room temperature. Serve with corn chips or fresh Italian bread.

Serves 10

Pita Wedges

2 large round pita breads
8 ounces herbed Brie or garlic/herb
   spreadable cheese

Slivered almonds
Garlic salt, to taste

Split breads open and lay flat on cookie sheet. Spread an even layer of desired
cheese on each circle and cut into eight pie-shaped wedges. Sprinkle each wedge
with slivered almonds and garlic salt. Bake at 375° for 10 minutes.

Makes 32 wedges

Caviar & Artichoke Dome

4 cans (14-ounce) artichoke hearts, drained well
16 ounces cream cheese, room temperature
¼ cup sour cream

2 tablespoons mayonnaise or salad dressing
½-1 cup onion, finely chopped
4 ounces black caviar, drained

Chop artichokes and shape into dome in center of serving dish. Set aside. Combine cream cheese, sour cream, mayonnaise and onion. With electric mixer, beat at medium speed for 1 minute, or until blended. Spread mixture evenly over artichoke dome, flattening top slightly. Spoon caviar on top of dome. Refrigerate. Serve with crackers.

Serves 20-30

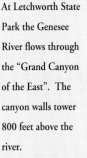

Aspara-guess

1 loaf party rye bread
½ cup mayonnaise
¼ cup sour cream
2 tablespoons lemon juice

2 cans (15-ounce) asparagus, drained and each spear cut into thirds
Melted butter
Parmesan cheese

Cut crusts from bread and roll each piece thin. Mix together mayonnaise, sour cream and lemon juice and spread mixture on bread. Top bread with one piece of asparagus. Fold and secure with toothpick. Dab with melted butter and sprinkle with Parmesan cheese. Bake at 400° for 12 minutes or until brown.

Makes 50 appetizers

Pesto Mushroom Caps

24 ounces mushrooms
4 tablespoons olive oil

1¼ cups mozzarella cheese, shredded
3 ounces pesto sauce

Preheat oven to 350°. Wash mushrooms and remove stems. Brush inside of caps with oil, then fill with mozzarella cheese. Top with pesto sauce. Bake for 10-12 minutes. May place under broiler briefly, if desired. Serve hot.

Serves 8-10

Mushroom Triangles

1 onion, finely chopped
1 teaspoon butter
¾ pound fresh mushrooms, finely chopped
¼ teaspoon salt
⅛ teaspoon pepper
12 ounces cream cheese, room temperature

½ teaspoon Worcestershire sauce
¼ teaspoon garlic powder
½ teaspoon seasoned salt
1 loaf white bread, thinly sliced
½ cup butter, melted

Sauté onion in butter until golden. Add mushrooms and sauté for 2 minutes. Remove from heat and season with salt and pepper. In medium-sized bowl, mix together cream cheese, Worcestershire sauce, garlic powder and seasoned salt. Stir in mushroom mixture and let stand. Cut crusts from bread and toast one side under broiler. Spread thick layer of mushroom mixture on untoasted side of bread and cut diagonally into quarters. Refrigerate or freeze. To serve, brush with melted butter and broil for 5-10 minutes. Serve immediately. (Note: If freezing before baking, spread untoasted side of bread with butter or margarine before topping with mushroom mixture.)

Makes 50-80

Pesto Sauce

¾ cup olive oil

4 cloves garlic

¼ teaspoon salt

2 cups fresh basil leaves, packed

2 tablespoons pine nuts or chopped almonds

1 cup Parmesan cheese, grated

Place oil, garlic, salt and basil in food processor or blender and purée. Add nuts and process until coarsely chopped. Transfer mixture to bowl and fold in cheese.

Approximately 1½ cups

Mock Mushroom Hors d'oeuvres

2-3 cups white Cheddar cheese, grated
2 cans (5-ounce) black olives, drained and
  chopped
1 cup mayonnaise

1 tablespoon scallions, chopped or
  ½ tablespoon onion flakes
¼ teaspoon curry powder
16 English muffin halves

Combine first five ingredients. Lightly toast English muffin halves and spread
with mixture. Broil for 3-5 minutes or until bubbly. Before serving, cut each
muffin half into quarters.

Makes 64 appetizers

Delicious Spinach Nibbles

2 packages (10-ounce) frozen chopped
  spinach, thawed and drained
2 cups herb-seasoned stuffing mix
2 onions, chopped
6 eggs, beaten
¾ cup margarine, melted

½ cup Parmesan cheese
½ teaspoon garlic powder
1 teaspoon pepper
1 teaspoon thyme
Dash of seasoned salt (optional)

Preheat oven to 350°. Grease cookie sheets. Combine all ingredients, mixing well.
Using rounded teaspoonfuls, roll mixture into balls and place on prepared cookie
sheets. Bake for 20 minutes and serve hot. (Note: Add more stuffing mix if
mixture is too moist to roll. Also, appetizers may be frozen and thawed before
baking.)

Makes 70-80

Bruschetta

Winter Bruschetta

If fresh basil is
unavailable, spread
toasted bread with
favorite pesto sauce
and add tomato
topping. If good
plum tomatoes are
not available, use
canned, drained and
seeded.

3 plum tomatoes, peeled (see p. 26)
3 medium scallions or ½ small onion,
   finely chopped
10 large fresh basil leaves, finely chopped
Salt, to taste

Pepper, freshly ground, to taste
1 clove garlic
1 loaf crusty country bread, cut in slices
   ½-inch thick
3 tablespoons olive oil

Seed tomatoes and chop fine. Place in bowl and mix with onion and basil. Add salt and pepper. Slice garlic clove in half and rub cut side over one side of each slice of bread. Drizzle with small amount of olive oil. Put slices on cookie sheet and broil until lightly toasted. Top with tomato mixture. Serve immediately.

Serves 6 or more, depending on size and number of bread slices

Sausage Puffs

12 ounces hot sausage
12 ounces mild sausage
4 ounces Swiss cheese, shredded
1 tablespoon Parmesan cheese, grated
3 eggs, beaten
1 teaspoon basil

1 tablespoon parsley
1 teaspoon garlic powder
1 package puff pastry, thawed but kept
   cold
½ cup Dijon mustard
2 tablespoons honey

Preheat oven to 350°. In large skillet, brown sausage. Drain off fat and let cool. Add Swiss cheese, Parmesan cheese, eggs (reserve 2 tablespoons), basil, parsley and garlic. Stir well to blend. Roll out one sheet of cold pastry to a 12x17-inch rectangle. Place one half of the sausage mixture down the center of rectangle and bring sides together. Pinch ends tightly. Repeat with remaining pastry and sausage mixture. Place on cookie sheet and brush with reserved egg. Bake for 30-40 minutes, then let cool for 10 minutes. Slice and serve with mixture of mustard and honey.

Makes 24 appetizers

Shrimp Antipasto

1-1½ pounds cooked shrimp, peeled and deveined
6 ounces Provolone cheese, cut into cubes
6 ounces pitted black olives, drained
1 cup vegetable oil
⅔ cup lemon juice
2 tablespoons Dijon mustard

2 teaspoons sugar
1-1½ teaspoons thyme leaves
1 teaspoon salt
4 ounces Genoa salami, cut into cubes
1 large red pepper, seeded and cut into square pieces

Place shrimp, cheese and olives in large shallow dish. Combine oil, lemon juice, mustard, sugar, thyme and salt, mixing well. Pour over shrimp mixture. Cover and refrigerate for 6 hours or overnight. Before serving, add salami and pepper. Toss, then drain thoroughly. Garnish as desired. (Note: Cooked scallops may be substituted for all or part of the shrimp.)

Serves 4-6

Crab Rangoon

8 ounces crabmeat
8 ounces cream cheese, room temperature
½ teaspoon steak sauce
¼ teaspoon garlic powder

1 package won ton skins
Water, for moistening edges
Peanut oil, for frying

Mix together first four ingredients. Place one teaspoon of mixture onto each won ton skin. Moisten two adjacent edges with water and fold moistened corner over opposite corner. Seal edges. Place in single layer in frying pan coated with ½-inch peanut oil. Fry until golden brown on one side, then turn over and fry on other side. Place on absorbent paper-lined cookie sheet in warm oven until ready to serve.

Makes 2-3 dozen

Satay Kambing Madura

½ cup Indonesian soy sauce (or ½ cup regular soy sauce mixed with 1 teaspoon dark molasses)
1 teaspoon ground hot red pepper
¾ cup hot water
⅓ cup peanut butter

½ cup roasted peanuts, ground
1 clove garlic, minced
Juice of one lemon
3 pounds lamb, well-trimmed and cut into 1-inch cubes
Hot Sauce Dip

Combine soy sauce, pepper, water, peanut butter, peanuts, garlic and lemon juice in saucepan. Bring to a boil and stir until smooth. Cool to room temperature. Place lamb in large dish and cover with half of the sauce. Mix well and let stand for 1 hour. Reserve remaining marinade for Hot Sauce Dip. Preheat broiler. Place lamb on broiling pan and broil for about 6 minutes per side until browned and thoroughly cooked. Serve immediately with toothpicks and Hot Sauce Dip.

Makes 50-60 pieces

Hot Sauce Dip

Hot Sauce Dip

Reserved marinade

4 ounces tomato sauce

¼ cup water

Juice of 1 lemon

1 teaspoon red pepper sauce

Combine all ingredients in saucepan. Bring to a boil and cook for 2-3 minutes. Serve warm in small bowl for dipping.

Zesty Cheese Dip

8 ounces cream cheese, room temperature
4 ounces feta cheese, room temperature (see p. 77)
¼ cup sour cream
1-2 tablespoons anchovy paste

6 sun-dried tomatoes, diced
1 orange bell pepper, diced
Salt, to taste
Cayenne pepper, to taste

Place all ingredients in food processor and process until smooth. Refrigerate for at least 6 hours before serving. Serve with breadsticks, crackers or raw vegetables.

Makes approximately 2 cups

Pork Satay

Satay

1 cup soy sauce
¼ cup dry sherry
⅓ cup sesame oil
¼ cup honey
3 tablespoons lemon juice

¼ cup onion, grated
2 large cloves garlic, crushed
¼ teaspoon cayenne pepper (optional)
2-3 pounds pork tenderloin, cut into
  ¾-inch cubes

Sauce

¾ cup peanut butter, smooth or crunchy
1½ tablespoons sesame oil
1 tablespoon chili paste with garlic, or to
  taste

½ cup cream of coconut
1½ tablespoons lemon juice
1 tablespoon soy sauce, or to taste

Combine satay ingredients in large bowl. Marinate, covered, for 3 or more hours
in refrigerator, turning meat occasionally to coat evenly. Combine sauce
ingredients in saucepan and cook, stirring constantly, until hot and well-blended.
(Add hot water as needed if too thick.) Broil pork for about 6 minutes per side
until browned and thoroughly cooked. Serve immediately with toothpicks and
sauce for dipping. (Note: This recipe is also delicious when made with chicken.
Chili paste with garlic and cream of coconut are available in the Oriental or
gourmet section of food stores.)

Makes 50-60 pieces

Coconut cream is the first thick liquid squeezed from the coconut while making coconut milk. It can curdle while cooking, so heat slowly and stir constantly. Leftover cream will last 2 days in refrigerator, or can be frozen for longer storage.

Chicken Wings in Sauce

1 cup sugar
3 tablespoons dry mustard
2 tablespoons crushed red pepper
1¼ cups ketchup

¼ cup prepared mustard
2 tablespoons lemon juice
1 tablespoon honey
5 pounds chicken wings

In medium saucepan, combine all ingredients, except chicken wings, mixing well. Simmer sauce for 60 minutes. Preheat oven to 350°. Line a baking sheet with aluminum foil and place chicken wings on it. Baste tops of wings with sauce and bake for 20 minutes. Remove baking sheet from oven, turn wings over and baste with remaining sauce. Bake for another 20 minutes. If desired, chicken wings may then be broiled to enhance color.

Serves 10-12

Grilled Chicken Oriental

¼ cup soy sauce
3 tablespoons dry white wine
2 tablespoons lemon juice
2 tablespoons vegetable oil
¾ teaspoon fines herbs, crushed

½ teaspoon ginger root, grated
1 clove garlic, minced
¼ teaspoon onion powder
Dash of pepper
3 boneless chicken breasts, skinned

Mix together all ingredients except chicken breasts. Set aside. Slice chicken breasts into strips, cover with marinade, and let sit in refrigerator for 2 hours. Skewer onto bamboo sticks and grill for 10-15 minutes.

Serves 4

Chicken Puffs

1 cup chicken broth
½ cup butter or margarine
1 cup flour
1 tablespoon fresh parsley, snipped
2 teaspoons seasoned salt
2 teaspoons Worcestershire sauce
½ teaspoon paprika

¾ teaspoon celery seed (optional)
⅛ teaspoon cayenne pepper (optional)
4 eggs
5 ounces cooked boneless chicken, chopped
   (drained, if using canned)
¼ cup toasted almonds, chopped

Combine broth and butter in saucepan and bring to a boil. Stir in flour, parsley, seasoned salt, Worcestershire sauce, paprika, celery seed and pepper (if using). Cook, beating rapidly, until mixture leaves sides of pan and forms a compact ball. Remove from heat and add eggs, one at a time, beating well after each addition. Stir in chicken and almonds. Drop by rounded teaspoonfuls onto greased baking sheet. Bake at 400° for 15-18 minutes, or until browned. (Note: To freeze, follow above directions to point of baking. Put baking sheets into freezer for 5-6 hours, then transfer puffs to plastic bags. Thaw slightly before baking.)

Makes 50-60

Caribbean Punch

6 ounces frozen lemonade concentrate,
   thawed
6 ounces frozen limeade concentrate,
   thawed

6 ounces frozen orange juice concentrate,
   thawed
1 quart cold water
1 quart ginger ale, lemon-lime soda, or
   club soda

Mix thawed juices in large punchbowl. Stir in water and carbonated soda. Add ice ring or ice cubes and serve.

Serves 25 punch cups

SOUPS & STEWS

In 1779, the Sullivan-Clinton

Campaign was sent by George Washington to cut off the British supplies of food from the Iroquois Indians. The soldiers from New England were astounded by the fertility of the land and the abundant wildlife in the Genesee Valley and Finger Lakes region. The naturally unforested plains on both sides of the Genesee River and the fertile hills spreading to Seneca Lake were very attractive to men accustomed to land littered with rocks and trees.

The Seneca Indians cultivated large fields of crops and orchards in every village and town. While their diet depended heavily on the "Three Sisters" (beans, corn and squash), they also enjoyed fruits, nuts and berries. Accounts were brought back to New England of ears of corn eighteen inches long and orchards with over fifteen thousand apple, peach and pear trees. The word was out about the area that would one day be considered the "bread basket of the country".

SOUPS & STEWS

Tomato & Herb Soup

This recipe was contributed by photographer Walter Colley.

To peel ripe tomatoes, immerse in boiling water for 20-30 seconds, then transfer to cold or ice water to stop the cooking process.

¼ cup butter
1 cup onion, sliced
4 cups tomatoes, peeled, cored and
    coarsely chopped
6 ounces tomato paste
1 tablespoon fresh basil, snipped or
    1 teaspoon dried, crushed

2 teaspoons fresh thyme, snipped or
    ½ teaspoon dried, crushed
1 teaspoon salt
½ teaspoon white pepper
4 cups chicken broth
Dill weed, for garnish

In large saucepan, heat butter until melted. Add onion and cook until tender, but not browned. Add remaining ingredients, except dill, stirring well. Bring mixture to a boil, reduce heat, cover and simmer for 30-40 minutes. Press through food mill or purée in blender. Return to saucepan and heat through. Garnish with dill weed before serving.

Serves 8

Pumpkin Soup

3½ tablespoons unsalted butter
½ medium onion, chopped
1 carrot, chopped
1½ stalks celery, chopped
½ green bell pepper, chopped
27 ounces pumpkin puree

4-6 cups chicken stock
1 tablespoon tapioca
Pinch of red pepper flakes
Salt, to taste
1 cup heavy cream
Ground nutmeg, for garnish (optional)

Melt butter in heavy pot and add onion, carrot, celery and green pepper. Sauté until soft. Place in blender and purée. Return to pot and add pumpkin, chicken stock, tapioca, and red pepper flakes. Simmer for 10 minutes, stirring occasionally, until thickened. Add salt. Just before serving, add cream and heat through. Garnish with nutmeg, if desired.

Makes 2 quarts

Curried Zucchini Soup

¼ cup butter
2 pounds zucchini, thinly sliced
5 tablespoons shallots or garlic, chopped
1 teaspoon salt
1½ teaspoons curry powder

¼ teaspoon cayenne pepper
4 cups chicken broth
Chives, for garnish
Croutons, for garnish

Melt butter in large frying pan. Add zucchini and shallots or garlic and cook until tender, approximately 10 minutes. In blender, purée half of the zucchini mixture with half of the spices and 2 cups of the chicken broth. Repeat process with remaining ingredients. Serve hot or cold, garnished with chives and croutons.

Serves 6-8

Cabbage Soup

1 tablespoon butter
1 tablespoon olive oil
1 cup onion, chopped
1 medium head of cabbage, shredded
8 cups chicken stock

¾ cup rice
2 tablespoons parsley
Salt and pepper, to taste
½ cup Parmesan cheese, grated

Melt butter and oil in large pan. Add onion and sauté until tender. Add cabbage and cook for approximately 5 minutes, until cabbage is well coated with butter and begins to soften. Stir in chicken stock and bring to a boil. Reduce heat and simmer for 15 minutes. Stir in rice, return heat to high, and bring to a second boil. Reduce heat to simmer and cook for another 15 minutes, stirring occasionally. Stir in parsley, salt and pepper. Spoon into individual bowls and garnish with Parmesan cheese.

Serves 4-6

Lettuce & Green Pea Soup

¼ cup margarine
4 cups lettuce, shredded
1 medium onion, chopped
2 tablespoons flour
¼ teaspoon coriander

20 ounces frozen peas
3 cans (14½-ounce) chicken broth
1 cup milk
1-2 tablespoons cream sherry

Melt margarine in large pot and sauté lettuce and onion until tender. Add flour and coriander and cook for 1 minute. Stir in peas and chicken broth. Cover pot and cook for 15 minutes, stirring often. Pour small batches of mixture into blender and process until smooth. Stir in milk and sherry. Serve hot.

Makes 9 cups

Lettuce Soup

1 head iceberg lettuce
4 tablespoons butter or margarine
¼ cup flour
29 ounces chicken broth
½ cup celery, sliced

2 tablespoons watercress, chopped
   (optional)
Salt and pepper, to taste
Grated carrot, for garnish

Core, rinse and thoroughly drain lettuce, then coarsely chop to equal 2 cups. Melt butter in large saucepan. Add flour and cook over low heat for approximately 5 minutes. Stir in chicken broth and cook over low heat until thickened. Add lettuce, celery and watercress. Continue to cook until vegetables are tender, but firm. Add seasonings and garnish with carrot.

Serves 4-6

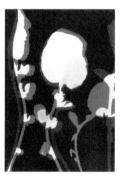

Cream of Broccoli Soup

10 ounces broccoli, chopped
1 large carrot, chopped
2 cups chicken broth
1 tablespoon butter or margarine
1 stalk celery, sliced

½ medium onion, chopped
½ teaspoon dried rosemary, ground
1 cup half-and-half
Salt, to taste (optional)
1 teaspoon lemon juice

Place broccoli, carrot and 1½ cups of the chicken broth in a medium saucepan.
Cover and cook until vegetables are tender. Melt butter in medium frying pan and
sauté celery and onion until soft. Allow both mixtures to cool slightly, then place
in blender. Add rosemary and blend to desired smoothness. (Note: Soup may be
refrigerated for several hours or frozen at this point.) Pour soup into large saucepan
and add remaining chicken broth, half-and-half, salt (if using) and lemon juice.
Heat thoroughly, but do not boil. Serve immediately.

Serves 4

Tortellini & Bean Soup

1 large stalk celery, chopped
1 small onion, chopped
1 tablespoon olive oil
2 medium cloves garlic, minced
16 ounces tomatoes
29 ounces chicken broth
½ teaspoon basil
¼ teaspoon pepper

1 bay leaf
½ cup water
1 large carrot, thinly sliced
9 ounces cheese tortellini, fresh or frozen
1 cup cut green beans, fresh or frozen
1 can (15-ounce) white kidney beans,
   rinsed and drained

In large saucepan, sauté celery and onion in olive oil for approximately 5 minutes,
or until tender. Add garlic and cook for 1 minute, stirring constantly. Add
tomatoes with their liquid, breaking them into small pieces with a spoon. Add
broth, basil, pepper, bay leaf and water. Bring to a boil. Reduce heat to low and
simmer for 15 minutes, stirring occasionally. Stir in remaining ingredients. Bring
to a second boil, then simmer on low heat for 10 minutes, or until tortellini and
beans are just tender.

Serves 4-6

Dried beans will
expand to three times
their size after
preparation. Two
cups of dried beans
will measure six cups
after soaking and
cooking.

Hearty Minestrone Soup

1 onion, chopped
2 cloves garlic, chopped
2 stalks celery, chopped
2 tablespoons olive oil
14½ ounces beef broth
14½ ounces chicken broth
28 ounces crushed tomatoes
29 ounces tomato puree
1-2 cups water
2 cups zucchini, cut into bite-sized pieces
2 cups yellow summer squash, cut into
   bite-sized pieces
2 carrots, peeled and sliced
2 small potatoes, peeled and chopped

1 pound Italian sausage links, cooked and
   thinly sliced
½ teaspoon oregano
1 tablespoon parsley
2 teaspoons basil
2 tablespoons sugar
Salt and pepper, to taste
1 can (16-ounce) kidney beans, drained
1 can (16-ounce) garbanzo beans, drained
6 ounces sweet corn
8 ounces waxed beans
8 ounces cut green beans
1 cup macaroni
Parmesan cheese, to taste

Sauté onion, garlic and celery in olive oil. In 10-12 quart kettle, add onion mixture, broths, tomatoes, tomato puree, water, zucchini, squash, carrots, potatoes, sausage, oregano, parsley, basil, sugar, salt and pepper. Cover and cook for 35 minutes. Add kidney beans, garbanzo beans, corn, waxed beans and green beans and cook for an additional 15 minutes. Add macaroni and cook just until tender. Serve immediately with Parmesan cheese sprinkled on top. (Note: Recipe can be made ahead but do not cook macaroni until just before serving.)

Serves 8-10

Major-General John Sullivan claimed to have destroyed at least 160,000 bushels of corn and large quantities of vegetables when he attacked the Iroquois Nations.

Herbed Lentil Rice Soup

5 cups chicken broth
3 cups water
1½-2 cups dry lentils
1 cup brown rice
32 ounces tomatoes, strained and juice
    reserved
4 carrots, quartered and sliced
1 onion, chopped
2 stalks celery, chopped

4 cloves garlic, chopped
½ teaspoon basil
½ teaspoon oregano
½ teaspoon thyme
1 bay leaf
2 tablespoons parsley
¼ cup apple cider or red wine vinegar
Salt and pepper, to taste

In large pot, combine all ingredients except parsley, vinegar, salt and pepper.
Bring to a boil, cover pot and simmer for 1 hour, or until lentils are tender. Stir in
remaining ingredients and remove bay leaf. (Note: If soup thickens, use reserved
tomato juice to thin.)

Serves 8

Outer Banks Soup ~ The Clark House

4 tablespoons butter or margarine
½ cup flour
½ cup onion, diced
⅓ cup celery, diced
24 ounces clam juice
1 cube fish bouillon
½ teaspoon lemon zest, grated
¼ teaspoon ground nutmeg

Dash of cayenne pepper
1 tablespoon tomato paste
2½ teaspoons Worcestershire sauce
6 ounces snow crab, thawed and excess
    water removed
10 ounces small shrimp, cooked
½-1 cup heavy cream
Sherry for garnish (optional)

In 2-quart saucepan, melt butter over medium heat. Stir in flour and cook for 5
minutes. Do not brown. Add onion and celery and cook 5 minutes longer. Add
next seven ingredients. Heat to boiling, then reduce heat and simmer for 10
minutes, stirring often. Add crab, shrimp and cream and return to a simmer.
Ladle soup into bowls and add sherry, if desired.

Serves 4-6

2 cups flour

¼ teaspoon salt

2 tablespoons margarine

⅔-1 cup milk

Preheat oven to 400°. In medium bowl, combine flour and salt. Cut in margarine, then add milk to make a fairly thick dough. Turn out onto floured board and knead briefly. Roll to desired thickness and cut with small biscuit cutter. Place crackers on ungreased cookie sheet. Poke each cracker 2 times with a fork. Bake for approximately 15 minutes, but check crackers after 10 minutes and turn over if getting too brown on bottom.

Makes approximately 4 dozen

Before using, leeks must be cleaned carefully to remove grit inside layers. Cut off tough, unusable green tops and stand leaf-end down in cold water for one hour. When ready to use, cut down center of leek, almost to the root, and spread the layers, rinsing briefly under lukewarm water. Cut off root end and strip off damaged outer layers.

Captain's Chowder

¼ cup margarine
1 large onion, finely chopped
1 large green pepper, finely chopped
2-3 potatoes, diced
12 ounces fresh mushrooms, sliced
2 pounds bay scallops or chopped fish fillets
2 cans (10¾-ounce) low-salt cream of mushroom soup

2½ soup cans milk
¾ soup can sherry or additional milk
2 ounces pimiento, drained and finely chopped
½ teaspoon black pepper
1 can (11-ounce) whole kernel corn (optional)
1 package (10-ounce) frozen peas, cooked (optional)

Melt margarine in large pot. Sauté onion and green pepper until tender. Add potatoes and mushrooms. Sauté for 8-10 minutes, stirring often. Add scallops or fish and cook for 10 minutes longer. Combine soup, milk and sherry in large saucepan. Simmer for 5 minutes, stirring until smooth. Slowly add soup mixture to fish mixture, stirring constantly. Add pimiento, black pepper, corn and peas (if using) and heat to just below boiling point. May serve at once or, for better flavor, refrigerate overnight.

Serves 8-10

Combo Chowder

2 cups water
2 cups potatoes, diced
½ cup carrots, sliced
½ cup broccoli, chopped
½ cup celery, chopped
½ cup leeks, chopped
¼ cup onion, chopped
1½ teaspoons salt

¼ teaspoon pepper
¼ cup margarine
¼ cup flour
2 cups milk
8 ounces orange Cheddar cheese, extra sharp, diced or grated
Ham or bacon, cooked and diced (optional)

In large saucepan, bring water to a boil. Add vegetables, salt and pepper, reduce heat and simmer for 10 minutes. Do not drain. In separate pan on medium heat, melt margarine, add flour and blend in milk until thick. Add mixture to chowder. Stir in Cheddar cheese and ham or bacon, if desired. Cook 10-15 minutes longer.

Serves 6-8

Vegetarian Chili

1 medium zucchini, cubed
1 medium onion, chopped
2-3 tablespoons vegetable oil
½ pound mushrooms, sliced
28 ounces crushed tomatoes

3 tablespoons chili powder
1 teaspoon basil
Salt and pepper, to taste
1 can (16-ounce) kidney beans, with liquid
6 ounces tomato paste

In 8-quart saucepan, sauté zucchini and onion in oil until slightly tender. Add mushrooms, tomatoes and seasonings, mixing well. Cover and simmer for 12-15 minutes. Add kidney beans and enough tomato paste to make a thick, but not pasty, consistency. Simmer 5 minutes longer.

Serves 4

Chili With a Twist

3 cups onion, chopped
½ cup vegetable oil
1 tablespoon garlic, minced
3 pounds beef chuck, cut into 1-inch cubes
¼ cup chili powder
1 tablespoon ground cumin
2 tablespoons paprika
1 tablespoon oregano
1½ tablespoons red pepper flakes
1 bay leaf

1½ teaspoons baking cocoa
16 ounces tomato sauce
1 cup chicken broth
3 tablespoons cider vinegar
32 ounces kidney beans, drained
2 green bell peppers, cut into pieces
1 red bell pepper, cut into pieces
6 scallions, sliced, for garnish
Sour cream, for garnish

In a large pan, cook onion in oil until tender. Add garlic and beef, cooking over medium heat until beef is browned. Add the next ten ingredients. Bring mixture to a boil, then cover and simmer on low for 1 hour. Stir in beans and peppers and cook 15 minutes longer. Store overnight in refrigerator to blend flavors. Serve hot and top with scallions and sour cream.

Serves 8-10

Danish Soup

Broth
21½ ounces beef consommé or broth
21½ ounces water
2 carrots, thinly sliced

1 stalk celery, chopped
1 bunch parsley, chopped
1 onion, chopped

Meatballs
⅔ pound lean ground beef
4 tablespoons dried bread crumbs
2 eggs

¼ teaspoon salt
¼ teaspoon pepper

Dumplings
⅓ cup butter
⅔ cup water
⅔ cup flour

½ teaspoon salt
3 eggs

Combine consommé, water and carrots in large pan. Put celery, parsley and onion into cheesecloth bag, add to pan and bring to a simmer. In medium bowl, mix together ground beef, bread crumbs, eggs, salt and pepper. Form into small meatballs and add to broth. Simmer for 40 minutes. Meanwhile, combine butter and water and bring to a boil. After butter has melted, add flour and salt, mixing well. Set aside to cool. Fill a 6-quart pan with water, add a small amount of salt, and bring water to a boil. Add eggs, one at a time, to the flour mixture and mix well. Slice out dumplings with side of a teaspoon and add to boiling water, approximately 15 at a time. Boil each batch for about 5 minutes, turning occasionally. Using a slotted spoon, remove dumplings from water and keep warm by placing them into another pot or soup tureen to which a small amount of hot broth has been added. When soup has simmered for the specified time, remove cheesecloth bag and add soup to the pot with dumplings. Serve hot.

Serves 4-6

Jambalaya

½ pound hot sausage, cut into ½-inch
   pieces
½ pound ham, cut into pieces
3 tablespoons vegetable oil
1 cup onion, chopped
1 cup green pepper, chopped
1 cup celery, chopped
3 cloves garlic, minced
1 bay leaf

½ teaspoon thyme
1 teaspoon basil
2 cups white rice
2 cups tomatoes, chopped
3 cups chicken broth
2 teaspoons salt
½ teaspoon black pepper
½ teaspoon red pepper sauce
1 pound fresh shrimp, peeled and deveined

Preheat oven to 350°. In large Dutch oven, sauté sausage and ham in oil. Remove from pan and set aside. In same oil, sauté onion, green pepper, celery, garlic, bay leaf, thyme and basil, until onion is soft. Add rice and sauté for 3-5 minutes longer. Stir in next five ingredients. Add sausage and ham. Bring mixture to a boil, reduce heat and simmer for 15 minutes. Stir in shrimp and bake in oven for 20 minutes, until shrimp become tender. Fluff rice and serve.

Serves 8

Beef Soup

1½ pounds stew beef, cut into bite-sized
   pieces
3 cups water
1 teaspoon salt
¼ teaspoon pepper
1 clove garlic, minced
1 bay leaf

2 medium carrots, sliced
1 cup celery, sliced
1 medium onion, cut into wedges
16 ounces tomato sauce
1 can (15-ounce) red kidney beans, with
   liquid
¼ cup small-to-medium sized macaroni

Place beef, water, salt and pepper into large kettle. Bring to a boil and skim. Add garlic, bay leaf, carrots, celery and onion. Cover pan and simmer for 1½ hours. Stir in remaining ingredients. Return to a boil, reduce heat and simmer for 6-8 minutes, stirring occasionally, until macaroni is tender. Serve.

Serves 6

Spicy Stew Italiano

2 tablespoons vegetable oil
1 cup onion, chopped
1 pound hot Italian sausage, cut into 1-inch pieces
1½ pounds skinless, boneless chicken thighs, cut into 1-inch pieces
1 tablespoon fennel seed
7 ounces spicy salsa
1¾ cups chicken stock

1 cup tomato puree
¼ cup tomato paste
1 tablespoon balsamic vinegar
1 tablespoon oregano
1 tablespoon ground cumin
1½ cups corn, fresh or frozen
1½ cups stewed tomatoes
Pinch of basil
Sour cream, for garnish

Heat oil in a Dutch oven and sauté onion for 5 minutes. Add sausage and chicken and cook for 10 minutes, stirring occasionally. Spoon off all but two tablespoons of the fat. Stir in next eight ingredients. Bring mixture to a boil, reduce heat and simmer, partially covered, for 30 minutes. Stir in corn, tomatoes and basil, and cook 5 minutes longer. Top each serving with sour cream.

Serves 6-8

Zuppa di Pollo Con Vino

Whole fryer chicken
3 carrots, halved
3 stalks celery, halved
1 onion, halved
Salt and pepper, to taste
¾ cup fresh parsley, chopped
2 cloves garlic
1 bay leaf

White pepper, to taste
½ cup white wine or white vermouth
2 carrots, chopped
2 stalks celery, chopped
1-1½ cups frozen tortellini
Sour cream, for garnish
¼ cup fresh parsley, chopped, for garnish

In Dutch oven, cover chicken with water and add next eight ingredients. Bring to a boil, then simmer on low for 2 hours. Remove chicken and set aside. Purée vegetables in blender and return to broth. Add next three ingredients and cook until chopped vegetables are tender. Bone chicken and add meat to soup. Meanwhile, cook tortellini according to package directions, drain and add to soup. Serve, garnished with sour cream and parsley.

Serves 6-8

Chicken Con Queso ~ Park Ave. Pub

Roux
⅔ cup vegetable oil   ½ cup flour

Soup Base
1½ pounds chicken breast, diced   2 quarts chicken stock
1 cup white onion, diced   1 pint heavy cream
3 cans (4-ounce) green chilies, diced 24 ounces beer
½ cup butter or margarine   1½ pounds Cheddar cheese, grated
                                       Salt and pepper, to taste

Combine oil and flour in small saucepan. Cook over low heat until a medium
brown roux is formed, about 25 minutes. Sauté chicken, onion and chilies in
butter in a 7-8-quart pot. Add chicken stock, half of the roux, and heavy cream.
Cook over medium-to-low heat, stirring occasionally, until mixture comes to a
boil. In a separate pan, heat beer and thicken with remainder of roux. Add to
soup mixture. Gradually add grated cheese, stirring with a whisk. Season with salt
and pepper. Serve immediately.

Serves 8-10

Gazpacho

¼ cup cider vinegar   3 cups tomatoes, chopped
1 large clove garlic, crushed   1 large cucumber, peeled
¼ cup olive oil   1 red bell pepper, chopped
2 teaspoons sherry   ½ cup onion, chopped
½ cup warm water   Salt, to taste
1 large heel of French bread, torn into Cayenne pepper, to taste
    pieces   1-2 cloves garlic, mashed

Combine vinegar, garlic, oil, sherry, water and bread in bowl. Let stand for several
hours. In food processor or blender, combine remaining ingredients and purée.
Add bread mixture and blend. Chill soup and serve as is or with desired
Accompaniments. (Note: Tomato juice may be added to reach desired
consistency.)

Serves 6-8

Accompaniments for
Gazpacho

Traditionally, several
foods are passed
around at the table
when serving
gazpacho. These
include corn, diced
avocado, cooked
crabmeat, diced
cucumbers, chopped
green peppers,
chopped onions,
chopped tomatoes
and croutons.

Chilled Strawberry Soup ~ The Spring House

1 quart fresh strawberries, hulls removed and some sliced, for garnish
1 quart heavy or light cream

1 cup sugar
½ cup rum
Lemon-lime soda

Place unsliced strawberries in blender and add cream, sugar and rum. Mix until smooth and creamy. Refrigerate until ready to serve. Just before serving, spoon soup into individual bowls and add a dash of lemon-lime soda. Garnish with sliced strawberries and serve.

Serves 6-8

Peach Soup

4 cups peaches, peeled and diced
2 cups sweet white wine
2 cups water
⅓-½ cup sugar

1 cinnamon stick
2 tablespoons lemon juice
⅛ teaspoon almond extract
Lemon slices, for garnish

In large saucepan, combine peaches, wine, water, sugar and cinnamon. Cover and simmer for 30 minutes. Remove cinnamon stick and discard. Pour half of the mixture into blender and purée until smooth. Repeat with remaining half. Return mixture to saucepan and add lemon juice and almond extract. Heat to boiling, stirring frequently. (Add additional sugar, if desired.) Serve hot or cold, garnished with lemon slices.

Serves 6-8

Chilled West African Soup

2 tablespoons butter
½ cup onion, chopped
1 tablespoon curry powder
1 cup leeks, chopped (see p. 32)
1 clove garlic, finely minced
½ cup bananas, diced
1½ cups apple, peeled and diced

1 cup tomatoes, peeled and chopped
  (see p. 26)
1 cup potato, peeled and cubed
Salt and black pepper, to taste
4 drops red pepper sauce, or to taste
3½ cups chicken broth
1 cup heavy cream
Chopped peanuts, for garnish

Melt butter in large pot and add onion. Sauté until translucent, and add curry,
stirring to coat onion. Add remaining fruits and vegetables. Stir well. Add salt,
black pepper, red pepper sauce and broth and simmer for 20 minutes. Pour into
food processor or blender and process until smooth. Chill thoroughly. Just before
serving, stir in cream. Garnish with chopped peanuts.

Serves 6-8

The first buildings erected

in what was to become Rochester were a sawmill and a flour mill, completed in 1789. Although the mills failed within two years, the energy waiting to be harnessed from the Genesee River induced future settlers to try milling again. By the 1830s, when the City of Rochester was chartered, it had become known as the "Flour City". It was, for a time, the largest wheat flour producing city in the world. Before the milling industry moved west, 36 mills were in operation and 700,000 barrels of flour per year were being sold worldwide.

The words "Genesee Flour" meant top quality and exceptional whiteness. Bags of flour from this region were earning top dollar at market and were on display at national and international expositions. It may have been the high quality of Genesee wheat that convinced Dr. Sylvester Graham to take up residence in Rochester in 1830. It was at this same time that his dietary ideas were becoming popular and Graham flour was becoming the first food fad of the nation.

Just a Few Notes...

The zest of the citrus fruit is the outer layer of rind containing the essential oils of the fruit. It can be removed with a fine grater or vegetable peeler. Try to avoid the bitter white portion of the peel.

BREADS & MUFFINS

Simply Scones

Glaze

---

1 tablespoon half-and-half

¼ teaspoon cinnamon

2 tablespoons sugar

Mix ingredients together and brush on scones.

When cutting scones, push straight down with biscuit cutter. Twisting the cutter may cause scones to bake lopsided.

3 cups flour
⅓ cup sugar
2½ teaspoons baking powder
½ teaspoon baking soda
¾ teaspoon salt (optional)

¾ cup margarine
1 cup plain nonfat yogurt
3 ounces raisins
Glaze

Preheat oven to 425°. Combine flour, sugar, baking powder, baking soda and salt (if using). Add margarine, cutting in with pastry blender or fork until mixture looks crumbly. Add yogurt and raisins and mix until ingredients are blended together. Place dough on floured surface and pat out until roughly ½-inch thick. Using a biscuit cutter, cut out scones. Place dough on ungreased cookie sheet and brush with Glaze. Bake for 12 minutes or until brown.

Makes 16 two-inch scones

Oatmeal Biscuits

1 cup rolled oats
2 cups white flour
1 cup oat flour
3½ teaspoons cream of tartar
1¾ teaspoons baking soda
1 teaspoon cinnamon
⅔ cup margarine

½ cup maple syrup
1 tablespoon fresh orange zest, grated or
    1½ teaspoons dried
1 cup milk
Milk, for topping
Oats, for topping

Preheat oven to 450°. In a bowl, mix oats, flours, cream of tartar, baking soda and cinnamon. Cut in margarine with pastry cutter or fork until mixture resembles coarse crumbs. Stir in maple syrup, orange zest and milk. Mix until a soft dough is formed. Turn dough onto lightly floured surface and knead 10-12 times. Pat dough to 1-inch thickness and cut out biscuits with floured biscuit cutter. Place biscuits ½-inch apart on ungreased cookie sheet. Brush tops with milk and sprinkle with a few oats. Bake for 12-15 minutes, or until golden. (Note: Regular flour may be substituted for the oat flour.)

Makes 12-15 two-inch biscuits

Cinnamon Rolls

Dough
1 package active dry yeast
¼ cup lukewarm water
½ cup scalded milk
⅓ cup shortening
¼ cup sugar

½ teaspoon salt
½ cup mashed potatoes
1 egg, beaten
3 cups flour

Topping
2 tablespoons butter, melted
½ cup brown sugar, packed

½ cup pecans or walnuts, chopped

Filling
3 tablespoons butter, melted
¾ cup brown sugar, packed

¾ teaspoon cinnamon

In small bowl, dissolve yeast in lukewarm water. Pour scalded milk into large bowl and add shortening, sugar, salt and potatoes. Let cool, then add yeast, mixing thoroughly. Stir in beaten egg and flour. (Dough will be stiff.) Refrigerate overnight. The next day, mix together topping ingredients in medium bowl. Sprinkle evenly in bottom of 13x9-inch baking dish and set aside. Punch down dough and divide into thirds. Place one piece of dough onto floured surface and roll out to a 12x9-inch rectangle. Brush with 1 tablespoon of the melted butter. In small bowl, mix together ¼ cup of the brown sugar and ¼ teaspoon of the cinnamon and sprinkle evenly over dough. Starting at narrow end of rectangle, roll up dough and cut into 1-inch slices. Place slices into prepared baking dish. Repeat entire process with second and third pieces of dough. Cover dish and let dough rise until doubled, approximately 30 minutes. Bake at 350° for 15-20 minutes. Remove baking dish from oven and invert onto serving plate. Serve immediately.

Makes 3 dozen

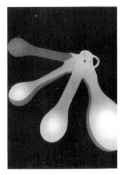

Updated Sally Lunn Bread

1 package active dry yeast
½ cup warm water
1 cup warm milk
½ cup margarine, room temperature
3 tablespoons brown sugar, packed
2 tablespoons white sugar

2 teaspoons salt
¼ teaspoon cinnamon
3 eggs, beaten, room temperature
2 cups whole wheat flour
3½-4 cups white flour

In large bowl, sprinkle yeast into water and stir until dissolved. Add milk, margarine, sugars, salt, cinnamon and eggs. Stir in whole wheat flour and 1 cup of the white flour. Beat until well blended, about 1 minute. Stir in enough of the remaining white flour to make a soft dough. Cover and let rise until doubled in bulk, about 1 hour. Stir batter down, and spoon into a well-greased and floured 10-inch tube pan. Cover and let rise again until doubled in bulk, about 1 hour. Bake at 375°-400° for approximately 30 minutes, or until done. Remove from pan and cool on wire rack. (Note: Two 9x5-inch loaf pans may also be used. Bake at 350°-375° for approximately 30 minutes, or until done.)

Makes 1 large or 2 small loaves

Buttermilk Bread

2 packages active dry yeast
2 teaspoons sugar
½ cup warm water
2 teaspoons salt

3 tablespoons corn oil
1½ cups buttermilk, room temperature or
    slightly warm
5½ cups unbleached flour

In large bowl, combine yeast, sugar and water and proof for 10 minutes. Mix in remaining ingredients, using flour as needed to make a smooth dough. Knead until dough is no longer sticky. Place dough in a large buttered bowl, cover with a towel, and let rise until doubled. Punch down dough and knead briefly to remove air bubbles. Divide dough in half and place in two greased 9x5-inch loaf pans. Cover pans and let dough rise until doubled. Bake at 375° for 30 minutes. Remove bread from pans and bake 10 minutes longer on oven rack. Let bread cool before slicing.

Makes 2 loaves

Potato Bread

¾ pound potatoes, peeled
2 cups water
5 cups white flour
1½ tablespoons honey
1 tablespoon active dry yeast

1 cup lukewarm water
2 cups whole wheat flour
1 tablespoon salt
¼ cup vegetable oil

Boil potatoes and water until potatoes become very soft. Stir water until potatoes disintegrate. Pour into large bowl and cool mixture slightly. Stir in 1 cup of the white flour, honey, yeast and lukewarm water. Cover and let proof for 1 hour. Add remaining white flour, the whole wheat flour, salt and oil. Turn dough onto floured surface and knead until dough loses its stickiness and springs back when touched. Place dough in large greased bowl, cover, and let rise in warm place for 1 hour. Punch dough down, divide in half and place into two greased 9x5-inch loaf pans. Cover and let dough rise again for 45 minutes. Slash top of dough with sharp knife. Bake in 400° oven for 45 minutes or until lightly browned.

Makes 2 loaves

Dill Bread

1 package active dry yeast
½ cup warm water
3 tablespoons sugar
1 tablespoon dillweed
1 cup evaporated milk

2 tablespoons butter or margarine, melted
1 teaspoon salt
3-3½ cups flour
Melted butter or margarine (optional)

Grease a 9x5-inch loaf pan. Dissolve yeast in warm water in large bowl. Stir in 1 tablespoon of the sugar and the dillweed. Let mixture stand at room temperature until bubbly, approximately 15 minutes. Stir in the remaining sugar, milk, butter and salt. Stir in enough flour to make a stiff dough. (Dough will be sticky.) Cover and let rise in warm place for 30-45 minutes. Stir dough down and place in prepared pan. Let pan sit in warm place until dough rises to 1½ inches above rim of pan, approximately 30 minutes. Bake at 350° for 35 minutes. If desired, brush top with melted butter. Let bread cool in pan for 5-10 minutes, then remove from pan and cool on wire rack.

Makes 1 loaf

Making indentations with your fingers in bread dough will indicate if the dough is ready. If the dough has been kneaded long enough, the indentations will spring back. The first rising is complete when the indentations remain in the dough.

The Erie Canal was responsible for Rochester becoming the first boom town in America. In 1822, 2,700 people lived in Rochesterville. In the next four years, the population nearly tripled.

Cracked Wheat Bread

1 cup cracked wheat
3 cups boiling water
½ cup butter or margarine
3 tablespoons salt
3 tablespoons molasses
5 tablespoons honey

1½ cups skim milk or water
2 packages active dry yeast
⅔ cup warm water
2 cups whole wheat flour
8 cups white flour

Cook cracked wheat in water until most of the liquid is absorbed. While still hot, mix in next five ingredients. In a large bowl, proof yeast in water for 10 minutes, then add cracked wheat mixture. Mix in wheat and white flours until a stiff dough is formed. Knead for 10 minutes, adding additional flour until dough is no longer sticky. Place dough in oiled bowl, turning to coat on all sides. Cover bowl and let dough rise until doubled. Punch down dough, shape into loaves, and place in four greased 8x4-inch loaf pans. Cover and let rise until dough reaches tops of pans. Bake at 375° for 30-35 minutes. Remove from oven and cool on wire racks.

Makes 4 loaves

Soft Breadsticks

¼ cup butter
2¼ cups flour
1 tablespoon sugar
1 tablespoon baking powder

1¼ teaspoons salt
1 cup milk
Sesame seeds, to taste

Preheat oven to 450°. Melt butter in 13x9-inch baking dish. Combine flour, sugar, baking powder, salt and milk in large bowl, stirring until mixture becomes stiff. Turn dough onto lightly floured surface and roll out to ¼-inch thickness. Cut dough into strips ¾-inch wide. Place in baking dish and turn over so that both sides are coated with butter. Sprinkle with sesame seeds and bake for 15-20 minutes, or until lightly browned, being careful not to overcook. (Note: Poppy seeds, dill, garlic, basil, or coarse salt may be substituted for sesame seeds.)

Serves 12

Herbed Tomato Bread

1 package active dry yeast
½ cup very warm water
1½ cups fresh tomatoes, peeled and
　chopped (see p. 26)
2 tablespoons sugar

2 tablespoons vegetable oil
2 tablespoons salt
1¼ tablespoons fresh herbs (basil, parsley,
　dill, oregano), chopped
3½ cups flour

In large bowl, dissolve yeast in warm water and set aside. Purée tomatoes and add to yeast, along with sugar, oil, salt and herbs. Stir in as much flour as can easily be absorbed. Knead dough for 5-6 minutes, adding flour as necessary, until dough is smooth. Place dough in greased bowl. Cover with plastic wrap and let rise until doubled, approximately 60-90 minutes. Punch down dough and turn out onto floured surface. Tear off ten golfball-sized pieces and form them into small rolls. Place on greased cookie sheet two inches apart. Form remaining dough into loaf shape and place in greased 9x5-inch loaf pan. Cover rolls and loaf with towel and let rise until doubled, approximately 30-40 minutes. Bake rolls and loaf at 400° for 15 minutes, then remove rolls from oven. Reduce oven temperature to 350° and continue baking 25-30 minutes longer. Cool breads on wire rack. (Note: If fresh tomatoes are unavailable, substitute 1½ cups canned plum tomatoes, with juice, and increase flour to 4½ cups.)

Makes 10 rolls and 1 loaf

Yankee Yorkshire Pudding

12 teaspoons butter
3 eggs
1 cup milk

1 cup flour
½ teaspoon salt

Preheat oven to 400°. Place one teaspoon butter in each of 12 muffin tins and place in oven until butter has melted. In large bowl, beat eggs, then add milk. Stir in flour and salt, then beat with electric mixer on slow speed for 2 full minutes. Pour mixture into 12 muffin tins, filling each approximately ¾ full. Bake for 30 minutes, leaving oven door closed to prevent batter from "falling".

Makes 12

Oatmeal Bread

2 cups quick oats
1 tablespoon butter or vegetable oil
1 teaspoon salt
¼ cup molasses
1¾ cups boiling water

1 tablespoon active dry yeast
¼ cup warm water
2 egg whites
5 cups unbleached flour

Combine oats, butter and salt in large bowl. Add molasses with boiling water. Mix well and let cool until lukewarm. In small bowl, dissolve yeast in warm water. Add yeast and egg whites to oatmeal mixture and stir. Add 4 cups of the flour, one cup at a time, stirring well after each addition. Place dough on lightly floured surface and knead in remaining flour. Knead, adding more flour if necessary, until dough is elastic and does not cling to hands. (Dough will be a bit sticky.) Place dough in lightly oiled bowl, turning to oil all surfaces. Cover bowl with plastic wrap and dry dish towel. Let dough rise until doubled, approximately 1½ hours. Punch down and knead for 2-3 minutes. Divide dough in half and shape into loaves. Place in two greased 9x5-inch loaf pans and let rise for 1 hour. Bake at 350° for 40-45 minutes. Remove bread from pans and cool on wire rack. (Note: Bread also may be formed into round loaves and baked on greased cookie sheet.)

Makes 2 loaves

Nutritious Banana Bread

4 over-ripe bananas
¼ cup sugar
1 egg
1 cup wheat flour
½ cup white flour

4 tablespoons butter, melted
1 teaspoon baking soda
1 teaspoon salt
¾ cup walnuts or pecans, chopped
¾ cup raisins

Preheat oven to 350°. Grease a 9x5-inch loaf pan. In a large bowl, mash bananas and mix in sugar. Add egg, mixing well, then stir in remaining ingredients. Pour batter into prepared pan and bake for 45 minutes.

Makes 1 loaf

Squash Corn Bread

½ cup margarine or butter, room
  temperature
¼ cup brown sugar, packed
2 eggs
1½ teaspoons lemon juice
1 cup Hubbard or butternut squash, baked
  and mashed or puréed

¼ cup milk
¾ cup corn meal
¾ cup flour
4 teaspoons baking powder
¼ teaspoon allspice
½ teaspoon cinnamon
½ teaspoon salt

Preheat oven to 350°. Grease a 9x5-inch loaf pan. Cream together margarine and
brown sugar. Beat in eggs, lemon juice, squash and milk. Set aside. In another
bowl, combine dry ingredients. Gradually add to squash mixture, mixing well.
Pour batter into prepared pan and bake for 50 minutes, or until toothpick inserted
near center comes out clean. Cool loaf in pan for 10 minutes, then remove from
pan and let cool on wire rack.

Makes 1 loaf

Apple Corn Bread

1 cup corn meal
1 cup flour
¾ cup sugar
1 tablespoon baking powder
1½ teaspoons salt

1 egg
1 cup milk
¼ cup butter, melted
1 tart apple, unpeeled, cored and shredded

Preheat oven to 425°. Grease a 9-inch square pan. Mix together dry ingredients
and set aside. Beat together egg, milk and butter and add to dry ingredients,
stirring just until moist. Stir in apple and pour into prepared pan. Bake for 20
minutes, or until done.

Serves 9

Carrot Bread

1½ cups sugar
2 cups flour
2 teaspoons baking soda
2 teaspoons cinnamon
½ teaspoon salt
½ teaspoon nutmeg
2 cups carrots, grated
1 cup vegetable oil

2 teaspoons vanilla extract
3 eggs
½ cup coconut, flaked
½ cup pecans, chopped
½ cup walnuts, chopped
½ cup dates, chopped
½ cup raisins

Line two 8x4-inch loaf pans with aluminum foil, which has been greased to prevent sticking. In large bowl combine first six ingredients. Stir in remaining ingredients, mixing well. Pour batter into prepared pans and let stand for 20 minutes. Preheat oven to 350°. Bake for 75 minutes, or until toothpick inserted near center comes out clean.

Makes 2 loaves

Fruit & Nut Bread

2¼ cups flour
1 cup sugar
1 teaspoon baking powder
1 teaspoon baking soda
¼ teaspoon salt
1 cup dates, chopped

1 cup pecans, chopped
¼ cup orange zest, grated
1 cup cranberries
1 cup buttermilk
¾ cup vegetable oil
2 eggs, beaten

Preheat oven to 350°. Grease a bundt pan. Combine first 5 ingredients in large bowl. Stir in dates, pecans, orange zest and cranberries. In smaller bowl, combine buttermilk, oil and eggs. Add to dry ingredients, stirring well to blend. Pour batter into prepared pan and bake for 1 hour. Remove pan from oven and let cool on wire rack for 20 minutes. Remove bread from pan and allow to cool completely.

Serves 12

Orange Fig Nut Bread

¾ cup boiling water
1 cup figs, finely chopped
2 tablespoons butter
1½ cups flour
½ cup sugar
3 teaspoons baking powder

1 teaspoon vanilla extract
1 egg, beaten
4 teaspoons orange zest, grated
⅓ cup orange juice
¾ cup whole-bran cereal
½ cup walnuts, chopped

Preheat oven to 350°. Grease a 9x5-inch loaf pan. In large bowl, pour boiling water over figs and butter and let stand for 10 minutes. In smaller bowl, combine flour, sugar and baking powder. Set aside. To the bowl with figs, add vanilla, egg, orange zest and orange juice. Beat well. Add dry ingredients and cereal, mixing just until combined. (Do not overbeat.) Stir in chopped nuts and pour into prepared pan. Bake for 45-50 minutes.

Makes 1 loaf

Orange Tea Loaf

1 cup sour cream
¾ cup sugar
½ cup butter, room temperature
2 eggs
1 tablespoon poppy seeds
1 tablespoon orange zest

2 tablespoons orange juice
2 cups flour
1 teaspoon baking powder
1 teaspoon baking soda
½ teaspoon salt

Preheat oven to 325°. Grease two 9x5-inch loaf pans. Combine sour cream, sugar and butter and beat with electric mixer until light and fluffy. Add eggs, poppy seeds, orange zest and orange juice, mixing well. Add flour, baking powder, baking soda and salt. Beat at low speed, scraping sides of bowl until all ingredients are combined. Divide batter in half and spoon into prepared pans. Bake for 50-55 minutes. (Bread is done if it springs back when touched.) Cool for 5 minutes, then remove from pans and cool completely on wire rack. Wrap in plastic wrap and let sit overnight.

Makes 2 loaves

Miniature Orange Muffins

1 cup sugar
½ cup unsalted butter, room temperature
2 eggs
1 teaspoon baking soda
1 cup buttermilk
2 cups flour

½ teaspoon salt
Zest of one orange
¾ cup currants (optional)
Juice of one orange
½ cup sugar (optional)

Preheat oven to 400°. Grease miniature muffin tins or line with paper cups. Cream sugar and butter, then add eggs and beat until fluffy. Mix together baking soda and buttermilk and set aside. Combine flour and salt, and add to egg mixture, alternating with buttermilk mixture. Add orange zest and currants, (if using), to batter. Stir in orange juice. Pour into prepared muffin tins and sprinkle with sugar, if desired. Bake for 15 minutes or until lightly browned.

Makes 4 dozen

Lemon Fruit Bread

Lemon Syrup

Juice of 1 lemon

¼ cup sugar

Stir lemon juice and sugar together. Bring to gentle boil, then drizzle over warm bread.

1 cup fresh fruit (blueberries, raspberries, strawberries, peaches, etc.)
2 tablespoons flour
6 tablespoons butter
1 cup sugar
2 teaspoons lemon zest

3 tablespoons fresh lemon juice
2 eggs
1½ cups flour
1½ teaspoons baking powder
⅓ cup milk or buttermilk
Lemon Syrup

Preheat oven to 350°. Grease and flour an 8x4-inch loaf pan. Combine fruit with flour, set aside. Cream butter and sugar until light and fluffy. Add lemon zest and juice, mixing well. Beat in eggs, one at a time. Combine flour and baking powder, then add to batter, a little at a time, alternating with milk. Mix only until batter is smooth. Fold in fruit mixture. Pour into prepared pan and bake for 45 minutes. Remove from loaf pan and place on wire rack. Drizzle with Lemon Syrup.

Makes 1 loaf

Little Applesauce Muffins

Batter
½ cup butter, room temperature
½ cup sugar
2 eggs
¾ cup applesauce

1¾ cups flour
1 tablespoon baking powder
½ teaspoon salt

Topping
½ cup sugar
½-1 teaspoon cinnamon

¼ cup butter, melted

Preheat oven to 425°. Grease miniature muffin tins or line with paper cups. In large bowl, cream butter and sugar. Beat in eggs, one at a time, until batter is light and fluffy. Stir in applesauce and set aside. In another bowl, combine flour, baking powder and salt. Add to applesauce mixture, stirring just enough to moisten. Fill prepared tins ⅔ full. Bake for 15 minutes or until golden. For topping, combine sugar and cinnamon. Dip tops of warm muffins into melted butter, then into cinnamon-sugar mixture. Serve warm.

Makes 3 dozen

The last active flour mill on the Genesee River at Rochester closed in 1942.

Rhubarb Bread

1½ cups brown sugar, packed
⅔ cup shortening, room temperature
1 egg
1 cup buttermilk
1 teaspoon salt
1 teaspoon baking soda

1 teaspoon vanilla extract
2½ cups flour
2 cups rhubarb, finely diced
½ cup white sugar (optional)
1 tablespoon butter or margarine
   (optional)

Preheat oven to 325°. Grease two 8x4-inch loaf pans. In large bowl, beat together brown sugar, shortening and egg. Blend in buttermilk, salt, baking soda, vanilla and flour. Add rhubarb, mixing well. Pour batter into prepared pans. If desired, make topping by mixing white sugar with butter until the texture is coarse. Sprinkle on top of batter. Bake for 50 minutes. (Note: Bread is very moist and is best when served immediately after cooling.)

Makes 2 loaves

Graham became a household word with his flour and crackers, Dr. James Caleb Jackson of Dansville, New York, was perfecting the first modern breakfast cereal. Jackson was a Graham disciple. He and his family operated a health resort featuring the water cure, fibrous foods and non-caffeine drinks. His cereal, produced in 1863, was called Granula, a mixture of Graham flour and water, double-baked and double-ground into small chunks. Granula had to be soaked for twenty minutes before eating. Jackson also developed a cereal-based "coffee" he called Somo.

These products were originally intended for resort use only, but they became so popular that the Jacksons finally opened the Our Home Granula Company. By 1883, sixty thousand pounds of the cereal were being produced yearly. The Jacksons eventually sold the company, and by 1920 Granula was no longer being made.

Several Seventh Day Adventists traveled from Battle Creek, Michigan, to stay at Dr. Jackson's resort. They returned home to start a water cure resort of their own, headed by Dr. J. H. Kellogg, who produced his first cereal in 1877. He called it Granola, before changing the name to Granose. He then introduced Corn Flakes in 1907. A patient at Kellogg's Sanitorium in 1891, C. W. Post eventually went on to develop Postum (1895), and a product very much like Jackson's Granula, called Grape Nuts (1898). ■   ■   ■   ■   ■   ■   ■   ■

EGGS & BRUNCH

Waffles with Apple, Pear & Raisin Sauce

1 egg white
1 cup flour
¼ teaspoon salt
½ teaspoon cinnamon
1 tablespoon sugar
½ cup milk

½ cup water
6 tablespoons vegetable oil
1 egg yolk
4 teaspoons baking powder
Apple, Pear and Raisin Sauce

In large bowl, beat egg white with electric mixer until stiff. In another bowl, combine next eight ingredients. Fold in egg white and add baking powder, stirring well. (If batter is too thick, add a few drops of water.) Cook according to waffle-iron instructions or pour batter into hot, greased waffle iron and cook until golden brown, about 3 minutes. Top with Apple, Pear and Raisin Sauce, and garnish with powdered sugar or whipped cream, if desired.

Makes 4-6

Apple, Pear & Raisin Sauce

4 apples, cored, peeled and diced

3 pears, cored, peeled and diced

¼ cup apple juice

½ cup raisins

1 teaspoon cinnamon

Dash of ginger

Dash of nutmeg

In large saucepan, cook apples and pears in apple juice until fruit is tender, approximately 10-15 minutes. Add remaining ingredients and cook for an additional 2 minutes, stirring occasionally. Spoon over hot waffles or pancakes.

Serves 4-6

Grandma's Griddle Cakes

2 cups cake flour
2 teaspoons baking powder
¼ cup sugar
1 teaspoon salt (optional)

1 egg
1 cup milk
¼ cup margarine, melted

In large bowl, combine flour, baking powder, sugar and salt (if using). Set aside. In smaller bowl, beat egg slightly, then stir in milk and margarine. Add to dry ingredients, stirring just until mixed. (Batter should be lumpy.) Pour desired amount of batter onto hot griddle or frying pan and cook until done, turning once. May be served with maple syrup or topped with Apple, Pear and Raisin Sauce.

Serves 2-4

Ginger Pancakes with Lemon Sauce

Pancakes

2 cups flour
2 teaspoons baking soda
½ teaspoon salt
2 tablespoons vegetable oil
¼ cup molasses

1 egg
1⅓ cups milk
1½ teaspoons ginger
1 teaspoon cinnamon
½ teaspoon cloves

Lemon Sauce

½ cup margarine
1 cup sugar
¼ cup water

3 tablespoons lemon juice
1 egg

Combine all pancake ingredients in large bowl, mixing well. Pour batter onto heated griddle and cook until bubbles form on top and underside is golden brown. Flip pancake and brown other side. Meanwhile, combine margarine, sugar, water and lemon juice in saucepan and bring to a boil. Beat egg in small bowl. Add 2 tablespoons of sugar mixture to egg, one tablespoon at a time, beating well after each addition. Add this mixture back to sugar mixture in saucepan, and bring to second boil. Continue cooking until sauce thickens slightly. Top pancakes with hot sauce and serve immediately.

Serves 4

Brunch is a meal eaten in late morning or around noon, and combines aspects of both breakfast and lunch.

Hot Fruit Compote

16 ounces frozen mixed fruit
1 can (15-ounce) mandarin oranges,
  with syrup
1 can (8-ounce) pineapple chunks,
  with syrup
1 banana, sliced

3 tablespoons brandy
½ pint sour cream
1½ tablespoons sugar
2 tablespoons heavy cream
½ cup toasted almonds, sliced

Preheat oven to 350°. Mix together fruits and brandy in 2-quart casserole dish. Bake uncovered for 35 minutes. Combine sour cream, sugar and heavy cream. Spoon hot fruit into individual bowls and serve with a dollop of sour cream topping and toasted almonds.

Serves 4-6

Elegant French Toast

1 loaf French bread, baguette size
2 eggs
¾-1 cup milk
1½ tablespoons sugar
2-3 tablespoons amaretto liqueur
1 can (20-ounce) peach halves
3 tablespoons sugar
3 tablespoons amaretto liqueur

2 tablespoons butter
2-3 tablespoons peach preserves (optional)
Butter, for sautéing
Sliced almonds, for garnish
Powdered sugar, for garnish
Fresh strawberries, for garnish (optional)
Fresh blueberries, for garnish (optional)

The night before serving, cut bread diagonally into 1-inch thick slices. Place in a shallow baking dish. In a bowl, beat together eggs, milk, sugar and amaretto. Pour mixture over bread slices, turn bread once and cover dish with plastic wrap. Refrigerate overnight. The next day, drain syrup from peaches and pour syrup into medium saucepan. Add sugar, amaretto, butter and preserves (if using). Boil mixture until reduced in volume and thickened. Reduce heat and add peach halves. Keep mixture hot, but not boiling. Meanwhile, in large skillet, sauté French bread slices in butter over medium heat until slices are uniformly golden brown, approximately 5-6 minutes. To serve, place 3-4 slices of French toast on each plate. Top with a small amount of peach syrup and sprinkle with almonds and powdered sugar. Place 2-3 peach halves on each plate, and add fresh strawberries or blueberries for garnish, if desired. Pour remaining peach syrup into server and serve at table.

Serves 2-4

Stuffed French Toast

8-10 slices day-old bread, crusts removed
16 ounces cream cheese, cut into cubes
2-3 bananas, sliced (optional)

12 eggs
2 cups milk
⅓ cup real maple syrup

Grease a 13x9-inch pan. Place 4-5 slices of bread in bottom of pan, then top with cream cheese and sliced bananas. Top with remaining bread and set aside. Beat together eggs, milk and maple syrup and pour mixture over bread. Cover pan with plastic wrap and refrigerate overnight. Preheat oven to 350°. Remove plastic wrap from pan and bake for 35-45 minutes, until top layer of bread is lightly browned. Serve with additional warmed maple syrup, if desired.

Serves 8

Canadian Cheese Scramble

Cheese Sauce
2 tablespoons butter, melted
2 tablespoons flour
½ teaspoon salt

¼ teaspoon pepper
2 cups milk
1 cup Cheddar cheese, grated

Scramble
1 cup Canadian bacon or ham, diced
¼ cup green onions, chopped
3 tablespoons butter
12 eggs, beaten

4 tablespoons butter, melted
2-2½ cups soft bread crumbs
½ teaspoon paprika

Grease an 11x7-inch baking dish. In medium saucepan combine melted butter, flour, salt and pepper. Cook for 1 minute, then slowly add milk, stirring constantly. When mixture is thick, add cheese and cook until cheese melts. Set aside. In large frying pan, sauté bacon or ham and onions in butter. Add eggs and cook until set. Add cheese sauce to egg mixture and pour into prepared baking dish. Combine melted butter, bread crumbs and paprika and sprinkle over egg mixture. Cover and refrigerate for 30 minutes or overnight. Bake uncovered at 350° for 30 minutes.

Serves 10

Huevos Rancheros

3 tablespoons butter or margarine
2 cloves garlic, chopped
8-12 green onions, chopped, reserving
    some tops for garnish
2 cans (14½-ounce) stewed tomatoes
½ teaspoon cumin

1 teaspoon oregano
2 tablespoons chili powder
12 eggs
2 cups Cheddar or Monterey Jack cheese,
    shredded
12 corn tortillas (6-inch), heated

Melt butter in large pan and lightly sauté garlic and onions. Add tomatoes, cumin, oregano and chili powder and let simmer for 20 minutes. (While sauce is simmering, mash tomatoes.) Make small "wells" in sauce with a spoon. Crack eggs into "wells", cover, and simmer until eggs have reached desired firmness. When eggs are 2-3 minutes from being done, top with cheese. Using slotted spoon, remove eggs from sauce and place on tortillas. Surround eggs with sauce and garnish with reserved onion tops.

Serves 6

Ham & Cheese Pastry Spirals

3 tablespoons butter or margarine
3 cups ham, finely chopped
1 green pepper, finely chopped
½ cup white or green onion, chopped

½ cup Swiss cheese, grated
½ cup mild Cheddar cheese, grated
1 package frozen puff pastry, thawed but
    kept cold

Melt butter in frying pan. Add ham, pepper and onion and sauté lightly. Drain excess liquid. Mix cheeses together in bowl. Remove one sheet of pastry dough from refrigerator and lay out on cutting board. Spread evenly with half of the ham mixture, leaving 1 inch of far edge bare. Cover with half of the cheese mixture. Roll up pastry and place seam side down. Cut into 1½-inch thick slices. Lay slices flat in 13x9-inch baking dish, leaving ½-1 inch space between each slice. Refrigerate baking dish. Repeat process with second pastry. Bake uncovered at 400° for 20-30 minutes, watching carefully so that spirals do not burn. When pastry is golden brown, remove from pan and set briefly on paper towel. Serve immediately.

Serves 8-16

The Alleghany County town of Cuba, New York, was known as the "Cheese Center of the World" in the early 1900s. Cheese produced there had a distinctive taste and sharpness, and aged faster than cheese made in other regions. Cheeses are still being produced there today.

Brunch Casserole

8 slices bread, torn into bite-sized pieces
¾ cup butter, melted
2 cups sharp Cheddar or Swiss cheese,
  shredded
2 cups broccoli, chopped and cooked
  (optional)

2 cups cooked chicken, tuna or ham in
  bite-sized pieces
4 eggs
2 cups milk
1 teaspoon salt
½ teaspoon pepper

In large bowl, toss bread pieces with melted butter. In bottom of greased 13x9-inch baking dish, layer ½ of the bread, ½ of the cheese, ½ of the broccoli (if using), and all of the meat. Top with remaining broccoli, cheese and bread. Set aside. In mixing bowl, beat together eggs, milk, salt and pepper. Pour mixture over top of casserole. Refrigerate for at least 2 hours or overnight. Bake uncovered at 350° for 60 minutes, watching it near end of cooking time so that it does not burn.

Serves 6-8

Breakfast Baked Potatoes

1 large onion, chopped
Vegetable oil, for sautéing
4 Idaho potatoes, scrubbed and baked
4 ounces ham, diced
4 eggs, hard-boiled and chopped
¾ cup sour cream
¼ teaspoon mustard powder

¼ teaspoon garlic powder
Salt and pepper, to taste
4 ounces Gruyère cheese, shredded
4 ounces pitted black olives, drained and
  sliced
2 tablespoons bacon bits

Lightly sauté onion in oil and set aside. Cut potatoes in half lengthwise and carefully scoop out potato. Place into food processor along with ham, eggs, sour cream, mustard powder, garlic powder, salt and pepper. Process until mixture is very fine. Transfer to a bowl and mix in onions. Spoon mixture into potato skins and top with cheese. Bake at 400° until cheese melts, approximately 10-15 minutes. Top with black olives and bacon bits and serve immediately.

Serves 4-8

Spinach & Cheese Quiche

1 package (10-ounce) frozen chopped
   spinach
2 eggs, beaten
1¼ cups cottage cheese
¼ cup sharp cheese, shredded
2 teaspoons Parmesan cheese, grated

1 teaspoon seasoned salt (optional)
¼ teaspoon pepper
Dash of onion powder
Dash of nutmeg
Dash of paprika

Cook spinach according to package directions and drain well. Set aside. Mix together remaining ingredients, then gently fold in spinach. Place mixture into a greased 8-inch pie plate and bake at 350° for 25 minutes.

Serves 4

Vegetable Quiche

2 tablespoons butter
1 small onion, chopped
1 green pepper, chopped
1 small zucchini, sliced
1 cup mushrooms, sliced
2 tablespoons flour

1 small tomato, diced
3 eggs
½ cup milk
1½ teaspoons seasoned salt
2 pie crusts (9-inch), unbaked
1 cup Cheddar cheese, shredded

Preheat oven to 375°. Melt butter in frying pan and add onion, pepper, zucchini and mushrooms. Sauté until vegetables wilt, approximately 7 minutes. Stir in flour and tomato and set aside. Beat together eggs, milk and seasoned salt. Place first crust into pie plate. Sprinkle with ½ cup of the cheese. Place second crust on top of cheese. Top second crust with vegetable mixture, then cover with egg mixture. Sprinkle with remaining cheese and bake for 40-45 minutes, or until knife inserted near center comes out clean. Let stand for about 10 minutes before serving.

Serves 6-8

In the early 1900s, Orator Woodward had started to produce a cereal beverage called Grain-O, but he dropped production when his other product, Jell-O, became popular.

Blueberry & Poppy Seed Brunch Cake

Cake

²⁄₃ cup sugar

½ cup butter or margarine, room
   temperature

2 teaspoons lemon zest, grated

1 egg

1½ cups flour

½ teaspoon baking soda

2 tablespoons poppy seeds

½ cup sour cream

Filling

2 cups fresh or frozen blueberries, drained

⅓ cup sugar

2 teaspoons flour

¼ teaspoon nutmeg

Powdered Sugar Glaze

Preheat oven to 350°. Grease and flour bottom and sides of 9 or 10-inch springform pan. In large mixing bowl, beat sugar and butter with electric mixer until light and fluffy. Add lemon zest and egg and beat for 2 minutes on medium speed. Set aside. In another bowl, combine flour, baking soda and poppy seeds. Add to butter mixture, alternating with sour cream. Pour batter into prepared pan. Set aside. In medium bowl, combine blueberries, sugar, flour and nutmeg, mixing well. Spoon over batter and bake for 45-55 minutes or until crust is golden brown. Cool slightly in pan, then remove sides. Drizzle with Powdered Sugar Glaze.

Serves 8

Powdered Sugar
Glaze

⅓ cup powdered
sugar

1-2 teaspoons milk

Combine powdered
sugar with enough
milk to reach desired
consistency. Blend
until smooth.

Orange Glazed Bowknots

2 cups flour

1 tablespoon baking powder

1 teaspoon salt

6 tablespoons shortening

²⁄₃ cup milk

Orange Glaze

Preheat oven to 450°. Combine flour, baking powder and salt in mixing bowl. Cut in shortening until mixture resembles coarse crumbs. Add milk and stir well with fork until mixture forms ball. Place on lightly floured surface and knead slightly. Roll dough to a thickness of ⅜-inch. Cut with doughnut cutter and twist dough into a figure 8. Place on cookie sheet and bake for 10-12 minutes. Allow bowknots to cool for approximately 5 minutes, then top with Orange Glaze. Serve immediately.

Makes 1 dozen

Orange Glaze

½ cup powdered
sugar

1 tablespoon orange
juice

2 teaspoons orange
zest, finely minced

Combine ingredients,
stirring until well
blended. Spread on
slightly cooled
bowknots.

Swedish Breakfast Biscuits

1½ cups sugar
1 cup butter, room temperature
3 eggs
Dash of salt

1 teaspoon baking powder
½ teaspoon cardamom
3 cups flour

Preheat oven to 350°. Grease a 13x9-inch pan. Cream sugar and butter in large bowl. Add eggs, one at a time, mixing well after each addition. Stir in remaining ingredients. Spread batter into prepared pan and bake for 30 minutes. Allow to cool, then cut into 1x3-inch slices. (Note: For a more traditional biscuit, bake slices again at 350° for 10 minutes.)

Makes approximately 3 dozen biscuits

Cinnamon Coffee Cake

2¼ cups flour
½ teaspoon salt
¾ cup vegetable oil
1 cup brown sugar, packed
¾ cup granulated sugar
¼ teaspoon ginger
2 teaspoons cinnamon

1 cup almonds, slivered, or walnuts or
  pecans, chopped
1 egg, beaten
1 teaspoon baking soda
1 teaspoon baking powder
1 cup buttermilk

Preheat oven to 350°. Grease a 13x9-inch baking dish. In large mixing bowl, combine flour, salt, oil, sugars, ginger and 1 teaspoon of the cinnamon. Mix with fork. To make topping, transfer ¾ cup of this mixture to a small bowl and add remaining cinnamon and nuts. Set aside. To mixture in large bowl, add egg, baking soda, baking powder and buttermilk. Beat with electric mixer until ingredients are well blended. Pour into prepared pan and cover with topping mixture. Bake for 35-40 minutes, or until toothpick inserted near center comes out clean.

Serves 10-12

Cranberry Coffee Cake

2 cups flour
1 teaspoon baking powder
1 teaspoon baking soda
½ teaspoon salt
½ cup butter or margarine, room
   temperature
1 cup sugar

2 eggs
1 teaspoon almond extract
1 cup sour cream
8 ounces whole cranberry sauce, broken up
½ cup almonds, chopped
Powdered sugar (optional)

Preheat oven to 350°. Grease 9-inch tube or 10-inch bundt pan. Mix together
flour, baking powder, baking soda and salt. Set aside. Beat butter until creamy,
then beat in sugar, ¼ cup at a time. Add eggs one at a time, beating well after each
addition. Stir in almond extract, then dry ingredients, alternating with sour
cream. Spoon half of the batter into prepared pan. Add half of the cranberry
sauce and swirl through batter. Spoon remaining batter over top of mixture, then
swirl in remaining cranberry sauce. Sprinkle with almonds and bake for 55
minutes. Cool on wire rack for 15 minutes, sprinkle with powdered sugar, if
desired, and serve.

Serves 10-12

SALADS

abandoned flour mills in Rochester became the home of the R. T. French Company. The company, owned by R. T.'s sons George and Francis, imported and ground spices as well as marketed herbs, extracts, coffee and tea. French's quickly became the largest manufacturer of mustard in Western New York. Mustard was not in great demand as a condiment for the home table until 1904, when French's developed a mild, golden-yellow prepared salad dressing with a true mustard flavor. French's Cream Salad Brand Mustard was first packaged with its own wooden serving paddle, at the cost of 10¢ for a nine-ounce jar. The mustard became an "overnight sensation", possibly helped by the introduction of hot dogs in buns at the Saint Louis World's Fair that same year. Mustard is now the second most widely used spice in the United States.

Because of the high-quality standards used in their business, George and Francis were asked to formulate the national standards for purity and labeling of spices for the Pure Food and Drug Act of 1906.

S A L A D S

Gemini Salad

This recipe was contributed by photographer Roxanne Malone.

Arugula is a slightly peppery-tasting plant from the mustard family. Watercress is also peppery to smell and taste, but it produces a cooling, refreshing effect in the mouth after eating.

Salad

1 small bunch watercress
1 small bunch arugula
1 medium Vidalia onion, thinly sliced
Juice of one lemon
Cold water, for soaking

1 clove garlic, whole
1 green sweet pepper, sliced
1 red sweet pepper, sliced
6 artichoke hearts, sliced
1 clove garlic, minced

Dressing

¼ cup cider or balsamic vinegar
Pinch of thyme
1 small bunch fresh basil, torn apart
⅛ teaspoon white pepper

⅛ cup olive oil
Pinch of salt (optional)
1 tablespoon honey (optional)

Soak watercress, arugula and onion in lemon juice and water in refrigerator for 1 hour. Thoroughly drain and pat dry. Rub sides of salad bowl with whole garlic clove. Combine salad ingredients in bowl. Combine dressing ingredients and pour over salad. Toss lightly and serve immediately.

Serves 4-5

Orange Dressing

2 teaspoons orange zest

1 teaspoon salt

1 teaspoon sugar

½ teaspoon dry mustard

⅓ cup wine vinegar

⅔ cup vegetable oil

1 clove garlic, minced

Combine all ingredients in large jar. Shake vigorously before serving on salad. (Note: Dressing may be made ahead and stored in refrigerator.)

Winter Salad Bowl

¼ bunch curly endive
1 medium head lettuce
½ onion, mild white or sweet red

1 ripe avocado, sliced
2 oranges, peeled and sliced
Orange Dressing

Wash, drain and tear apart endive and lettuce. Slice onion in rings. Arrange vegetables and fruit in large salad bowl, reserving several orange slices for garnish. Top with Orange Dressing.

Serves 8-10

Claremont Salad

Dressing
1½ cups sugar
1½ teaspoons celery seed
1½ teaspoons mustard seed

¾ cup white vinegar
¼ cup water

Salad
1 small-to-medium head of cabbage, quartered and thinly sliced
1 medium onion, white or red, thinly sliced
2 peppers, red or green, thinly sliced

1 cucumber, peeled and thinly shredded
2 carrots, thinly shredded
1 tablespoon salt
1 teaspoon pepper

Mix dressing ingredients in saucepan and bring to a boil. Reduce heat to simmer and cook for 10 minutes. Remove from heat and allow to cool. Combine salad ingredients in large bowl. Toss well with dressing. Refrigerate for at least 24 hours before serving, stirring occasionally. (Note: This salad keeps well for several weeks in the refrigerator.)

Serves 10-12

Tomato, Mozzarella & Basil Salad

2 tablespoons red wine vinegar
1 clove garlic, minced
½ teaspoon salt
¼ teaspoon dry mustard
Generous dash of pepper

⅓ cup olive oil
4 large Italian plum tomatoes
6 ounces mozzarella cheese
8-10 fresh basil leaves

Combine vinegar, garlic, salt, mustard and pepper in small bowl. Add oil and stir with whisk until oil is blended. Set aside. Slice tomatoes and cheese into ¼-inch slices. Place into shallow bowl or baking dish. Pour dressing mixture over slices, cover, and refrigerate for 30 minutes-3 hours, turning occasionally. Slice basil into strips. Arrange tomato and cheese slices alternately on serving plate, sprinkle with basil strips, and drizzle with dressing.

Serves 4-6

Jicama Salad

Salad

8 cups lettuce (iceberg, red or butter), torn
    into bite-sized pieces
1½ cups jicama, cut into thin strips
1 medium mild red onion, cut into rings

1 grapefruit (optional)
1 can (11-ounce) mandarin oranges,
    drained
½ pound cherry tomatoes, halved

Dressing

1 tablespoon cider vinegar
2 tablespoons lime juice
6 tablespoons olive oil
1 clove garlic
½ teaspoon salt

½ teaspoon cumin
⅛ teaspoon crushed red pepper
Black pepper, to taste
1 large avocado

In large salad bowl, mix lettuce and jicama. Arrange onion rings on top. If using grapefruit, remove peel and white membrane and cut into sections. Arrange over onions, along with mandarin oranges and tomatoes. Cover and refrigerate for 1-2 hours. Prepare dressing by combining all ingredients, except avocado, in blender or food processor. Blend well at high speed. Just before serving salad, peel, pit and slice avocado. Arrange on salad, add dressing and mix gently. (Note: Sliced water chestnuts may be substituted for the jicama.)

Serves 6-8

Zero Dressing

1 tablespoon onion, finely diced
1 tablespoon green pepper, finely diced
1 tablespoon cucumber, finely diced
3 tablespoons lemon juice
1-1½ cups tomato juice

1 teaspoon salt
Black pepper, to taste
1 clove garlic, finely minced
1 teaspoon thyme
⅛ teaspoon cayenne pepper

Combine onion, green pepper and cucumber. Add remaining ingredients, mix well, and refrigerate.

Makes 1¾ cups

This recipe is called Zero Dressing because it has no oil. It keeps for only four days, but if the green pepper and cucumber are eliminated, it will keep for one week. Experimenting with dehydrated vegetables and other herbs will add variety to this recipe.

Fennel Salad

2 fennel bulbs
3 tablespoons olive oil
2 tablespoons red wine vinegar
⅛ teaspoon salt

Pepper, freshly ground, to taste
1 teaspoon fresh mint, chopped
Orange slices, for garnish

Remove hair-like ends and outer layer of fennel bulb. Cut bulb into quarters and remove center core. Chop fennel into small pieces. Add remaining ingredients and toss well. Garnish with orange slices.

Serves 4

Sweet Pepper Salad

6 tablespoons white vinegar
2 tablespoons sherry
1 tablespoon Worcestershire sauce
6 tablespoons olive oil
½ teaspoon salt
¼ teaspoon black pepper

2 teaspoons sugar
1 teaspoon paprika
4 green peppers, cut into thin strips
4 red peppers, cut into thin strips
12 pitted black olives, drained and halved
8 ounces feta cheese, cubed

Feta cheese can be very salty. To get rid of some of the salt, rinse carefully in water or soak in milk for at least one hour.

In large bowl, combine first eight ingredients, mixing well. Stir in green and red pepper strips. Marinate in refrigerator for 24 hours. To serve, drain peppers, reserving a small amount of marinade. Place in shallow serving dish and top with olives and cheese. Spoon reserved marinade over top of salad.

Serves 10-12

Curried Spinach Salad

Dressing

¼ cup white wine vinegar

¼ cup vegetable oil

2 tablespoons mango chutney, chopped

2 teaspoons sugar

½ teaspoon salt

1½ teaspoons curry powder

1 teaspoon dry mustard

Salad

10 ounces fresh spinach, stems removed, torn into pieces

½ cup cucumber, peeled and thinly sliced

1½ cups apples, unpeeled and thinly sliced

½ cup seedless red grapes, halved

½ cup peanuts

2 tablespoons scallions, sliced

Combine all dressing ingredients in jar with tight-fitting lid. Mix well and chill. In large bowl, combine salad ingredients. Shake dressing, pour over salad, and toss.

Serves 6

Spinach Salad Dressing

1 cup sugar

2 teaspoons salt

1 teaspoon dry mustard

1 teaspoon celery seed

1 small onion, grated

¾ cup vinegar

2 cups vegetable oil

Combine all ingredients in large jar with lid. Refrigerate. Shake well before serving.

Makes 2¾ cups

Raspberry Spinach Salad

10 cups fresh spinach, trimmed, washed and drained

1 cup fresh raspberries

1 cup macadamia nuts or chopped walnuts

3 kiwi fruit, peeled and sliced

Raspberry Dressing

Tear apart spinach. Combine with remaining salad ingredients and top with Raspberry Dressing. (Note: Red lettuce may be substituted for part of the spinach.)

Serves 8-10

Raspberry Dressing

4 tablespoons raspberry vinegar

4 tablespoons raspberry jam

1 cup vegetable oil

Place raspberry vinegar and jam in blender and mix. Add oil and blend.

Spinach Combo Salad

7 ounces cheese-filled tortellini, frozen
6 cups fresh spinach, washed and lightly
   packed
1 cup red cabbage, coarsely shredded

6 slices crisp bacon, drained and crumbled
4 green onions, sliced
Chutney Dressing

In large saucepan, cook tortellini according to directions. Drain and rinse in cold
water. Drain again. In large salad bowl, toss together tortellini, spinach, cabbage,
bacon, and onions. Cover and chill. Serve with dressing.

Serves 12

Chutney Dressing

¼ cup chutney

⅓ cup prepared red
wine vinegar and oil
salad dressing

Pepper, freshly
ground, to taste

Cut smaller any large
pieces of chutney.
Combine all
ingredients in
covered jar and chill.
Shake well just before
serving and toss with
salad.

Pea Salad

Salad
20 ounces frozen peas, thawed
1 cup dry roasted peanuts
½ cup celery, chopped

1 can (5-ounce) sliced water chestnuts,
   drained
2 tablespoons onion, chopped

Dressing
½ cup favorite Italian dressing
½ cup sour cream

¼-½ teaspoon curry powder

Mix together salad ingredients in large serving bowl. In smaller bowl, combine
dressing ingredients. Pour dressing over salad and chill before serving.

Serves 10-12

Curry Dressing

2 cups mayonnaise
3 tablespoons ketchup
3 tablespoons honey
3 tablespoons onion, grated

1 teaspoon lemon juice
1 tablespoon curry powder
7-8 drops red pepper sauce

Combine all ingredients. Let stand for several hours to blend flavors. Serve as a
dressing for chicken salad, as a dip with vegetables or as a sauce for chicken or
pork.

Makes 2-2½ cups

Black Bean & Fresh Corn Salad

Dressing
4 tablespoons red wine vinegar
1 tablespoon sugar

1 tablespoon water
½ teaspoon ground cumin

Salad
1 red bell pepper, chopped
½ green bell pepper, chopped
2 tablespoons red onion, chopped
4 tablespoons fresh cilantro, chopped

5 ears corn, cooked and cut off cob
1 can (16-ounce) black beans, drained and rinsed well
Salt and pepper, to taste

Mix together dressing ingredients. In large bowl, combine salad ingredients. Add dressing and mix well. (Note: May substitute 2 cups canned or frozen corn.)

Serves 6-8

Crunchy Broccoli Salad

2 bunches broccoli
½ cup celery, chopped
½ cup raisins
½ pound crisp bacon, crumbled
½ cup walnuts, peanuts, almonds, or sunflower seeds, whole or chopped

½ cup onion, chopped
8 ounces water chestnuts, sliced and drained
Broccoli Salad Dressing

Broccoli Salad Dressing

1¼ cups mayonnaise

⅔ cup sugar

¼ cup + 2 tablespoons vinegar

2 tablespoons lemon juice

Combine ingredients and mix with salad.

Rinse broccoli well in cold water and peel stalks. Chop into bite-sized pieces. Add remaining ingredients and mix with dressing. Refrigerate and serve cold.

Serves 4-6

Cucumber & Radish Salad

2 cucumbers, peeled
6 radishes, finely julienned
1 scallion, thinly sliced
4 teaspoons balsamic vinegar
1 teaspoon sugar

Salt, to taste
2 tablespoons cashew or macadamia nuts,
    coarsely chopped
1 kiwi fruit, peeled, sliced and halved

Quarter cucumbers lengthwise and run a knife under seeds to remove. Slice cucumbers at an angle into ½-inch-thick pieces. Place in serving bowl and toss with radishes, scallion, vinegar, sugar and salt. Chill until ready to serve. Arrange salad on four serving plates and garnish with nuts and kiwi slices.

Serves 4

Fresh Vegetable Relish

1 pound summer squash, cut into strips
    1-inch long
1½ cups bell and chili peppers, assorted
    colors, cut into thin strips 1-inch long
½ cup green onion, sliced
½ cup celery, cut into thin strips
    1-inch long
2 cloves garlic, minced

¼ cup fresh basil leaves, thinly shredded
⅔ cup red wine vinegar
⅓ cup sugar
1 teaspoon salt
Pepper, to taste
¼ cup olive oil
3 plum tomatoes, cut into quarters
    and halved

Combine squash, peppers, onion, celery, garlic and basil in large bowl. In measuring cup or small bowl, combine vinegar, sugar, salt and pepper. Stir to dissolve solids. Add oil. Toss vegetables and dressing together. Cover and refrigerate for at least 30 minutes, or up to 8 hours. Just before serving, add tomatoes and toss.

Serves 6-8

Marinated Sesame Asparagus

3 teaspoons sugar
3 teaspoons sesame oil
6 teaspoons soy sauce

1 pound asparagus spears, trimmed and
  blanched
1 tablespoon roasted sesame seeds

Blend sugar, sesame oil and soy sauce. Add asparagus and marinate in refrigerator for at least 4 hours, turning one or more times. To serve, arrange asparagus on individual plates. Pour a small amount of marinade over asparagus and sprinkle with sesame seeds.

Serves 6-8

Jellied Asparagus Salad

1 can (10¾-ounce) cream of asparagus
  soup, undiluted
3 ounces lemon-flavored gelatin
8 ounces cream cheese, room temperature
½ cup cold water

½ cup mayonnaise
¾ cup celery, chopped
1 tablespoon green onion, chopped
½ cup green pepper, chopped
½ cup pecans, chopped

In large saucepan, heat soup to boiling, then remove from heat. Add gelatin, stirring until dissolved. Add cream cheese and mix until melted. Add water and mayonnaise, beating until blended, then stir in remaining ingredients. Pour into twelve individual 3-ounce molds, or one 40-ounce mold. Refrigerate until set, at least 3 hours.

Serves 12

Dilled Asparagus

1½ pounds fresh asparagus or 3 packages
   frozen
¼ cup mayonnaise
½ cup plain yogurt

¼ cup Dijon mustard
1 tablespoon fresh dill weed, minced
1 tablespoon fresh chives, minced
Salt and pepper, to taste

Cook asparagus for 5 minutes, or just until tender. Cool. Mix together remaining ingredients and pour over asparagus. Chill overnight.

Serves 6-8

Dilly Potato Salad

5 pounds potatoes
¼ cup prepared French dressing
1 cup sour cream
2 cups mayonnaise
½ cup sweet onion, minced

½ cup green pepper, minced
1-2 tablespoons dill weed
1 teaspoon salt
1 teaspoon pepper, freshly ground
Fresh dill weed, for garnish

Boil potatoes in large kettle. Allow potatoes to cool slightly and cut into large chunks. In bowl, combine remaining ingredients, except dill weed for garnish. Pour mixture over hot potatoes. Let mixture sit for 30 minutes so potatoes absorb marinade. Transfer to serving bowl and garnish with dill. Cover and refrigerate for several hours.

Serves 10

Warm Tortellini Almond Salad

Dressing

12 ounces marinated artichokes, with
  liquid
½ cup fresh Parmesan cheese, grated

1 tablespoon Dijon mustard
¼ teaspoon dill weed

Salad

1 cup whole almonds
1 pound meat or cheese-filled tortellini
1 small head iceberg lettuce, chopped into
  bite-sized pieces

1 cup mushrooms, sliced
1 red pepper, cut into strips
¼-½ cup green onions, sliced

Remove artichokes from marinade and set aside. Combine marinade with cheese, mustard and dill weed. Preheat oven to 350*. Spread almonds on baking pan and toast for 15 minutes. Cook tortellini according to package directions and drain. Chop artichokes and mix with hot tortellini, almonds, lettuce, mushrooms, pepper and onions. Toss with dressing and serve warm. (Note: Leftovers served cold are also delicious!)

Serves 4-6

Fiesta Pasta Salad

Dressing

½ cup orange juice
½ cup vegetable oil
1 tablespoon orange zest, grated
1 tablespoon sugar

1 tablespoon basil, crushed
¼ teaspoon pepper, freshly ground
⅛ teaspoon nutmeg

Salad

1 can (20-ounce) pineapple chunks,
  drained and halved
½ pound pasta shells, cooked
2 navel oranges, peeled and cubed
1 red bell pepper, julienned

1-2 carrots, julienned
1 cup frozen peas, thawed
3-4 scallions, chopped
1 cup cashews

Combine dressing ingredients, blending well. Set aside. Combine salad ingredients in large bowl. Pour dressing over salad and toss well. Cover and refrigerate for at least 4 hours, or overnight.

Serves 6-8

Tuscan Chicken & White Bean Salad

Dressing

1 clove garlic, minced

¼ teaspoon salt

3 tablespoons fresh lemon juice

1½ tablespoons Dijon mustard

1¼ teaspoons thyme

¼ cup extra-virgin olive oil

Salad

3 cups chicken breast, cooked and cut into chunks

15 ounces white kidney beans, drained

1½ cups celery, chopped

¾ cup Vidalia or Bermuda onion, chopped

⅓ cup fresh parsley, chopped

Mash garlic with salt. Stir in lemon juice, mustard and thyme. Add olive oil and stir with whisk until thick. Set aside. Combine salad ingredients and mix with dressing. Chill until ready to serve.

Serves 4-6

Chilled Chicken & Rice Salad

¾ cup wild rice

2½ cups chicken broth

¾ cup long-grain white rice

¾ cup broccoli florets

¾ cup carrots, julienned or thinly sliced

2½ cups chicken breast, cooked and cut into bite-sized pieces

3 green onions (including tops), sliced

½ pound mushrooms, sliced

1 large red pepper, sliced

1½ cups fresh spinach, cut into strips

2 tablespoons parsley, chopped

White Wine Dressing

Combine wild rice and chicken broth in saucepan. Bring to a boil, cover, and simmer for 15 minutes. Add white rice and continue simmering for another 20-25 minutes, until liquid is absorbed. Chill. Steam broccoli and carrots and chill. Combine rice, broccoli, carrots and remaining salad ingredients in large bowl. Mix with White Wine Dressing just before serving.

Serves 6-8

White Wine Dressing

⅔ cup dry white wine

¼ cup olive oil

4 teaspoons sugar

1 teaspoon dry mustard

½ teaspoon salt

½ teaspoon pepper

Combine all ingredients in jar with tight-fitting lid. Shake well before serving.

Oriental Chicken Salad

Dressing

6 tablespoons soy sauce

½ cup water

3 tablespoons sesame oil

¾ cup red wine vinegar

½ teaspoon sugar

Salad

3 cups Romaine lettuce, torn into bite-sized pieces

1 cup chicken, cooked and cubed

Red onion, sliced, to taste

6-8 mushrooms, sliced

¼ cup toasted almonds, slivered

Combine dressing ingredients and set aside. In large salad bowl, combine lettuce, chicken, onion and mushrooms. Cover with dressing and toss. Sprinkle with almonds. Serve slightly chilled or at room temperature.

Serves 4-8

Oriental Tuna Salad

Salad

1 pound fresh tuna, cooked and cut into chunks

5 ounces frozen peas, thawed

6 ounces cocktail onions

⅔ cup celery, chopped

⅓ cup sliced water chestnuts, halved

2 ounces toasted almonds, slivered

Dressing

1 cup mayonnaise

½ teaspoon lemon juice

1 teaspoon soy sauce

½ teaspoon curry powder

In large bowl, mix together salad ingredients. In smaller bowl, combine dressing ingredients. Pour dressing onto salad and carefully mix together. Refrigerate until ready to serve. (Note: Three cans (6½-ounce) of chunk-style tuna, drained, may be substituted for fresh.)

Serves 6-8

Artichoke & Shrimp Pizzazz

Marinade

1 cup vegetable oil
½ cup vinegar
4 tablespoons Dijon mustard

4 tablespoons fresh parsley, chopped
4 tablespoons onion, chopped
Salt and pepper, to taste

Salad

1 pound shrimp, cooked, peeled and
  deveined

1 can (28-ounce) artichoke hearts, drained
  and quartered
Lettuce leaves

Blend marinade ingredients in blender. Place shrimp and artichoke hearts in bowl, cover with marinade, and marinate overnight in refrigerator. Drain and serve on individual plates lined with lettuce leaves.

Serves 8

Shrimp Salad

1½ pounds shrimp, cooked, peeled and
  deveined
4 eggs, hard-boiled and chopped
1 teaspoon dry mustard
2 tablespoons parsley, chopped
2 tablespoons green pepper, chopped
1 teaspoon onion, grated

8 stuffed olives, thinly sliced
4 teaspoons anchovy paste
⅛-¼ teaspoon Worcestershire sauce
1 cup mayonnaise
Lettuce, for serving
Green olives, for garnish

Cut shrimp in half, if large. Combine with eggs, mustard, parsley, green pepper, onion and olives. Set aside. Mix together anchovy paste, Worcestershire sauce and mayonnaise. Gently combine with shrimp mixture and serve in lettuce-lined bowl. Garnish with additional olives, if desired.

Serves 4-5

Salmon Mousse

1 can (14¾-ounce) red salmon, drained and flaked
1 cup mayonnaise
2 tablespoons lemon juice
2 tablespoons onion, grated

2 tablespoons horseradish
2 tablespoons celery, chopped
4 drops red pepper sauce
1 envelope unflavored gelatin
¼ cup water

Combine salmon, mayonnaise, lemon juice, onion, horseradish, celery and red pepper sauce in large bowl. Stir gelatin and water in saucepan over medium heat until gelatin dissolves. Pour gelatin over salmon and mix well. Coat one 3½-cup or several smaller molds with oil or mayonnaise and fill with salmon mixture. Refrigerate until set.

Serves 6-8

Strawberry Salad

Honey-Mint Dressing
3 tablespoons olive oil
1 tablespoon honey
1 tablespoon tarragon white wine vinegar
1 clove garlic

½ teaspoon salt
¼ teaspoon mint leaves, dried
⅛ teaspoon pepper, freshly ground

Salad
1 head Boston lettuce
1 ripe avocado, pitted, pared and cut lengthwise into slices

1 pint strawberries, washed and hulled
½ cup seedless green grapes
¼ cup walnut pieces

Mix all dressing ingredients in jar and shake well. Let stand covered at room temperature for 3 hours. Before serving, remove garlic clove and discard. Arrange lettuce leaves in salad bowl. Arrange remaining salad ingredients over lettuce. Pour dressing over salad and toss.

Serves 8

Mustard and horseradish are both members of the diverse Cruciferae family of plants. Some other vegetables from the family are cabbage, cauliflower, rutabaga and watercress. Both mustard seeds and horseradish root need to be crushed or broken to release the oils that give off their unique flavors.

Orange & Poppy Seed Salad

Scant ½ cup sugar
¼ teaspoon salt
1 tablespoon honey mustard
   (or ½ teaspoon dry mustard and
   1 teaspoon honey)
2 teaspoons frozen orange juice
   concentrate

¼ cup cider vinegar
½ cup vegetable oil
¼ cup avocado or olive oil
1 tablespoon poppy seeds
1 tablespoon orange zest, freshly grated
Chilled lettuce
Toppings (see below)

Mix together sugar, salt, mustard, orange juice concentrate, and vinegar. Add the
two oils, beating constantly until dressing is slightly thickened. Add poppy seeds
and orange zest. Store covered in refrigerator. To serve, lightly spoon dressing
over chilled lettuce topped with one of the following possibilities:

   Fresh orange slices, purple onion rings, toasted pecan pieces
   Diced apples, celery, grape halves, toasted pecan pieces
   Orange sections, pitted prune halves, toasted pecan pieces
   Strawberries, purple onion rings, toasted pecan pieces
   Shredded red and green cabbage, apple or pineapple bites
   Pear slices, pitted prune halves

Makes approximately 1 cup dressing

Light & Fruity Tossed Salad

Dressing
½ cup vegetable oil
1 cup cider vinegar
1¼ teaspoons salt

1 cup sugar
½ teaspoon pepper
1 clove garlic

Salad
1 large bunch red leaf lettuce, washed and
   torn into bite-sized pieces
2 scallions, sliced

1 can (15-ounce) mandarin oranges,
   drained
¼ cup almonds, sliced or walnuts, chopped

Mix dressing ingredients together in blender at least one day in advance
(dressing improves with age). Combine salad ingredients and toss sparingly with
dressing, since flavor is strong. (Note: For variety, substitute one pint fresh
strawberries for oranges.)

Serves 8-10

Cranberry Mousse

1 cup cranberry juice cocktail
3 ounces raspberry-flavored gelatin

1 can (16-ounce) whole cranberry sauce
1 cup heavy cream, whipped

Heat cranberry juice cocktail to boiling in medium saucepan. Remove from heat and add raspberry gelatin, stirring until dissolved. Stir in cranberry sauce. Refrigerate until mixture has thickened. Fold in whipped cream and pour into a 3½-cup mold. Chill until firm. Garnish with raspberries or additional whipped cream, if desired.

Serves 6-8

Frozen Fruit Salad Cups

1 can (20-ounce) crushed pineapple, drained
1 pint sour cream
½ cup sugar
⅛ teaspoon salt
Red food coloring

1 banana, sliced
2 tablespoons lemon juice
1 can (16-ounce) pitted dark sweet cherries, drained
¼ cup pecans, chopped
Lettuce leaves

Combine pineapple, sour cream, sugar, salt and a few drops of food coloring in large bowl. Stir in banana, lemon juice, cherries and pecans, mixing well. Spoon into paper-lined muffin tins and freeze. When frozen, remove from tins and store in plastic bag in freezer. Remove from freezer 20 minutes before serving. Remove paper liner and serve on lettuce-lined plate.

Serves 12

Stuffed Peach Salad

Celery Seed Dressing
½ cup sugar
2 tablespoons flour
1 teaspoon paprika
½ cup vinegar
½ teaspoon onion, grated

1 teaspoon salt (optional)
½ cup vegetable oil
Boiling water
1 teaspoon celery seed

Filling
½ cup dates, chopped
¼ cup pecans, chopped
½ cup celery, finely chopped
⅓ cup Celery Seed Dressing

5 fresh peach halves, pitted and peeled
  (see p. 38)
Lemon juice
Lettuce leaves

Mix sugar, flour and paprika in saucepan. Blend in vinegar. Cook over low heat until thick, stirring constantly. Add onion and salt (if using). Remove from heat and allow mixture to cool. Gradually add oil, beating until thoroughly blended. Pour a small amount of boiling water over celery seed and let stand for 30 seconds. Drain off water and add seed to dressing, mixing well. Chill. Combine dates, pecans, celery and dressing. Sprinkle peach halves with a small amount of lemon juice and place on individual plates lined with lettuce leaves. Spoon filling into peach halves and serve. (Note: One can (16-ounce) peach halves, drained, may be substituted for fresh peaches.)

Serves 5

MEATS

the 19th century, the owners of a saloon on Front Street in Rochester offered a free lunch with a nickel beer. The centerpiece of the lunch was a grayish-white bratwurst sausage made with stale bread and pork. The sausage became so popular that Rochester Packing Company soon began to mass-produce the "white hot". When the company later became the Tobin Packing Company, the white hot was dropped. However, consumer demand soon brought it back, with dried fresh bread replacing the stale. In 1942, Tobin was the first sausage company in Rochester to undergo United States Government Inspection, with the result that they could no longer use bread in any sausage product. The white hots, also known as pork hots, are now made with pork, milk and eggs and are only available in the Rochester area.

Tobin was the first company to parboil hot dogs to insure their quality for the consumer. They also produced the Texas hot, a fat red hot dog that is often paired with the white hot. In 1926, Zweigle's Inc., another local producer of white and Texas hots, sold the first hot dog in a baseball park in Rochester.

MEATS

Grilled Pork Marinade

This recipe was contributed by photographer Woody Packard.

3 tablespoons olive oil
3 tablespoons Dijon mustard
3 tablespoons fresh rosemary or marjoram, minced, or 1 tablespoon dried
6 tablespoons lemon juice

3 tablespoons soy sauce
3 cloves garlic, minced
Black pepper, freshly ground, to taste
6 pork chops

Combine all ingredients except meat, mixing well. Pour over pork chops and marinate in refrigerator for at least 1 hour. Grill meat over hot fire to desired doneness. (Note: This marinade works equally well for lamb chops.)

Serves 6

Stuffed Pork Chops

6 pork chops (2-inches thick), with pockets
Salt and pepper, to taste
2 tablespoons onion, chopped
¼ cup celery, chopped
1 tablespoon butter
3 slices whole wheat bread, cubed one day ahead
2 slices white bread, cubed one day ahead
3 ounces mushrooms, chopped

¼ teaspoon poultry seasoning
¼ teaspoon ground sage
⅛ teaspoon salt
Dash of pepper
2 tablespoons chicken broth or orange juice
½ apple, cored, peeled and shredded
1 egg
Orange juice

Preheat oven to 350°. Sprinkle inside and outside of pork chops with salt and pepper. Brown chops and set aside. Sauté onion and celery in butter. In a large bowl, mix onion and celery with remaining ingredients, except orange juice. Stuff pork chops and secure with wooden toothpicks. Arrange meat in 13x9-inch baking dish and add enough orange juice to cover bottom of dish. Cover and bake for 1 hour. Uncover dish and bake for an additional 15 minutes.

Serves 6

White Hots & Cabbage

6 slices bacon
1 head savoy cabbage, cut up
2 cloves garlic, minced
1 large onion, sliced
Salt and pepper, to taste

1-2 tablespoons sugar (optional)
½ cup water
1 teaspoon seasoned salt
1 pound white hot dogs, cut into bite-sized
   pieces

In large frying pan, cook bacon and remove from pan to absorbent paper. Add
cabbage, garlic, onion, salt, pepper, sugar (if using), water and seasoned salt to
bacon fat in frying pan. Cover and cook for 20 minutes over medium-low heat,
stirring occasionally. Add hot dogs, cover pan, and cook for an additional 10
minutes. Crumble bacon and sprinkle over mixture. (Note: If white hot dogs are
not available, Kielbasa sausage may be substituted.)

Serves 6

Roast Loin of Pork with Apple Cream

Pork loin roast (4 pounds)
½ teaspoon garlic powder
½ bay leaf, crushed
Salt and pepper, to taste
1 cup dry white wine

1 cup applesauce
2 apples, cored, peeled and sliced
¼ cup brown sugar, packed
½ cup heavy cream

Preheat oven to 350°. Rub roast with garlic powder, bay leaf, salt and pepper and
place in roasting pan. Pour wine over roast and bake for 60 minutes, basting
frequently. Skim off excess fat. Spread applesauce over meat, place apples in
bottom of pan and sprinkle roast with brown sugar. Continue to baste frequently.
Bake for another 40-60 minutes, or until roast reaches internal temperature of
160°-165°. Remove from pan. Add cream to mixture in bottom of pan, bring to
a boil to heat through, and serve over roast.

Serves 8

Oriental Pork Tenderloin

¼ cup soy sauce
1 tablespoon fresh ginger, grated
2 tablespoons honey

1 teaspoon garlic powder
Pork tenderloin (1½ pounds)

Mix first four ingredients in large bowl. Add pork and marinate at room temperature for 4 hours. Place under broiler. Cook until done, approximately 20-30 minutes, occasionally basting pork with marinade.

Serves 4-6

Grilled Leg of Lamb

2 cups dry vermouth
½ cup vegetable oil
2 tablespoons tarragon vinegar
⅓ cup onion, finely chopped
1 tablespoon parsley, finely chopped
1 teaspoon basil leaves
1 teaspoon garlic powder

1 bay leaf, crumbled
½ teaspoon pepper
½ teaspoon Worcestershire sauce
Leg of lamb (6-7 pounds), trimmed, boned
   and butterflied
1 lemon, thinly sliced

Combine all ingredients except lamb and lemon slices. Pour into large shallow dish or roasting pan. Add meat, cover pan and refrigerate for 2 days, turning meat occasionally. Remove meat from marinade and place on grill over medium-hot coals. Reserve marinade. Grill lamb for approximately 50 minutes, turning every 10-15 minutes. Brush occasionally with marinade. Cut crosswise into thin slices, garnish with lemon slices and serve.

Serves 10

Sosaties (Lamb Kebabs)

3 onions, cut in thick slices
1-2 tablespoons vegetable oil
5 tablespoons apricot jam
2 tablespoons vinegar
2 tablespoons brown sugar, packed
2 bay leaves
3 cloves garlic, chopped

2½ teaspoons salt
1 teaspoon pepper
2 tablespoons curry powder, or to taste
Leg of lamb (1 pound), cut into 1-inch
   squares
9 ounces dried apricots

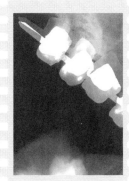

Separate onion slices into rings. Heat oil in frying pan and sauté onion rings for
1-2 minutes, making sure that rings stay whole. Remove rings from oil and drain
well on paper towel. Make marinade by mixing apricot jam, vinegar, brown sugar,
bay leaves, garlic, salt, pepper and curry powder in bowl. Add onion rings and
lamb, coating each piece of meat. Marinate for 24 hours in refrigerator, turning
meat 2-3 times. Soak apricots in water until plump. Remove meat and onion
rings from marinade. Place on skewers, alternating with apricots. Grill on
barbecue or broil in oven to desired doneness, turning for even cooking. Place
marinade in saucepan and bring to a boil. Serve sosaties and sauce separately with
potatoes or rice.

Serves 3-4

Garlic Lamb Kebabs

1 cup olive oil
⅓ cup lemon juice
¼ cup mild prepared mustard
2 cloves garlic, minced
1-2 teaspoons cumin

2 pounds boneless lamb, cut into chunks
Green pepper, cut into squares
Cherry tomatoes
Fresh mint leaves or parsley, for garnish
Garlic Sour Cream

Combine first five ingredients, mixing well. Place lamb in large dish and cover
with marinade. Marinate overnight in refrigerator. Place lamb and vegetables on
skewers and broil or grill until lamb is pink, about 15 minutes. Garnish with mint
or parsley, and serve with Garlic Sour Cream.

Serves 4

Garlic Sour Cream

2 cups sour cream

4 cloves garlic,
minced

½ teaspoon salt

Combine ingredients
and refrigerate for
several hours.

Butterflied Lamb with Cilantro

Leg of lamb (5 pounds), trimmed, boned and butterflied
½ cup fresh cilantro, packed
3 large cloves garlic
4 tablespoons olive oil (preferably extra-virgin)

3 tablespoons vinegar, balsamic or red wine
⅛ teaspoon pepper, freshly ground
1 bunch fresh cilantro, for garnish

One day ahead, score meat and lightly pound to insure uniform thickness. Combine cilantro, garlic, oil, vinegar and pepper in food processor. Process until finely chopped. Place lamb in large, shallow dish and cover with marinade. The next day, remove dish from refrigerator and bake lamb at 350° for 20 minutes per pound. Garnish with fresh cilantro and serve.

Serves 8

Veal Spedini

This recipe came from New York State's Executive Mansion.

1 pound veal, cut for spedini into 3-inch squares
32 ounces crushed tomatoes
2 cups bread crumbs
½ cup locatelli or Parmesan cheese, grated
6 sprigs parsley, chopped

9 tablespoons corn oil, divided
¼ pound Italian fontina cheese, cut into 1-inch pieces
2 medium onions, sliced
12 bay leaves

Marinate veal spedini in crushed tomatoes overnight or at least two hours before preparing. Combine bread crumbs with cheese and parsley in a bowl. Put 6 tablespoons of the oil in frying pan and cook bread crumb mixture until golden. Set aside to cool. Lightly coat bottom of a 13x9-inch baking dish with remaining oil. Remove spedinis from tomatoes and set tomatoes aside. Coat each spedini on both sides with bread crumb mixture. Place one piece of fontina cheese in center of each spedini square. Overlap opposite sides of veal over cheese. Place spedini in rows in baking dish, covering each with 1 onion slice and 1 bay leaf. Spread crushed tomatoes over spedini. Bake at 375° for 30 minutes.

Serves 6

Veal French ~ The Rio

6 veal slices (2 ounces each), top round
Flour seasoned with salt and pepper,
   for dredging
2 eggs, lightly beaten
2 tablespoons vegetable oil

1 teaspoon shallots, minced
¼ cup + 2 tablespoons medium dry sherry
1 tablespoon fresh lemon juice
2 tablespoons unsalted butter
2 teaspoons fresh parsley, minced

Pound veal slices between layers of plastic wrap to ⅛-inch thickness. Dredge veal
in flour, shaking off excess and dip in eggs, letting excess drip off. In large non-
stick skillet, heat 1 tablespoon of the oil over moderately high heat until oil is hot
but not smoking. Sauté veal in batches until golden, approximately 1 minute on
each side. Add remaining oil as necessary and transfer veal to serving platter. Keep
warm. Add shallots and sherry to skillet and carefully ignite. Reduce heat to
moderately low and cook mixture, stirring constantly, until flames go out. Add
lemon juice and butter, stirring until butter is melted. Pour sauce over veal and
sprinkle with parsley.

Serves 2

Veal Goulash

¼ cup margarine
2-3 yellow onions, chopped
2 pounds veal shoulder, cubed
½ teaspoon salt
½ teaspoon pepper
1 tablespoon paprika

1 cup water
¼ cup cream or water
1 tablespoon flour
1 teaspoon vinegar
1 teaspoon tomato paste

Melt margarine in large frying pan and sauté onions until soft. Reduce heat to
simmer and add veal, salt, pepper and paprika. Cook, covered, for approximately
1 hour, adding water ¼ cup at a time as necessary. Remove meat from pan and set
aside. In small bowl, mix together cream and flour until mixture is smooth. Pour
into liquid in frying pan and cook slightly. Add vinegar and tomato paste, mixing
well. Return veal to pan and coat with sauce. Serve hot.

Serves 4

Veal Tarragon

1 pound veal cutlets
¼ cup flour
1 teaspoon salt
½ teaspoon pepper
¼ cup olive oil

14½ ounces chicken broth
1 teaspoon tarragon
1 tablespoon lemon juice
1 tablespoon cold water

Place cutlets between pieces of waxed paper and pound to make them thin. Put flour, salt and pepper into a plastic bag and shake cutlets, one or two at a time, to coat. Save remaining flour mixture. Place oil in frying pan, add cutlets, and brown them over medium heat. Remove veal from pan and drain excess oil. Pour chicken broth into pan and bring to a boil, stirring often to loosen browned bits. Return cutlets to pan and sprinkle with tarragon. Reduce heat, cover pan, and simmer for 10 minutes. Add lemon juice. Remove cutlets from pan and keep warm. Mix reserved flour mixture with cold water and add to pan to make thick gravy. Pour over cutlets and serve immediately. (Note: This recipe also works well with turkey cutlets.)

Serves 5-6

Summer Casserole

1 pound ground beef
1 pound mild Italian sausage
1 large onion, chopped
1 green pepper, cut into strips
1 quart spaghetti sauce

4-5 medium yellow squash or zucchini, sliced
½ pound mozzarella cheese, thinly sliced
½ cup Parmesan cheese

Brown meats in heavy skillet. Add onion and pepper and sauté until tender. Drain off and discard excess liquid. Add spaghetti sauce and simmer for 1-1½ hours. Put half of the squash or zucchini into 13x9-inch pan. Cover with half of the sauce and meat mixture, then with half of the mozzarella cheese. Make second layer, using remaining ingredients. Top with Parmesan cheese and bake at 350° for 45 minutes.

Serves 6-10

Boboti

1 slice white bread, crust removed
⅓ cup milk
2 pounds ground lamb or beef
1 medium onion, chopped
½ cup raisins
½ cup blanched almonds, whole or halved
2 tablespoons apricot jam
2-3 tablespoons fruit chutney, or to taste

2-4 teaspoons curry powder, or to taste
5 teaspoons lemon juice
1 teaspoon turmeric
2 teaspoons salt
2 teaspoons vegetable oil
3 eggs
½ cup milk
Fresh bay leaves, for garnish

Soak bread in milk. Drain milk from bread, squeezing bread to remove excess. Crumble bread and mix with all ingredients except oil, eggs, milk and bay leaves. Heat oil in pan and lightly brown meat mixture. Place in 2-quart casserole, smoothing top. (Boboti may be frozen at this point, then defrosted before continuing with next steps.) Beat eggs and milk together and pour over meat mixture. Garnish with bay leaves. Bake at 350° for approximately 50 minutes. May be served with rice, chopped fresh tomatoes, sliced bananas, coconut, chutney and vegetables.

Serves 6-8

Spicy Slow-Cook Barbecue

1½ pounds stew beef
1½ pounds pork, cubed
2 cups onions, chopped
3 green peppers, chopped
6 ounces tomato paste
½ cup brown sugar, packed

¼ cup cider vinegar
¼ cup chili powder
2 teaspoons salt
2 teaspoons Worcestershire sauce
1 teaspoon dry mustard

Combine all ingredients in 3½ to 5-quart crockpot. Cover and cook on high for 8 hours, stirring occasionally. Before serving, stir mixture with wire whisk until meat is shredded. Serve on sandwich rolls.

Makes 12 sandwiches

Pot Roast Braised in Ginger Plum Sauce

Chuck roast (3½-4 pounds)
1-2 tablespoons olive oil
3 tablespoons green onions, finely minced

Ginger Plum Sauce
1 tablespoon olive oil
2 tablespoons fresh ginger root, grated or
    finely chopped
2-3 cloves garlic, finely chopped
2 shallots, finely chopped
1-1½ cups beef stock

30 ounces plums, pitted and coarsely
    chopped
2 tablespoons cider vinegar
¼ cup teriyaki sauce
½ cup plum wine (or ¼ cup water and
    ¼ cup plum juice)

Preheat oven to 350°. Brown roast in hot oil. Add onions and lightly brown.
Transfer all to large roasting pan. Put oil in large frying pan and sauté ginger root,
garlic and shallots until translucent. Slowly add remaining ingredients, stirring
well. Pour over pot roast. Braise uncovered in oven for 3 - 3½ hours. Before
serving, flour may be added to sauce to thicken, if desired. (Note: If canned plums
are used, drain off liquid before using.)

Serves 6

Burgundy Beef Stew

Dumplings

2 cups flour

4 teaspoons baking
powder

½ teaspoon salt

1 cup milk

In large bowl,
combine dry
ingredients, then
gradually add milk.
Drop by rounded
teaspoonfuls into
gravy of stew or pot
roast. Cook, covered,
for the last 12
minutes of cooking
time.

4 pounds sirloin steak, cut into
    1-inch cubes
4 cups carrots, sliced
2 cups celery, sliced
4 medium onions, sliced
10 ounces water chestnuts, sliced and
    drained

¾ pound fresh mushrooms, sliced
⅓ cup flour
1¼ tablespoons salt
2 tablespoons sugar
1 can (32-ounce) whole tomatoes, broken up
2 cups Burgundy wine

Preheat oven to 325°. In large roasting pan or Dutch oven, mix meat, carrots,
celery, onions, water chestnuts and mushrooms. In small bowl mix together flour,
salt and sugar and stir into meat mixture. Stir in tomatoes and wine. Cover and
bake for approximately 4 hours, stirring occasionally.

Serves 12

Brazilian Beef

2 cups wine vinegar
1 cup water
1 cup Burgundy or other hearty red wine
¼ cup gin
1 bay leaf, crushed

3 cloves garlic, crushed
1 teaspoon tarragon
5 drops red pepper sauce
Eye of round or tip roast (3 pounds)
Salt, coarse or rock

In large bowl, combine all ingredients except meat and salt, mixing well. Add meat and place in refrigerator overnight, occasionally turning meat. Remove bowl from refrigerator and let stand at room temperature for 2-3 hours before roasting meat. Preheat oven to 275°. Remove meat from marinade and dust with salt. Cook roast for 1 hour, then baste every ½ hour with a few tablespoons of marinade. Cook roast until a meat thermometer reads almost 140° for medium-rare. For more well-done meat, cook at 350° until thermometer reads 150°. Let roast rest for 15 minutes before carving. (Note: May substitute 2 cups tarragon vinegar for tarragon and wine vinegar.)

Serves 6

Savory Pot Roast

1 cup red wine
½ cup soy sauce
1 cup orange juice
1 tablespoon thyme
1 tablespoon rosemary
¼ teaspoon Worcestershire sauce

1 cup onion, chopped
1 tablespoon pepper
4 cloves garlic, minced
Favorite cut of beef for pot roast
   (4 pounds)

In large container with tight-fitting lid, mix together all ingredients except beef. Cut roast into 3-4 pieces (to allow marinade to penetrate more thoroughly) and place in container with marinade. Refrigerate for 24 hours. Transfer meat and marinade to large pot, cover and cook on top of stove over low heat for approximately 4 hours, or until tender. (Note: Juice may be used as gravy or as soup base.)

Serves 8

Grilled Marinated Flank Steak

Red Pepper
Marmalade

_____

2 large, sweet red
peppers

½ cup prepared
pimientos

1 cup apricot
preserves

Juice of one lemon

Wash peppers,
discard seeds and cut
into thin strips.
Place peppers,
pimientos and
preserves into small
saucepan. Bring to a
boil and simmer for
20 minutes or until
mixture thickens.
Let cool, then stir in
lemon juice.

½ cup soy sauce
½ cup water
1½ tablespoons garlic, crushed
1 tablespoon sesame oil
2 teaspoons chili powder

1 tablespoon fresh ginger root, peeled
   and grated
3-4 pounds flank steak, trimmed of
   visible fat
Red Pepper Marmalade

Mix soy sauce, water, garlic, oil, chili powder and ginger root in a large plastic bag
or a marinating container which can be flipped. Add meat, seal bag or container,
and turn so that the marinade is distributed all around the meat. Refrigerate for 12
hours, turning bag or container 2-3 times. Remove steak from marinade. Grill
steak for 4-5 minutes on each side, then slice into thin strips, cutting at an angle.
Serve immediately with Red Pepper Marmalade.

Serves 6-8

Mexican Pie

1 pound ground beef
2½-3 teaspoons chili powder
½ teaspoon oregano leaves
¼ teaspoon ground cumin seed
2 tablespoons instant minced onion
¼ teaspoon instant minced garlic

2 teaspoons dried sweet pepper flakes
10 ounces frozen chopped spinach, thawed
½ pint cottage cheese
1 loaf frozen bread dough, thawed
½ cup Cheddar cheese, shredded
1 egg, beaten

Grease a 9-inch springform pan. In skillet, brown ground beef combined with
next six ingredients. Drain off fat. Squeeze moisture from spinach and place in
mixing bowl. Add cottage cheese and mix well. Divide bread dough into three
equal parts. Roll each piece of dough into 9-inch round. Place one round into
prepared pan. Spread meat on top of dough, almost to edge. Top with second
bread round. Cover with spinach mixture and sprinkle with Cheddar cheese. Top
with third bread round. Cover pan with damp cloth and let bread rise in warm
place until doubled in size. Preheat oven to 350°. Brush top of bread with egg,
place on lower rack of oven and bake for 40 minutes.

Serves 6-8

Cajun Seasoned Burgers

1 tablespoon garlic powder
1 tablespoon chili powder
1 tablespoon onion powder
1 tablespoon oregano
1 tablespoon paprika
1 tablespoon thyme
1 tablespoon ground cumin

2 teaspoons white pepper
2 teaspoons black pepper
2 teaspoons cayenne pepper
Salt, to taste (optional)
2 pounds ground beef
Monterey Jack cheese, shredded, for
  topping

Make Cajun Seasoning Mixture by combining herbs and spices. Blend 2 tablespoons of seasoning mixture into ground beef, form into hamburger patties, cook to taste and top with cheese. (Note: Leftover seasoning mixture can be stored for future use.)

Serves 6-8

Beerbecue Sauce

28 ounces ketchup
12 ounces chili sauce
⅓ cup prepared mustard
1 tablespoon dry mustard
1½ cups brown sugar, packed
2 tablespoons pepper, coarsely ground
1½ cups wine vinegar with garlic
1 cup lemon juice

½ cup thick steak sauce
Dash of red pepper sauce, to taste
¼ cup Worcestershire sauce
1 tablespoon soy sauce
2 tablespoons vegetable oil
12 ounces beer
Flank steak

Combine all ingredients, except meat, and mix well. Marinate flank steak in sauce for several hours. Broil or grill to desired doneness. (Note: This sauce can be stored in the refrigerator for a long period and works equally well for pork or chicken.)

Makes 6 pints

Cajun Seasoning for Chicken or Shrimp

½ cup water

½ cup margarine, melted

2 tablespoons Cajun Seasoning Mixture

3 whole chicken breasts, cut into bite-sized pieces or 2 pounds medium-sized shrimp

Combine water, margarine and seasoning mixture to make sauce. Place chicken or shrimp in single layer in shallow casserole dish. Cover with sauce and broil 12-15 minutes, until browned. Serve over fried rice.

in France in 1809 as a safe, practical way to preserve food for Napoleon's army. In 1810, the process was enhanced with the invention in England of a tin-coated, steel container. When this product crossed the Atlantic in 1818, the American canning industry was born, enabling poultry, fish and meat, as well as fruits and vegetables to be preserved.

In 1881, Amos Cobb and his sons opened the Cobb Preserving Company in Fairport, New York. By 1897, the Cobbs were packing and shipping more than two million cans of produce annually. The cans were formed and soldered by hand, and the food to be preserved was forced through a small "cap hole" in the top. The hole was then sealed and the cans were processed in boiling water. If the cans did not swell and burst, the contents (complete with lacerations from the cap hole and dark specks from the hot solder), were enjoyed by consumers across the country.

In 1899, the Cobb Preserving Company began to manufacture open-top cans for their food producers. By 1904, the company had perfected the first tin-plated, air-tight can made without using solder. In that year alone the company packed and shipped six million cans of produce.

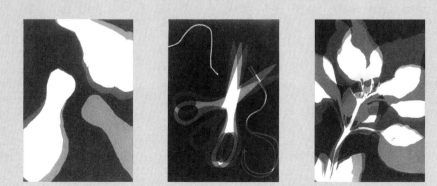

POULTRY

Chicken Marsala

This recipe, authored by Stacy Zamudio, was contributed by photographer Robert Barker.

¼ cup flour
¼ cup cornstarch
Salt and pepper, to taste
½ teaspoon oregano
½ teaspoon basil
4 boneless chicken breasts, sliced into thin
   pieces

3-5 tablespoons olive oil and butter
½ cup shallots or onion, finely chopped
2 cloves garlic, finely chopped
1 pound fresh mushrooms, thinly sliced
½-¾ cup Marsala wine
¼-½ cup chicken broth
2 tablespoons fresh parsley, chopped

Combine flour, cornstarch, salt, pepper, oregano and basil in bowl and dredge chicken pieces in mixture. Place mixture of olive oil and butter in large frying pan and sauté shallots, garlic and mushrooms until tender. Remove vegetables from pan and set aside. Turn up heat and cook chicken pieces just until cooked through. Stir in vegetables, Marsala wine and chicken broth. Allow to cook until sauce has thickened. Sprinkle chicken with parsley and serve over rice or pasta. (Note: If sauce does not thicken by itself, add a small amount of cornstarch mixed with water to achieve desired thickness.)

Serves 4

Chicken ~ The Clark House

Cream Substitute

¼ cup skim milk

½ teaspoon cornstarch

Mix together to make a low-fat substitute for heavy cream.

1 tablespoon olive oil
2 whole boneless chicken breasts, skinned
   and halved
Flour
2-3 cloves garlic, minced
¼ teaspoon basil
⅛ teaspoon rosemary
⅛ teaspoon thyme

½ cup white wine
½ cup mushrooms, sliced
¼ cup sun-dried tomatoes in oil, rinsed
   and julienned or ⅓ cup tomato, peeled,
   seeded and diced (see p. 26)
Salt and pepper, to taste
½ cup heavy cream or Cream Substitute

In a pan large enough to hold chicken in one layer, heat oil over medium heat until hot, but not smoking. Dredge chicken in flour, add to oil and cook for 4-5 minutes, turning once. Add remaining ingredients, except cream, and cook until wine is reduced by half. Add cream and simmer until sauce thickens, about 5 minutes longer. Serve with rice or noodles.

Serves 4

Grilled Chicken Breasts Provençal

6 boneless chicken breasts, skinned
½ teaspoon fresh thyme, minced
Pepper, freshly ground, to taste
2 tablespoons fresh lemon juice
2 tablespoons extra-virgin olive oil
½ cup Niçoise or Kalamata olives, pitted
  and chopped
¼ cup green onion, minced

½ teaspoon fresh lemon juice
1 clove garlic, minced
1-2 teaspoons capers, drained
¼-½ teaspoon tomato paste
6-12 bacon slices, thinly sliced
6 bay leaves
6 fresh thyme sprigs

Pound chicken breasts to thickness of ¼-inch. Place in single layer in 13x9-inch baking dish. Sprinkle both sides with thyme, pepper, lemon juice and olive oil. Cover and refrigerate for 8 hours, turning occasionally. Make filling by combining olives, onion, lemon juice, garlic, capers and tomato paste in bowl. Set aside. Blanch bacon slices in boiling water for 5 minutes. Drain, rinse and pat dry. Remove chicken breasts from marinade and place 2 rounded teaspoons of filling mixture in center of each breast. Fold sides over filling, then fold in ends to form compact cylinders. Wrap 1-2 bacon strips around each breast and secure with toothpicks. Slip one bay leaf and one sprig of thyme under bacon. Grill until meat is springy to the touch, approximately 10 minutes per side. Remove and discard toothpicks. Serve chicken whole, or slice thickly across grain of meat. (Note: Instead of grilling, chicken may be broiled for approximately 23 minutes.)

Serves 6

Chicken in Lemon Yogurt Sauce

4 tablespoons margarine
4 chicken breasts, skinned and halved
2 tablespoons flour
½ cup chicken bouillon
¾ cup plain yogurt
¼ cup white wine

2 teaspoons lemon zest, grated
½ teaspoon salt
½ teaspoon pepper
½ cup mushrooms, sliced
Chopped parsley or dill, for garnish

Preheat oven to 350°. Melt 2 tablespoons of the margarine in a shallow baking dish. Add chicken, turning each piece once to coat with margarine. Bake uncovered for 30 minutes. After chicken has cooked for 20 minutes, melt remaining margarine in saucepan. Add flour and cook briefly over medium heat, stirring constantly. Add bouillon and continue to stir constantly until mixture is thickened. Add yogurt, wine, lemon zest, salt and pepper, mixing well. Remove pan from heat. Remove chicken breasts from oven and cover each breast with sliced mushrooms. Pour sauce over chicken, and bake uncovered for 15-20 minutes longer, until chicken is tender. Sprinkle with parsley or dill before serving.

Serves 8

Tangy Chicken Crunch

2 cups nonfat yogurt
Juice of one lemon
1 teaspoon garlic powder
Salt and pepper, to taste

1-2 teaspoons Worcestershire sauce
6 boneless chicken breasts, halved
8 ounces herb-seasoned stuffing, crushed
¼-⅓ cup butter, melted

Mix together yogurt, lemon juice, seasonings and Worcestershire sauce. Add chicken and marinate overnight in refrigerator. Remove breasts, one at a time, retaining as much of the marinade as possible. Roll chicken in crushed stuffing mix. Place in greased, shallow baking dish and drizzle melted butter lightly over top of chicken. Bake uncovered at 350° for 45 minutes or until chicken juices run clear when chicken is pierced with fork.

Serves 6-12

French Country Chicken & Vegetables

Roasting chicken (3½-4 pounds)
½ cup margarine, room temperature
¼ teaspoon garlic, minced
¼ teaspoon thyme, crushed
6 medium carrots, cut into 1-inch pieces

3 large potatoes, peeled and cut into
   quarters
6 small onions, peeled
¼ cup dry red wine
2 tablespoons water
Minced parsley, for garnish

Preheat oven to 375°. Wash and dry chicken. Blend 2 tablespoons of the margarine with garlic and spread inside chicken. Truss chicken and rub outside with 2 more tablespoons of the margarine. Place chicken in roasting pan and bake for 30 minutes. In large skillet, melt remaining margarine with thyme. Add carrots, potatoes and onions, and sauté for about 5 minutes, stirring often. Arrange vegetables around chicken in roasting pan. Combine wine and water and pour over vegetables. Continue roasting chicken and vegetables for another 60-75 minutes, basting every 20 minutes. Remove chicken from roasting pan, and arrange on platter with vegetables sprinkled with parsley.

Serves 4

Elegant Chicken

4 boneless chicken breasts, halved
Seasoned salt, to taste
¼ cup butter
14 ounces artichoke hearts, drained and
   halved

½ pound mushrooms, sliced
3 tablespoons flour
1½ cups chicken broth
⅓ cup sherry

Sprinkle chicken with seasoned salt, and brown in butter in large frying pan. Arrange chicken in single layer in shallow baking dish. Add artichokes and set aside. Sauté mushrooms in frying pan until tender, adding additional butter if necessary. Sprinkle flour over mushrooms, and stir until blended. Gradually add chicken broth and sherry, stirring constantly. Simmer for 5 minutes, then pour over chicken. Bake covered at 375° for 30 minutes.

Serves 8

Baked Apricots

2 cans (17-ounce) apricot halves, drained

1 cup brown sugar, packed

2 stacks crackers, round, butter-flavored, crushed

½ cup butter or margarine, melted

Arrange apricots in 8-inch square baking dish. Sprinkle with sugar, then cracker crumbs. Drizzle with butter and bake at 300° for 30 minutes, or until browned and bubbly.

Serves 6-8

Curtice Brothers of Rochester was founded in 1868. By 1906, the company had become the largest canning factory in the country.

Mediterranean Chicken

6 chicken breast fillets, skinned and boned
¼ cup olive oil
½ red pepper, julienned
½ yellow pepper, julienned
½ cup onions, chopped
1 cup fresh mushrooms, sliced
½ cup pitted black olives, drained and sliced
2 small fresh tomatoes, diced
2 cups canned whole tomatoes
Minced garlic, to taste
1 teaspoon thyme
Salt and pepper, to taste

Flatten fillets and sauté in olive oil until golden, approximately 5-8 minutes. Add peppers, onions, mushrooms, olives and fresh tomatoes. In blender, liquefy canned tomatoes and seasonings. Pour tomato and seasoning mixture over chicken and simmer until vegetables are tender, approximately 15-20 minutes. Serve immediately.

Serves 6

Lemon Herb Chicken

Chicken (3½-pound), skinned and cut-up
½ cup olive oil
¼ cup lemon juice
2 small cloves garlic, crushed
3 tablespoons fresh oregano, chopped
⅛ teaspoon salt
⅛ teaspoon pepper
Lemon slices, for garnish
Fresh oregano, for garnish

Place chicken meaty side down in a 13x9-inch pan. Combine next six ingredients, mixing well. Pour over chicken and marinate in refrigerator for 2 hours, turning chicken several times. Bake uncovered at 350° for 30-40 minutes. Broil chicken 6 inches from heat for 5 minutes, until lightly browned. Garnish with lemon slices and oregano.

Serves 4-6

Poulet Dijonnaise

Wedge of onion
2-3 cloves garlic
4 tablespoons Dijon mustard
4 tablespoons red wine vinegar
½ teaspoon basil

½ teaspoon pepper
2-4 drops hot sauce (optional)
½ cup vegetable oil
4 whole chicken breasts, skinned, boned
  and halved

Preheat oven to 350°. Chop onion and garlic in food processor. Add remaining ingredients, except chicken, and blend well. Pour sauce over chicken and bake for 1 hour. (Note: The sauce can be prepared 2-3 days ahead and refrigerated.)

Serves 8

Chicken Breast Mandarin Orange

2 cans (11-ounce) mandarin oranges
¼ cup raisins
¼ cup sherry
5 boneless chicken breasts, skinned and
  halved
2 teaspoons paprika
Pepper, to taste
¼ cup butter
2 tablespoons vegetable oil

1 cup chicken bouillon
2 cloves garlic, minced
2½ cups fresh mushrooms, sliced
Butter, for sautéing
2 tablespoons cornstarch
1 teaspoon ground ginger
1½ tablespoons soy sauce
½ teaspoon water
½ cup plain yogurt

Drain mandarin oranges, reserving juice, and set both aside. In small bowl, let raisins soak in sherry. Sprinkle chicken breasts with paprika and pepper. Melt butter and oil in preheated electric skillet or large frying pan, and brown chicken on both sides. Add chicken bouillon, reserved juice from mandarin oranges, garlic, raisins and sherry. Cover and simmer for 30 minutes. In small skillet, sauté mushrooms lightly in small amount of butter. Set aside. Remove chicken breasts to preheated serving dish and keep warm. Blend cornstarch, ginger, soy sauce and water and add to skillet, cooking until thickened, stirring constantly. Add oranges and mushrooms to skillet, and gradually stir in yogurt. Pour sauce over chicken and serve immediately.

Serves 6-8

Hoisin sauce can be used in stir-frying, as a dipping sauce, and in marinades for poultry. For a slightly spicier version of the sauce, look for Chee How Sauce in the Oriental food section of the supermarket.

Chicken with Hoisin Sauce & Cashew Nuts

4 tablespoons vegetable oil
½ cup unsalted cashews
2 whole boneless chicken breasts, cut into
 1-inch cubes
1 tablespoon soy sauce
1 tablespoon sugar

1 tablespoon cornstarch
½ teaspoon salt
½ pound fresh mushrooms, sliced
1 green pepper, cut into 1-inch pieces
½ cup water chestnuts, sliced
2 tablespoons Hoisin sauce

Put 1 tablespoon of the oil into large wok or frying pan and roast cashews until browned. Remove cashews from pan and set aside. In large bowl, mix together cubed chicken, soy sauce, sugar and cornstarch. Set aside. Heat another tablespoon of the oil in the same pan. Add salt, mushrooms and pepper and cook until vegetables are tender. Add water chestnuts, heat through, and remove from heat. Remove vegetables from pan. Add remaining oil and, when hot, add chicken mixture and cook until chicken pieces turn white and are completely cooked. Add Hoisin sauce, vegetables, and cashews, stirring well until hot. Serve immediately.

Serves 4

Chicken Champignon

1 pound fresh mushrooms, sliced
Chicken (3-pound), skinned and cut up
2 tablespoons cornstarch
¼ cup water
2 tablespoons olive oil
¾ cup rosé wine

¼ cup soy sauce
1 clove garlic, minced
2 tablespoons sugar
2 sprigs fresh rosemary,
 removed from stem

Preheat oven to 350°. Lightly grease a 13x9-inch baking dish. Place mushrooms in dish, then top with chicken pieces. Combine cornstarch and water in bowl, stirring until smooth. Stir in remaining ingredients and pour over chicken. Bake uncovered for 1 hour.

Serves 4

Bakmi Goreng

½ pound thin egg noodles
Dried onion flakes, to taste
Vegetable oil, for sautéing and frying
2 cloves garlic, peeled and finely chopped
1 large onion, peeled and finely chopped
4 ounces fresh shrimp, peeled and
  deveined
4 ounces chicken, shredded

1 fresh red chili pepper, chopped
8 green onions, sliced
2 cups Chinese cabbage, sliced
2 tablespoons soy sauce
2 teaspoons sugar
1 teaspoon salt
½ teaspoon pepper
1 egg, beaten

Soak noodles for 10 minutes in cold water. Drain and spread on a tray to dry,
about 2 hours. In a small amount of oil, sauté onion flakes until brown and drain
on paper towel. Set aside. Stir-fry garlic and chopped onion in small amount of
oil until soft. Add shrimp and chicken and cook for 5 minutes. Add chili pepper,
green onions, and Chinese cabbage and stir-fry for 3 minutes. Mix together soy
sauce, sugar, salt and pepper and pour over vegetables. Remove from heat and
keep warm. Pour 2-3 tablespoons vegetable oil into frying pan, and when hot, fry
noodles on high heat until lightly browned and slightly crisp. Drain noodles on
paper towel and place on serving platter. Arrange vegetable and meat mixture over
noodles. In small frying pan, heat a small amount of oil and fry egg to make a
thin, flat omelette. Cool slightly and shred. Garnish noodles with egg and onion
flakes, and serve hot.

Serves 3-4

Tandoori Chicken

Chicken pieces (2-3 pounds), skinned
2 tablespoons salt
½ cup lemon juice
6 cloves garlic
½ ounce fresh ginger root
1 cup plain yogurt
¼ cup lemon juice
2 tablespoons vinegar
2 tablespoons vegetable oil

1-2 tablespoons hot pepper flakes
¼ cup Tandoor Masala
2 tablespoons salt
1 teaspoon ground cumin seeds
1 teaspoon ground mango powder
1 teaspoon paprika
1 tablespoon vegetable oil
Fresh lemon and onion slices, for garnish

Wash chicken and pat dry. Make several cuts on surface of chicken and rub with mixture of salt and lemon juice. Refrigerate for 30-45 minutes. In blender, grind garlic and ginger. Mix with yogurt, lemon juice, vinegar, oil, hot pepper flakes, Tandoor Masala, and salt. Remove chicken from refrigerator and drain. Rub chicken with yogurt marinade and refrigerate for several hours or overnight. At time of cooking, place chicken and marinade in large baking dish and bake at 350° for 30-45 minutes. Remove pan from oven, drain off marinade, then return to oven and bake 30-40 minutes longer. Remove pan from oven and drain off excess juices. Mix together cumin seeds, mango powder, paprika and oil and spread on chicken. Broil for 8-10 minutes. Serve immediately, garnished with lemon and onion slices.

Serves 4-6

Mango powder, or amchoor, is made from dried unripe mango. It is used to give acidity to Indian dishes. It can be substituted in some recipes for lemon juice. One teaspoon of amchoor equals two tablespoons of lemon juice.

Curried Chicken with Crystallized Ginger

Frying chicken (2½-3 pounds), with or without skin, cut into pieces
3 tablespoons fresh lime juice
3 tablespoons flour
⅛ teaspoon pepper
3 tablespoons vegetable oil
1 tablespoon butter
1 large onion, chopped
1-3 tablespoons curry powder
1 cup water
1 cup evaporated skim milk or cream
1 teaspoon chicken bouillon granules
1 Granny Smith apple, cored and chopped
2 tablespoons crystallized ginger, chopped
½ cup dry roasted peanuts
1 papaya, peeled and cut into wedges, for garnish (optional)
8 lime wedges, for garnish (optional)

Sprinkle chicken with lime juice and let stand for 30 minutes. Pat dry. Mix together flour and pepper. Dredge chicken. Heat oil and butter in large skillet. Sauté chicken, including remaining flour mixture, until browned. Remove chicken from pan. Add onion and sauté until golden. Add curry, cook for 2 minutes, then gradually stir in water and milk. Stir until thick. Add bouillon granules and chicken to skillet. Cover and simmer for 30 minutes. Stir in apples and ginger. Cover and simmer for 10 minutes longer. Stir in peanuts and serve, garnished with papaya and lime wedges, if desired.

Serves 5-6

Chicken & Rice Hawaiian

3 tablespoons butter
1 cup celery, chopped
½ cup onion, chopped
½ pound fresh mushrooms, chopped
3 cups rice, cooked
2 ounces dried vermicelli, broken into pieces
5 cups steamed chicken, chopped into large pieces
1 cup water chestnuts, sliced
4 tablespoons soy sauce
1 teaspoon basil
¼ teaspoon turmeric
½ teaspoon curry powder
2 cups almond halves
1 cup chicken broth

Melt butter in frying pan. Sauté celery, onion, and mushrooms until soft. Combine rice, vermicelli and chicken in 13x9-inch dish. Add celery mixture and remaining ingredients. Bake covered at 350° for 20 minutes, or until hot and bubbly. If casserole becomes dry, stir in additional chicken broth.

Serves 10-12

Athenian Chicken Rolls

¾ cup butter
2 medium onions, finely chopped
1 celery stalk, finely chopped
2 cups chicken, cooked and chopped
1 cup chicken broth
2 tablespoons parsley, minced

1 teaspoon oregano
½ teaspoon salt
⅛ teaspoon pepper
½ pound feta cheese, crumbled (see p. 77)
2 eggs, beaten
12 sheets phyllo dough

Melt 2 tablespoons of the butter in a skillet. Cook onions and celery for 5 minutes, or until tender. Stir in chicken, broth, parsley, oregano, salt and pepper. Cook until all liquid is absorbed. Stir in feta cheese. Remove from heat and let cool completely. Stir in eggs. Set aside. Preheat oven to 350°. Melt remaining butter. Place long side of one sheet of phyllo dough facing you, and brush with small amount of butter. Place a second sheet of phyllo dough on top of the first and brush with butter. Repeat process with 4 more sheets, using no more than ⅓ of the butter. Spread ½ of the chicken mixture over length of one long side. Roll up, jelly-roll fashion, beginning with filling side. Tuck in ends to enclose filling. Repeat entire process with remaining phyllo dough and chicken mixture. Place chicken rolls on large baking sheet with sides. Brush tops with remaining butter. Bake for 20-30 minutes, or until well-browned and crisp. Cool slightly and cut into thick slices.

Serves 6

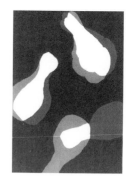

Marinated Drumsticks

½ cup ketchup
2 tablespoons horseradish
¼ cup lemon juice
¼ cup soy sauce

⅓ cup vegetable oil
Chicken drumsticks and thighs (8 each),
    partially cooked

Combine all ingredients, except chicken. Place chicken in shallow dish and cover with marinade. Cover dish and refrigerate for 4 hours or overnight, occasionally spooning marinade over chicken. Drain marinade and reserve. Grill chicken pieces for 20 minutes, baste with reserved marinade, then grill 10 minutes longer. Serve immediately.

Serves 6-8

Turkey Burgers in a Pocket

1 envelope onion mushroom or beefy
    onion soup mix
1 pound ground turkey
1 teaspoon chili powder
½ cup bread crumbs
½ cup tomato, finely chopped (optional)
¼ cup green pepper, finely chopped
    (optional)

Vegetable oil spray
1-2 tablespoons soy sauce, or to taste
2 tablespoons water
4 pita breads
Mozzarella or Cheddar cheese, shredded
Shredded lettuce

Combine soup mix, turkey, chili powder, bread crumbs, tomato and green pepper (if using) in a large bowl. Mix well, and shape into patties. Spray frying pan with vegetable oil spray and add soy sauce. Fry burgers for 1 minute on each side. Add water and simmer, covered, for 3 minutes. Turn burgers over and add an additional 1-2 tablespoons water, if needed. Cover and simmer for another 3 minutes. Place in pita breads, top with cheese, and heat in microwave oven for 35 seconds. Add lettuce and serve immediately.

Serves 4

Cornish Game Hens with Mandarin Glaze

1 package (6¼-ounce) long-grain and
   wild rice
1 cup pitted black olives, drained and sliced
4 tablespoons butter
½ cup onion, chopped
½ cup celery, chopped

1 can (11-ounce) mandarin oranges
6 Cornish game hens (1-1¼ pounds each),
   thawed and rinsed
¼ cup teriyaki sauce
1 teaspoon cornstarch
1 tablespoon butter

Prepare rice according to package directions and add olives. Melt butter and sauté onions and celery until limp. Add to rice. Drain oranges, reserving ¼ cup of the juice and 12 orange segments, for garnish. Add oranges to rice. Preheat oven to 350°. Rub each hen cavity with salt and stuff with ¾ cup rice mixture. Truss and place in shallow baking dish. Roast for 40-50 minutes. While hens are roasting, combine reserved orange juice and remaining ingredients in saucepan. Heat, stirring constantly, until glaze is no longer cloudy and is slightly thickened. Brush glaze over hens and cook 20 minutes longer. Garnish with reserved orange segments and serve.

Serves 6

Game Hens with Pineapple-Cornbread Stuffing

¼ cup butter or margarine
½ cup celery, chopped
½ cup green onion, chopped
1 can (8-ounce) crushed pineapple, drained
¼ cup peanuts or pecans, chopped
3 tablespoons dry sherry

¼ teaspoon salt
¼ teaspoon thyme, crushed
2 cups cornbread stuffing mix
6 Cornish game hens (1-1¼ pounds each),
   thawed and rinsed
¼ cup butter or margarine, melted

Melt butter in skillet and add celery and onion. Cook until tender, but not brown. Stir in pineapple, nuts, sherry, salt and thyme. Transfer mixture to large bowl and toss lightly with stuffing mix. Preheat oven to 350°. Rub each hen cavity with salt and fill with approximately ⅔ cup stuffing. Cover opening with foil and brush hens with melted butter. Roast for 1¼-1½ hours.

Serves 6

Roast Honey-Lime Duck~ Richardson's Canal House

2 ducks (4½ pounds each), excess fat
  removed
Salt and freshly ground pepper
1 medium onion, sliced

½ orange, unpeeled and sliced
1 lemon, unpeeled and sliced
Honey-Lime Sauce

Preheat oven to 450°. Pat ducks dry. Sprinkle inside and out with salt and pepper. Stuff each with onion, orange and lemon. Prick skin around thighs, back and lower breast. Arrange ducks, breast side up, on racks in large, deep roasting pan. Roast for 45 minutes. Drain off fat. Continue roasting until juices run clear when thickest part of thigh is pierced, about 45 minutes. Cool ducks to room temperature. Preheat oven to 400°. Split ducks in half, cutting down backs and through breasts. Pull out all exposed bones and discard. Halve each piece by cutting between breast and thigh. Arrange pieces skin side up in another large roasting pan. Roast duck until skin is crisp, about 15 minutes. During this time, prepare Honey-Lime Sauce. Arrange duck on plates, crossing wings and legs. Spoon sauce over and serve.

Serves 4

Honey-Lime Sauce

1 teaspoon cornstarch
½ teaspoon water
½ cup honey
¼ cup fresh lime juice
1½ teaspoons lime zest, grated

Dissolve cornstarch in water, set aside. Combine honey, lime juice and zest and bring to simmer in small saucepan over medium heat, stirring frequently. Add cornstarch and whisk until sauce thickens and clears.

Cranberry Walnut Sauce

12 ounces fresh cranberries
2 medium apples, peeled and chopped into
  bite-sized pieces
1 cup orange juice
1-1½ cups sugar

½ teaspoon cinnamon
⅛ teaspoon allspice
⅛ teaspoon ground cloves
½ cup walnuts, coarsely chopped

Wash cranberries in cold water, then combine with apples and orange juice in saucepan. Cover and cook until skins pop on cranberries. Cook for 8-12 minutes longer, until cranberries and apples are soft. Add desired amount of sugar and spices, mixing well. Let cool and add walnuts.

Makes 2 pints

farms are not as original as they may seem. Men raised fish in aquatic farms as early as the 5th century, B.C. in China. But it was not until the work of Seth Green that the idea of artificially propagating fish became practical and commercially successful. Green was born in Rochester in 1817. He had a thriving fish business by the time he was in his twenties, and was a keen observer of his crop. He developed his method of propagating fish as a hobby, and in 1864 opened the first fish hatchery in North America in Caledonia, New York. There he bred lake trout, salmon, sturgeon, shad, whitefish and striped bass.

Green had great success in restocking rivers that had been depleted by over-fishing and he received medals from France, Germany and the United States for his efforts. In 1871, he stocked the Sacramento River in California with Atlantic shad and introduced that fish to the Pacific Ocean. He was also an avid sports fisherman and inventor of fishing equipment. From his first efforts, the fish culture industry around the world has exploded and now produces well over ten million tons of fish annually.

SEAFOOD

Fillets Maltaise

This recipe was contributed by illustrator Mary Hazelwood.

Fillets

2 pounds fresh asparagus, or 2 packages (10-ounce) frozen spears, thawed

6 sole or flounder fillets (2½-3 pounds)
¼ cup butter, melted

Quick Orange-Hollandaise Sauce

2 tablespoons cornstarch
2 tablespoons vegetable oil
1 cup chicken broth
½ cup orange juice
2 egg yolks, lightly beaten

2 teaspoons orange zest
Dash of red pepper
1-2 tablespoons lemon juice
Salt, to taste

Wash and remove tough ends from asparagus. Cook until barely tender, 5-7 minutes. Place 3-4 asparagus spears crosswise on each fillet, wrap fillet around asparagus and place seam side down in baking dish. Cover with melted butter and bake at 350° for 20 minutes, or until fish flakes easily with a fork and asparagus is tender. While fish is baking, combine cornstarch and oil in small saucepan. Add broth and orange juice and cook over medium heat, stirring constantly, until thickened. Remove pan from heat. Add a small amount of sauce to egg yolks and pour egg mixture slowly back into sauce. Cook sauce over low heat for 1 minute, stirring constantly, while adding orange zest and red pepper. Remove from heat and stir in lemon juice and salt. Remove baking dish from oven and spoon a small amount of sauce over fish. Brown briefly under broiler and serve immediately. Pass remaining sauce at table.

Serves 6

No Salt Herb and Spice Mix

3 tablespoons dried summer savory

2 teaspoons whole peppercorns

1 teaspoon fennel seeds

1 teaspoon ground ginger

⅛ teaspoon garlic powder

Stir all ingredients together until mixed. Spoon into a peppermill. Grind on fish, chicken or pork before cooking, or serve at table on vegetables or salad.

Fish Fillets with Herb & Spice Sauce

1 medium onion, chopped
1 green pepper, chopped
14½ ounces stewed tomatoes

1 teaspoon No Salt Herb and Spice Mix
1 pound catfish or haddock fillets

Combine first four ingredients, mixing well. Cook over medium heat for 3 minutes. Add fish fillets and poach for 5 minutes.

Serves 3-4

Rolled Stuffed Fillet of Sole

½ cup margarine
1½ cups Italian-style bread crumbs
Juice of ½ lemon
6 sole fillets, thinly cut
¼ pound shrimp or ½ cup crabmeat,
   cooked and chopped (optional)

Paprika
Fresh parsley, snipped
½ cup milk
Lemon, thinly sliced, for garnish
Parsley sprigs, for garnish

Preheat oven to 350°. Grease a 12-inch round baking dish. Melt margarine in skillet over low heat. Add bread crumbs and lemon juice, stirring until mixture resembles moist sand. Reserve ⅓ cup. Spoon remaining crumb mixture onto fillets. If desired, cut shrimp or crabmeat into small pieces and place on top of crumbs. Roll up fillets, beginning at narrow end. Place rolls in prepared baking dish. Top with reserved bread crumbs and dust with paprika. Top with fresh parsley. Pour milk into baking dish and bake for 20-30 minutes. Remove rolls to serving platter and garnish with lemon slices and parsley sprigs.

Serves 6

Baked Cod

1 cup butter-flavored cracker crumbs
¼ cup Parmesan cheese
½ cup butter, melted
1 tablespoon lemon juice
1 tablespoon white wine

¼ teaspoon garlic powder
¼ teaspoon pepper
Fresh parsley, chopped, to taste
1½ pounds cod or favorite white fish

Preheat oven to 350°. Mix together all ingredients except fish. Lay fish in shallow baking dish and coat with desired amount of crumb mixture. Bake uncovered for 25-30 minutes.

Serves 4

To cook fish without a specific recipe, measure the fish at its thickest point and cook for 10 minutes per inch. Test to see if the fish is opaque and flakes at its thickest spot. If not, continue cooking. When poaching, start timing when the poaching liquid returns to a slight boil after adding fish.

Orange Roughy Almondine

½ cup almonds, slivered
1 tablespoon butter
1 tablespoon white wine
1½ teaspoons lemon juice

3 tablespoons butter, melted
1-1½ pounds orange roughy or other firm
white fish fillets
Paprika

In small skillet, lightly brown almonds in butter. In small bowl, stir together wine, lemon juice, and butter. Arrange fillets, skin side down, in shallow baking pan. Sprinkle tops with paprika, then cover with wine mixture. Broil fillets for 3-5 minutes on one side only. Add browned almonds and butter, and broil for an additional 2 minutes.

Serves 2-3

Baked Haddock with Stuffing

3 tablespoons butter
½ cup onion, chopped
¼ cup celery, chopped
½ cup mushrooms, chopped
2 cups soft bread crumbs

Dash of salt, pepper, tarragon and
rosemary
2 pounds haddock fillets
Juice of ½ lemon
3-4 tomatoes, thinly sliced

Preheat oven to 375°. Melt butter in large frying pan and sauté onion, celery and mushrooms for 5 minutes. Stir in bread crumbs and seasonings. Arrange haddock fillets in large, greased baking dish. Sprinkle with lemon juice and spread stuffing mixture over fillets. Top with tomato slices. Bake for 25-30 minutes, or until done.

Serves 6

Snapper with Summer Fruits ~ Edwards

½ cup flour
Salt and pepper, to taste
4 snapper or grouper fillets (7 ounces each)
2 tablespoons clarified butter
2 shallots, minced
2 tablespoons butter
2 cup combination of summer fruits
    (peaches, nectarines, grapes, apricots,
    mangoes, bananas, berries, plums,
    melons, pineapple, cherries, etc.)

Orange juice
½ cup Riesling wine
1 tablespoon fresh parsley, chopped, for
    garnish
Salt and pepper, to taste (optional)
Lemon juice, to taste (optional)

Mix together flour, salt and pepper. Dredge fillets in seasoned flour and shake off excess. Sauté in clarified butter. Starting with flesh side down, cook 4-5 minutes, until golden brown. Turn fish over and continue to cook until done. (Do not overcook.) Sauté shallots in 1 teaspoon of the butter. Seed fruit, if necessary, and cut into bite-sized pieces. Moisten with a small amount of orange juice so that fruit will not turn brown. Place fruit in sauté pan and add wine. Bring to a boil and add the remaining butter, swirling butter in pan to melt. Pour mixture over fish and garnish with parsley. Add salt, pepper and lemon juice, if desired.

Serves 4

Prepare clarified butter by melting one pound of butter slowly over low heat. Skim off the foam on top, then carefully pour off the clear yellow liquid, leaving the white milk solids in the bottom of the pan. Discard the foam and milk solids. The "clarified" yellow liquid is also known as "drawn" butter or ghee.

Balsamic-Broiled Scrod with Mint

3 tablespoons balsamic vinegar
1½ tablespoons honey
¾ teaspoon olive oil

1 pound scrod fillets
½ cup fresh mint leaves, minced
Lemon slices, for garnish

Stir together vinegar, honey and oil. Place scrod in lightly greased baking pan. Drizzle fillets with half of the vinegar mixture. Broil 6 inches from heat, brushing with remaining vinegar, until fillets are flaky. Transfer to warm platter and drizzle with cooking juices. Sprinkle with mint and garnish with lemon slices.

Serves 4

Orange Pepper Trout

2 onions, finely chopped
Olive oil
2 cloves garlic, finely minced
2 large orange or yellow peppers, sliced
    into thin strips
1 teaspoon sugar

¼ cup rum
Zest and juice of 2 oranges
¼ cup parsley, finely chopped
¼ teaspoon white pepper
Salt, to taste
4 trout fillets

In frying pan over low heat, sauté onions in oil until just browned. Add garlic and peppers, increase heat to medium, and sauté until garlic is soft. Add sugar, increase heat to high, and add rum. After rum has evaporated, add orange zest and juice, parsley, white pepper and salt. Reduce heat to medium and cook for 2-3 minutes. Add trout fillets, simmering mixture for 2 minutes on each side. Remove fillets, top with pepper mixture and serve with couscous or rice.

Serves 4

Baked Scallops

2 eggs
2 tablespoons water
½ teaspoon thyme
½ teaspoon dill weed

2 pounds large scallops, washed in cold
    water and dried
Cracker crumbs
¼-½ cup butter or margarine, melted
Lemon slices, for garnish

Grease a 13x9-inch baking dish. Beat together eggs, water, thyme and dill weed. Dip scallops in egg mixture and coat with cracker crumbs. Arrange scallops in single layer in baking dish and drizzle with melted butter. Bake at 425° for 15-20 minutes. Garnish with lemon slices.

Serves 4-6

Fish & Vegetable Stir-Fry

2 tablespoons vegetable oil
1 large clove garlic, minced
2 teaspoons fresh ginger, finely minced
1 pound red snapper fillets (or catfish, bass, perch), cut into ½-inch strips
¼ cup scallions, finely chopped
½ cup carrots, diagonally sliced into ⅛-inch pieces
½ cup bamboo shoots, sliced
½ cup celery, diagonally sliced into ¼-inch pieces
½ cup water chestnuts, sliced
½ cup mushrooms, sliced
⅓ cup stock (fish, vegetable or chicken)
1 tablespoon soy sauce
1 teaspoon hot sesame oil
1 teaspoon cornstarch
1 tablespoon cold water
1 tablespoon toasted sesame seeds, for garnish
¼ cup scallions, chopped, for garnish

Heat 1 tablespoon of the oil in a wok or large skillet. Sauté garlic and ginger for 30 seconds. Add fish and, over high heat, fry rapidly, turning fish carefully to cook it for approximately 1 minute per side. Remove fish, garlic and ginger from pan and keep warm. Add remaining oil to pan and, over high heat, stir-fry scallions, carrots, bamboo shoots, celery, water chestnuts and mushrooms for approximately 1 minute. Add stock, soy sauce and oil, cover pan, and let mixture boil for 5 minutes. Meanwhile, mix cornstarch and water. When vegetables are done, add cornstarch to them, along with reserved fish. Stir-fry mixture until sauce is thickened. Sprinkle with sesame seeds and scallions, and serve immediately.

Serves 4

Spinach for the Halibut

⅓ cup butter
¼ cup shallots, chopped
1 cup fresh mushrooms, chopped
⅓ cup flour
1 teaspoon salt
¼ teaspoon pepper
⅛ teaspoon nutmeg, grated

2 cups milk
½ cup Parmesan cheese, grated
½ teaspoon Worcestershire sauce
2 packages (10-ounce) frozen chopped
 spinach, cooked and drained
2 pounds halibut steak, skinned and boned
Paprika, to taste

Grease a 9-inch square baking dish. Melt butter in frying pan and sauté shallots
and mushrooms for 3-4 minutes. Add flour, salt, pepper and nutmeg and combine
completely. Slowly stir in milk to make cream sauce. When sauce begins to
thicken, add cheese and Worcestershire sauce. Remove from heat. Combine ½ of
the sauce with the spinach. Spread mixture in bottom of prepared baking dish.
Arrange halibut on top of spinach. Pour remaining sauce over halibut and sprinkle
with paprika. Bake at 450° for 10-15 minutes. (Note: Other types of fish can also
be used.)

Serves 6

Broiled Halibut

4 ounces olive oil
2 cloves garlic, minced
⅛ teaspoon cayenne pepper
1-2 green onions, including greens,
 chopped

2 tablespoons fresh parsley, chopped
1 teaspoon rosemary
1 teaspoon salt
2 pounds halibut steaks

Combine all ingredients, except halibut, in bowl, mixing well. Place halibut steaks
in dish and spread with mixture. Marinate in refrigerator for 1 hour. Remove
halibut from dish and place on broiling pan. Broil to desired doneness,
approximately 10 minutes per inch of thickness. Serve immediately.

Serves 6

Grilled Salmon

⅓ cup butter, room temperature
2 tablespoons lemon juice
2 teaspoons Dijon mustard
⅛ teaspoon red pepper

1 tablespoon fresh parsley, minced
6 large, thick salmon steaks
Olive oil

Cream butter and gradually beat in lemon juice, mustard, pepper and parsley. Set aside. Brush salmon with small amount of olive oil. Grill 6 inches above coals or broil until fillets flake in center, approximately 10 minutes. Top each fillet with butter mixture and serve immediately.

Serves 6

Poached Salmon

1½ tablespoons unsalted butter
3 tablespoons shallots, finely chopped
4 salmon fillets, boneless and unskinned
Salt and black pepper, to taste
½ cup dry white wine
2 sprigs fresh parsley
1 bay leaf

½ cup heavy cream
½ cup fresh basil, chopped
1 teaspoon lemon juice
⅛ teaspoon cayenne pepper
Capers, thoroughly rinsed, for garnish
   (optional)

Rub large skillet with 1 teaspoon of the butter. Scatter shallots over bottom of skillet. Arrange salmon over shallots without crowding. Sprinkle with salt and pepper. Drop remaining butter over each steak. Add wine, parsley and bay leaf. Cover and simmer for 10 minutes. Transfer salmon to serving platter and set aside, keeping warm. Boil liquid in pan down to ¼ cup. Add cream and bring back to a boil. Strain sauce into a saucepan, discarding parsley and bay leaf. Bring sauce to boil over high heat, adding any liquid that has accumulated around salmon on platter. Cook for approximately 2 minutes, until sauce is slightly thickened. Add basil, lemon juice and cayenne pepper. Pour sauce over salmon, garnish with capers, if desired, and serve immediately.

Serves 4

Salmon with Two Sauces ~ The Gateway

Crème Fraîche

½ cup sour cream

½ cup heavy cream

Combine ingredients
in bowl and mix. Let
stand at room
temperature for 6
hours.

2 pounds salmon fillets, with skin

Salt, to taste

Mustard-Cream Sauce
1 cup Crème Fraîche

1 tablespoon grainy French mustard

Tomato-Butter Sauce
3 tablespoons olive oil
2½ pounds ripe tomatoes, peeled, seeded
   and finely diced (see p. 26)
1 tablespoon fresh thyme, minced or
   1 teaspoon dried
Salt and pepper, to taste

3 tablespoons dry white wine
3 tablespoons white wine vinegar
1½ tablespoons shallots, finely chopped
½ cup Crème Fraîche
6 tablespoons unsalted butter, cut into
   small pieces

Green stocked the
Connecticut,
Hudson, Potomac
and Susquehanna
Rivers.

Green also set up the
Cold Spring Harbor
Fish Hatchery on
Long Island, New
York.

Lay salmon on cutting board, skin side down. With a long, thin, flexible knife, cut
at a 30° angle into ½-inch thick slices. Discard the skin. Put salmon on well-
greased, heavy baking sheet and sprinkle lightly with salt. Refrigerate until ready to
bake. Combine crème fraîche with mustard and set aside. Heat olive oil in a
medium skillet and sauté tomatoes over moderately high heat, stirring for
approximately 7 minutes, until thick and reduced well. Add thyme, salt and
pepper. Remove from heat and set aside. Put wine, wine vinegar and shallots into
a non-aluminum saucepan. Boil over medium-high heat until almost all liquid is
evaporated. Whisk in crème fraîche and quickly reduce by half. Add butter, one
piece at a time, whisking constantly. When mixture becomes a thick and foamy
sauce, combine with tomato mixture. Keep warm. Preheat oven to 500°. Remove
salmon from refrigerator and bake for 4 minutes. Meanwhile, warm mustard sauce
in a saucepan. To serve, spoon tomato-butter sauce onto warmed dinner plates.
Put 2 slices of salmon on top of the sauce and spoon the mustard-cream sauce over
the salmon. Serve immediately.

Serves 5-6

Swordfish Piccata ~ The Gateway

4 swordfish steaks (6 ounces each)
Flour, for dredging
1 egg, beaten
½ cup Parmesan cheese
½ cup parsley flakes

¼ cup butter
½ cup white wine
Juice of 1 lemon
1 tablespoon capers
Lemon zest, for garnish (optional)

Preheat oven to 350°. Dredge swordfish in flour, then in egg, then in mixture of
Parmesan cheese and parsley. Melt 2 tablespoons of the butter in a frying pan and
sauté fish until golden brown on both sides. Transfer fish to baking sheet and
bake for approximately 10 minutes, or until thoroughly cooked. Put remaining
butter into same frying pan and add wine, lemon juice and capers. Cook until
sauce is reduced by half. Place fish on serving plate and top with sauce. Garnish
with lemon zest, if desired, and serve immediately.

Serves 4

Grilled Swordfish Steaks with Almond Butter

Marinade
½ cup soy sauce
2 cloves garlic, pressed
2 teaspoons fresh lemon juice
½ cup orange juice

½ teaspoon lemon zest
½ teaspoon orange zest
6 large swordfish steaks, ¾-inch thick

Almond Butter
½ cup butter, room temperature
⅓ cup almonds, finely chopped

Whole almonds, for garnish
Lemon and orange slices, for garnish

Combine soy sauce, garlic, juices and zests in bowl. Place swordfish in glass dish
and cover with marinade. Marinate for 3-4 hours, turning once. While fish is
marinating, combine butter and almonds. Fill shell-shaped butter molds and chill
until serving time. Grill or broil fish for 20 minutes, until fish flakes easily with
fork, turning once and basting often. Place fish on plates, add 2 butter molds, and
garnish with whole almonds and/or fruit slices.

Serves 6

Creole Seafood Supreme

8 ounces cream cheese, room temperature
½ cup butter
1½ pounds shrimp, peeled and deveined
1 onion, chopped
1 red bell pepper, chopped
3 stalks celery, finely chopped
1 can (10¾-ounce) cream of mushroom
  soup, undiluted
1 can (6-ounce) sliced mushrooms, drained

1 teaspoon garlic salt
1 teaspoon Worcestershire sauce
¾ teaspoon cayenne pepper
1 pound crabmeat
1 tablespoon lemon juice
3 cups rice, cooked
2½ cups Cheddar cheese, grated
Cracker crumbs
Paprika

Preheat oven to 350°. Grease a 3-quart rectangular casserole dish. Melt cream cheese and 6 tablespoons of the butter in top of a double boiler or in microwave oven. Set aside. Sauté shrimp, onion, pepper and celery in the remaining 2 tablespoons of butter. In large bowl, combine mushroom soup, mushrooms, garlic salt, Worcestershire sauce, and cayenne pepper. Add cream cheese and shrimp mixtures, stirring to combine. Sprinkle crabmeat with lemon juice, then carefully stir into shrimp mixture. Stir in cooked rice. Spoon into prepared dish and top with cheese, cracker crumbs and paprika. Cover and bake for 30 minutes, or until heated through and bubbly.

Serves 10-12

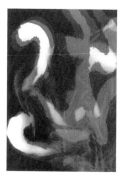

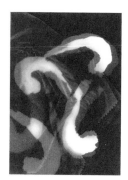

Seafood Madeira

2 salmon steaks
½ pound scallops or shrimp
Bottled Italian salad dressing
4 tablespoons margarine
1-2 shallots, minced
1-2 green onions, minced
12 ounces mushrooms, sliced

½ cup Madeira wine
¼ teaspoon tarragon
3 tablespoons fresh parsley, minced
2 tablespoons tomato paste
½ cup half-and-half
Parmesan cheese, grated

Marinate salmon steaks and scallops or shrimp in Italian dressing (enough to cover) for at least 1 hour. Place on grill in heavy-duty foil or in pan under broiler and cook for approximately 5 minutes, or until slightly browned. Set aside. Melt margarine in large skillet, and add shallots, green onions and mushrooms. Sauté over low heat for about 5 minutes, until mushrooms are lightly browned. Add wine, tarragon, parsley and tomato paste. Simmer for 5 minutes. Meanwhile, remove skin and bones from salmon, break gently into small pieces, and add to sauce in skillet. Add scallops and half-and-half, heat through, and serve over favorite pasta or rice. Sprinkle with Parmesan cheese. (Note: If large sea scallops are used, cut them in half horizontally before adding to recipe.)

Serves 4-6

Mango Shrimp

3 tablespoons olive oil
1 onion, finely chopped
4 cloves garlic, finely chopped
1 jalapeño pepper, minced
1 tablespoon fresh ginger, chopped
2 tablespoons sugar

¼ cup white wine
4 mangoes, pitted and sliced into
 1-inch cubes
Salt and pepper, to taste
¼ cup fresh basil, finely chopped
1 pound shrimp, peeled and deveined

Pour oil into large frying pan. Add onion and sauté until translucent. Add garlic, jalapeño pepper, ginger and sugar and sauté until garlic is soft. Add wine, mangoes, salt, pepper and basil. Cook for 3 minutes over medium heat. Add shrimp and cook until shrimp is just pink, approximately 1-2 minutes. May be served with basmati rice.

Serves 4

For a milder chili taste, use Anaheim, California or New Mexico chilies. Moderately hot peppers would be jalapeño, Fresno, and some Hungarian. For a fiery flavor, try habanero or Serrano.

Basmati rice is a short-grained aromatic rice used in Indian cooking. It can be purchased in supermarkets or Indian specialty shops.

Shrimp à La Mikrolimano

1 carrot, finely chopped
1 small onion, finely chopped
1 small green pepper, seeded and finely
  chopped
4 stalks celery, finely chopped
4 tablespoons butter
30 medium shrimp, peeled and deveined

⅓ cup white wine
16 ounces whole tomatoes, drained or 3
  medium tomatoes, chopped
1 teaspoon oregano
Salt and pepper, to taste
6 ounces feta cheese, crumbled (see p. 77)
4 ounces Parmesan cheese, grated

Sauté carrot, onion, green pepper and celery in medium-sized saucepan in 2
tablespoons of the butter until onion is golden. Remove vegetables and set aside.
Put remaining butter in same pan. Add shrimp and cook for 2-3 minutes, stirring
constantly. Add wine and continue cooking on medium heat for 2-3 minutes
longer. Return vegetables to pan, along with tomatoes and oregano. Add salt and
pepper. Transfer contents of pan to an oven-proof dish. Sprinkle with feta and
Parmesan cheeses. Place dish in 450° oven for 5 minutes or until cheese melts.
Serve over pasta or rice.

Serves 6

Virginia-Style Crab Cakes

½ cup fine bread crumbs, seasoned
5 tablespoons mayonnaise
1 egg, beaten
1 tablespoon fresh parsley, finely chopped
2 teaspoons Worcestershire sauce
1 teaspoon prepared mustard
1 teaspoon salt

¼ teaspoon white pepper
¼ cup celery, finely chopped
¼ cup onion, finely chopped
1 teaspoon lemon juice
1 pound crabmeat
Peanut oil, for frying

Combine bread crumbs, mayonnaise, egg and parsley in large bowl. Stir in
Worcestershire sauce and mustard. Add salt, pepper, celery, onion and lemon
juice, blending well. Stir in crabmeat. Chill slightly, then form mixture into
cakes. Place small amount of peanut oil in heavy skillet. Fry crab cakes over
medium-high heat until brown and crispy, approximately 5 minutes per side.

Serves 4

Maryland Crab Cakes

Seasoning Mix

2 teaspoons salt
2 teaspoons paprika
1 teaspoon garlic powder
1 teaspoon onion powder
1 teaspoon dry mustard

1 teaspoon basil
¾ teaspoon white pepper
½ teaspoon black pepper
½ teaspoon thyme

Crab Cakes

5 cups soft bread crumbs
7 tablespoons unsalted butter
2 cups onion, chopped
1 cup green bell peppers, chopped
1 cup celery, chopped
1 cup fresh parsley, chopped
1 tablespoon Worcestershire sauce

1 teaspoon red pepper sauce (optional)
1 teaspoon fresh garlic, minced
½ cup seafood stock
1 pound crabmeat, in lumps
3 eggs, lightly beaten
1 cup evaporated skim milk or heavy cream

Sauce

1 cup heavy cream

½ cup green onion tops, chopped

1 cup vegetable oil, for frying

Combine seasoning mix ingredients in small bowl. Set aside. Toast 3 cups of the bread crumbs in a 12-inch skillet over high heat, shaking occasionally, until the crumbs are light brown. Remove bread crumbs from pan, place in large bowl and set aside. Return skillet to high heat and add butter, onion, peppers and celery. Cook until vegetables start to brown, stirring constantly. Stir in 2 tablespoons of the seasoning mix, ½ cup of the parsley, Worcestershire sauce, red pepper sauce (if using), and garlic. Cook until mixture sticks to bottom of pan. Add seafood stock and scrape up crusted mixture from bottom of skillet. Remove from heat. To bowl with bread crumbs, add crabmeat, remaining seasoning mix, remaining parsley, vegetable mixture, eggs and milk or cream. Stir gently, without breaking up lumps of crabmeat. Reserve ½ cup of the mixture for use in sauce, and refrigerate both portions of mixture for 1½ hours. To make sauce, combine cream and reserved crab mixture in 8-inch skillet. Cook over high heat for approximately 3 minutes, whipping constantly. Add green onions and bring sauce to a boil, stirring occasionally. Remove from heat and keep warm. Remove crab mixture from refrigerator. Pour remaining 2 cups of bread crumbs into a pie plate and heat vegetable oil in skillet. Form crab mixture into cakes, dip into bread crumbs and fry until browned. Drain on paper towel and serve, garnished with sauce.

Makes approximately 14 crab cakes

VEGETABLES

The remarkable agricultural

climate of the Genesee Valley and the Lake Ontario growing plain helped Rochester to become the center of the nursery and seed industry in America. Once called the "Flour City", eventually Rochester became known as the "Flower City". In the late 1800s, seed companies, like those run by Charles Crosman, James Vick and Joseph Harris, all took turns at being first in their industry. They supplied seeds and bulbs to the self-sufficient vegetable gardener, the home flower gardener and the hearty souls moving west.

A secondary set of businesses grew up around the seed and nursery business. Companies thrived producing shipping materials, acting as mail-order centers and printing agricultural magazines. Artists and engravers provided beautiful color illustrations of vegetables, fruits, berries, trees and flowers for catalogues, which are highly regarded as works of art today.

VEGETABLES

Asparagus with Lemon Crumbs

1 pound asparagus, cut into 2-inch pieces
3 tablespoons butter
1 clove garlic, chopped
Juice of one lemon
½ teaspoon lemon zest

½ teaspoon dill
½ teaspoon pepper
1 tablespoon fresh parsley, chopped
¼ cup dry bread crumbs, unseasoned

Cook asparagus to desired tenderness. Melt butter in frying pan and sauté garlic.
Add lemon juice, lemon zest, dill, pepper and parsley, mixing well. Stir in bread
crumbs. Place asparagus in serving dish and toss with crumb mixture.

Serves 6

Asparagus with Cashews

2 pounds asparagus
2 tablespoons butter
2 tablespoons onion, chopped

¼ cup unsalted cashews
Dash of pepper

Cook asparagus to desired tenderness. Melt butter in frying pan and sauté onions
until translucent. Stir in cashews and pepper. Toss with asparagus and serve.

Serves 6-8

Rochester's location on the edge of the West put seedmen and the nursery industry at a great advantage. They were at least five days ahead of their competitors from Long Island in delivering their products.

Artichoke Stuffed Tomatoes

8 small tomatoes
14 ounces artichoke hearts, drained
1 clove garlic, minced
1 cup mayonnaise
1 cup Parmesan cheese, grated

1 tablespoon soy sauce
Dash of red pepper sauce
Pepper, to taste
Parmesan cheese
Paprika

Preheat oven to 350°. Cut tops off tomatoes and scoop out pulp. Coarsely chop artichokes and combine with remaining ingredients, except additional Parmesan cheese and paprika. Stuff tomatoes with mixture, sprinkle with Parmesan cheese and garnish with paprika. Bake uncovered for 20 minutes or until stuffing is heated through.

Serves 8

Stuffed Summer Tomatoes

6 large, ripe tomatoes
10 ounces frozen chopped spinach, thawed
2 tablespoons olive oil
¾ cup onion, finely chopped

½ cup Italian-style bread crumbs
¼ teaspoon salt
⅛ teaspoon pepper
¼ cup Parmesan cheese, grated

Preheat oven to 375°. Grease a 10x6-inch baking pan. Cut a ½-inch slice from top of each tomato. Scoop out pulp. Chop pulp and set aside. Place tomato shells upside down to drain. Squeeze excess water from spinach and set spinach aside. In skillet, heat olive oil and sauté onion for 2 minutes. Stir in bread crumbs, salt, pepper, tomato pulp and spinach. Cook until heated through, stirring constantly. Spoon hot mixture into tomato shells. Sprinkle each with 2 teaspoons Parmesan cheese and place in prepared pan. Bake uncovered for 10-12 minutes, until tomatoes are slightly soft. Place under broiler for a few seconds to slightly brown cheese, if desired.

Serves 6

Tomato Cheese Casserole

2-3 cups seasoned bread crumbs
5-6 cups tomatoes, peeled and sliced
  (see p. 26)
3 tablespoons margarine, melted
2-3 cups onions, thinly sliced and sautéed
1 tablespoon sugar

2 teaspoons oregano
Garlic salt, to taste
Garlic powder, to taste
2 cups sharp Cheddar cheese, shredded
2 cups mozzarella cheese, shredded

In 13x9-inch baking dish, layer above ingredients in order listed, pressing each layer down firmly as next one is added. Cover and bake at 350° for 40-50 minutes, removing cover near end of baking time to slightly brown top.

Serves 8-10

Zucchini & Tomato Casserole

2 tablespoons olive oil
1 large onion, cut into small chunks
1 large green pepper, cut into small chunks
3 stalks celery, cut into small chunks
¾ pound mushrooms, quartered
1 pound zucchini, cut into ¼-inch
  semicircles

¼ teaspoon basil
¼ teaspoon oregano
½ teaspoon salt
2 cloves garlic, minced
14½ ounces stewed tomatoes
Buttered bread crumbs, for topping

In large frying pan, heat olive oil and sauté onion, green pepper, celery and mushrooms for 5-7 minutes. Decrease heat to low and add zucchini and seasonings. Cover pan and steam for 15 minutes. Drain off and discard liquid. Put vegetable mixture into 2-quart casserole dish and cover with tomatoes. Top with buttered bread crumbs. Bake uncovered at 400° for 30 minutes.

Serves 4-6

Zucchini Parmesan Pancakes

2 pounds zucchini, grated
1 pound potatoes, grated
1½ tablespoons lemon juice
1 cup scallions, chopped
¾ cup Parmesan cheese, grated
1 teaspoon garlic, chopped

2 teaspoons sugar
¼-½ cup flour
2 eggs
Pepper, to taste
½ teaspoon salt
Peanut oil

Drain zucchini and potatoes very well to remove excess liquid. Place vegetables in large bowl and add remaining ingredients, except oil. Mix thoroughly, adding additional flour if mixture is too runny. Heat ½-inch oil in frying pan over medium-to-high heat. Drop spoonfuls of vegetable mixture into oil. Cook until golden brown and crispy. Remove from oil and drain thoroughly on paper towel before serving.

Serves 6-8

Squash Pancakes

1 egg, beaten
1 cup winter squash, cooked and mashed
½ cup flour
1½ - 2 tablespoons sugar
¼ teaspoon salt

½ teaspoon baking powder
¼ teaspoon cinnamon
¼ teaspoon nutmeg
1 tablespoon butter, melted
1 tablespoon milk

Mix egg with squash in large bowl. In another bowl, sift together dry ingredients. Add to squash mixture. Stir in butter and milk. Mix well and spoon desired amount of mixture onto heated griddle or frying pan. Cook on one side until bubbles appear, then turn over and cook on other side.

Makes 6-8 small pancakes

Squash & Apples

2 large Granny Smith apples, cored and
   peeled
3 pounds winter squash
¼ teaspoon cinnamon

¼ cup brown sugar, packed
1½ teaspoons flour
Dash of salt
¼ cup butter

Cut apples and squash into bite-sized cubes and place in 2-quart casserole dish.
Combine cinnamon, sugar, flour and salt. Sprinkle mixture over apples and
squash and top with pats of butter. Bake uncovered at 350° for 40 minutes.

Serves 4-6

Vegetable & Walnut Casserole

20 ounces favorite frozen vegetable or
   vegetable mixture
¼ cup butter or margarine
¼ cup flour
1½ teaspoons chicken bouillon granules

2 cups milk
⅔ cup water
3 tablespoons butter or margarine
3 cups stuffing mix
⅔ cup walnuts, chopped

Grease a 2-quart casserole dish. Cook vegetables, drain well, and put into prepared
dish. Melt butter and blend in flour and bouillon. Gradually add milk, stirring
until thick and smooth. Pour over vegetables and mix. Heat water and butter,
until melted, and mix in stuffing and walnuts. Cover vegetables with stuffing
mixture and bake at 350° for 35 minutes.

Serves 8

Spinach with Sesame Seeds

5 cups water
1 teaspoon salt
10 ounces fresh spinach, washed well
1 clove garlic, crushed
1 tablespoon soy sauce

1 green onion, minced
1 tablespoon roasted sesame seeds
1 tablespoon sesame oil
¼ teaspoon pepper

In large pot, heat water and salt to boiling. Add spinach, stirring frequently. Just before water comes to a second boil, remove pan from heat, drain and rinse spinach in cold water. Squeeze spinach to drain well. Mix remaining ingredients together and pour over spinach. May be served immediately or refrigerated.

Serves 4

Spinach Surprise

4 packages (10-ounce) frozen chopped
    spinach
8 ounces cream cheese, room temperature
½ cup butter or margarine, room
    temperature

Salt and pepper, to taste
14 ounces artichokes, drained and halved
5 ounces water chestnuts, drained and
    sliced
¼ cup bread crumbs

Cook and drain spinach, set aside. Melt cream cheese and butter, add spinach, salt and pepper, and blend well. Place artichokes and water chestnuts on bottom of 13x9-inch dish. Pour spinach mixture on top and sprinkle with bread crumbs. Bake uncovered at 350° for 20 minutes, or until heated through.

Serves 12

Escarole & Sausage Sauté

1 large head escarole
¼-½ cup water
1 large clove garlic, minced
2-4 tablespoons olive or vegetable oil

¼ pound Italian sausage
10-15 medium to large mushrooms, sliced
Fresh bread crumbs
½ cup Parmesan cheese, grated

Wash escarole well in cold water and drain. Cook in water until tender. Drain and set aside. Sauté garlic in oil and set aside. Remove sausage from casing, chop and brown until almost cooked. Add mushrooms and simmer until sausage is fully cooked (mushrooms should be limp). Place escarole in 2-quart baking dish, top with garlic, oil, sausage and mushrooms. Sprinkle with bread crumbs and Parmesan cheese. Bake at 350° for 10 minutes or until hot.

Serves 4-6

Marvelous Mushrooms

⅓ cup butter or margarine, room
  temperature
1 tablespoon dried minced onion
1 tablespoon dried minced parsley or
  cilantro
1 tablespoon Dijon mustard

Pinch of cayenne pepper
Pinch of nutmeg
1½ tablespoons flour
1 pound mushrooms, left whole
1 cup heavy cream

Preheat oven to 375°. Cream butter with next six ingredients. Place mushrooms in 1-quart casserole dish and dot with butter mixture. Pour cream over mushrooms and bake uncovered for 45 minutes. Stir mushrooms a few times during baking. As mushrooms are stirred, butter will blend with cream to form a sauce. Additional milk may be added if sauce is too thick.

Serves 4-6

Divine Leek Casserole

1½ pounds leeks, halved (see p. 32)
1 cup chicken broth
1 tablespoon butter
1 medium onion, chopped

8 slices pancetta (Italian bacon), cooked
  and crumbled
½ cup Parmesan cheese, grated

Cut leeks into 3-inch pieces and braise lightly in chicken broth until tender. In another pan, melt butter and sauté onion until translucent. Arrange leeks on a flat, oven-proof platter. Sprinkle with onion and bacon, then top with cheese. Broil until lightly browned and serve immediately.

Serves 5-6

Onion Pie

1 cup cracker crumbs, saltine or
  butter-flavored
¼ cup margarine
2 large onions, sweet white or yellow,
  sliced
2 eggs

¾ cup milk
¾ teaspoon salt
2-4 drops hot pepper sauce (optional)
1-2 ounces Cheddar cheese, grated
Paprika, for garnish (sweet or hot, to taste)

Place cracker crumbs in bottom of 9 or 10-inch pie plate. Sauté onions in margarine until soft. Place over cracker crumbs. Blend eggs, milk, salt and pepper sauce (if using). Pour over onions. Sprinkle with grated cheese and paprika. Bake uncovered at 350° for 30 minutes, until knife inserted near center comes out clean.

Serves 5-6

Fennel with Olives & Tomatoes

1 large onion, chopped
2 tablespoons olive oil
2 cloves garlic, minced
1 can (28-ounce) tomatoes, with juice
½ cup water
1 fennel bulb (1½ pounds), chopped

1 teaspoon fresh orange zest or scant
    ½ teaspoon dried
1 can (6-ounce) pitted black olives, drained
1 teaspoon fennel seeds (optional)
Salt and pepper, to taste
1 tablespoon lemon juice

Sauté onion in olive oil until soft, approximately 5 minutes. Add garlic and cook 3 minutes longer. Add remaining ingredients, except lemon juice. Bring to a boil and simmer, covered, for 15 minutes. Uncover and simmer for another 30 minutes. Add lemon juice. Serve hot or at room temperature.

Serves 4-6

Rainbow of Peppers & Almonds

5 tablespoons olive oil
1 cup almonds, sliced
2 red peppers, cut into ½-inch strips
2 green peppers, cut into ½-inch strips

2 yellow peppers, cut into ½-inch strips
6 tablespoons red wine vinegar
¼ cup sugar
Salt, to taste

Heat oil in large skillet. Add almonds and cook until lightly browned, approximately 4 minutes, stirring constantly. Add remaining ingredients. Increase heat to medium-high, cover and cook for 10 minutes, stirring occasionally. Uncover and continue to cook until peppers are tender, approximately 7 minutes longer. (Add water if necessary.) Serve warm or at room temperature.

Serves 8

Tuscan Vegetable Sandwiches

⅓ cup olive oil
¼ cup white wine vinegar
1 clove garlic, minced
Salt and pepper, to taste
1 eggplant, sliced lengthwise in ½-inch
   slices
1 medium zucchini, sliced lengthwise in
   ½-inch slices

1 large sweet red pepper, julienned
1 large sweet green pepper, julienned
1 large sweet red onion, peeled and sliced
   in ½-inch thick rings
1 loaf French bread, sliced lengthwise and
   cut in half crosswise
Garlic butter
8 ounces mozzarella cheese, shredded

Combine oil, vinegar, garlic, salt and pepper in bowl as marinade. Place vegetables in dish large enough to hold them and cover with marinade. Marinate for 1 hour. Remove vegetables from marinade and grill for 5 minutes on each side, turning once. Meanwhile, spread pieces of bread with garlic butter and toast lightly. Divide vegetables into 4 equal portions, then stack on toasted bread in order listed. Place on baking sheet, top with cheese, and broil until cheese melts. Serve immediately.

Serves 4

Sweet & Sour Beets

¼ cup water
1 tablespoon cider or wine vinegar
3 tablespoons sugar
Juice and zest of one orange

2 teaspoons cornstarch
3 medium beets, cooked, peeled and diced
Pepper, to taste

Heat water in saucepan. Add vinegar, sugar, orange juice and zest. Stir well to dissolve sugar. Add cornstarch, stirring until sauce is smooth. Add cooked beets and coat with sauce. Add pepper and serve immediately.

Serves 6

Cajun Ratatouille

6 tablespoons olive oil
1 large red onion, quartered and sliced
1 medium eggplant, peeled and cut into
 ¾-inch cubes
1 red pepper, chopped
1 green pepper, chopped
4 large cloves garlic, mashed
1 zucchini squash, cut into ¾-inch cubes
1 summer squash, cut into ¾-inch cubes
6 ounces small mushrooms, quartered

1½-2 pounds fresh tomatoes, or 28 ounces
 canned tomatoes, drained and chopped
½ cup fresh parsley, chopped
¼ cup fresh basil, chopped or 1 tablespoon
 dried
¼ cup fresh thyme, or 1 tablespoon dried
3 tablespoons cayenne pepper sauce or
 2 teaspoons dried cayenne pepper
2 teaspoons salt (3 teaspoons if dish is
 served cold)
1 teaspoon black pepper, freshly ground

Heat oil in wok or large, heavy frying pan. Sauté onions over medium-high heat
for 2-3 minutes, until almost soft. Add eggplant, peppers and garlic and sauté for
another 2-3 minutes. Add zucchini, summer squash and mushrooms and sauté 2-3
minutes longer. Stir in tomatoes and remaining ingredients, blending well.
Reduce heat, cover and simmer for 7-10 minutes. Serve hot or cold.

Serves 8-10

Corn Pudding

4 eggs
1 cup canned cream-style corn
1 cup canned whole-kernel corn, drained
2 tablespoons green pepper, finely chopped
2 tablespoons mushrooms, chopped
1 tablespoon flour

1 tablespoon sugar
1 teaspoon salt
¼ teaspoon pepper
1 cup milk
1 tablespoon butter, melted
3 tablespoons Cheddar cheese, grated

Grease a 1½-quart casserole dish. Beat eggs until thick. Add corn, green pepper
and mushrooms. Set aside. Combine flour, sugar, salt and pepper in mixing bowl.
Stir in milk and butter. Combine with corn mixture, beating well. Pour into
prepared dish and sprinkle with cheese. Bake at 325° for approximately 1 hour
and 20 minutes.

Serves 8-10

Tomatoes were grown in Rochester for the first time in 1825.

Broccoli 'N' Cheese Pita ~ The Crystal Barn

¾ pound phyllo pastry
¼ cup butter
½ cup onion, finely chopped
3 packages (10-ounce) frozen chopped
   broccoli, thawed and well-drained
3 eggs, beaten

½ pound feta cheese, crumbled (see p. 77)
¼ cup fresh parsley, chopped
2 tablespoons fresh dill, chopped
1 teaspoon salt
⅛ teaspoon pepper
½ cup butter, melted

Follow thawing directions on phyllo label. Preheat oven to 350°. Melt butter in medium skillet and sauté onion until golden. In large bowl, mix onion with next seven ingredients. Line inside of 9-inch springform pan with 4 phyllo pastry leaves, overlapping and brushing top of each with melted butter. (Keep unused pastry leaves covered with damp paper towels to prevent drying out.) Pour filling mixture into pan and fold overlapping edges of pastry leaves over top of filling. Cut four 9-inch circles from remaining phyllo leaves. Brush each with butter and layer one over the other on top of pie. With scissors, cut through leaves to make eight sections. Pour any remaining butter on top and place on jelly roll pan to catch drippings. Bake for 40-45 minutes, or until top crust is puffy and golden. Serve warm. (Note: As a lower fat alternative, spray pastry leaves with vegetable oil spray, then use 1 tablespoon melted butter on top of pita before baking.)

Serves 8

Broccoli with Water Chestnuts

2 packages (10-ounce) frozen chopped
   broccoli
8 ounces water chestnuts, drained and
   chopped
1 cup pecans, chopped

2 tablespoons butter or margarine
¼ cup Parmesan cheese, grated
½ cup cracker crumbs
¼-⅓ cup chicken or beef broth
2 tablespoons onion flakes

Place all ingredients in large microwave-safe serving dish. Cover dish and cook on high power for 5-8 minutes, stirring every 2-3 minutes, until broccoli is cooked.

Serves 6-8

Quick-Fried Green Beans in Garlic Sauce

⅔ cup chicken broth
1 pound fresh green beans, cut into bite-
    sized pieces
3 tablespoons peanut oil
2 tablespoons butter
4 cloves garlic, minced

2 scallions, sliced diagonally
Salt, to taste
1 tablespoon soy sauce
1 teaspoon sugar
1 tablespoon pale dry sherry

Put chicken broth in saucepan over medium heat. Add beans and simmer until nearly all liquid has evaporated, stirring frequently. Heat oil and butter in skillet or wok. Add garlic, scallions and salt. Stir-fry for 30 seconds. Add beans and toss until well-coated. Sprinkle with soy sauce, sugar and sherry. Stir-fry for 1 minute longer. Serve hot.

Serves 4

Herbed Green Beans

1 pound fresh green beans
¼ cup margarine
¾ cup onion, minced
¼ cup celery, minced
1 clove garlic, minced

¼ teaspoon basil
¼ cup fresh parsley, snipped
⅛ teaspoon rosemary
¾ teaspoon salt (optional)

Wash beans and pat dry. Remove ends, then slice beans diagonally into short pieces. In large covered saucepan, cook beans in ½-inch boiling, salted water for 15 minutes or until tender. Drain. Meanwhile, melt margarine in another saucepan. Add onion, celery and garlic and cook for 5 minutes. Stir in remaining ingredients, cover pan, and simmer for 10 minutes. Add mixture to cooked beans and toss well to coat.

Serves 4

Gingered Green Beans

1 pound fresh green beans, cut into
  bite-sized pieces
1 clove garlic, chopped

3 tablespoons butter or margarine
1 teaspoon fresh ginger, peeled and grated
⅛ teaspoon pepper, or to taste

Cook green beans to desired tenderness. Sauté garlic in butter. Stir in ginger and pepper. Add cooked beans to mixture, stirring to coat well. Serve immediately.

Serves 6

Braised Carrots & Celery

3 cups bouillon (chicken, vegetable
  or beef)
2-3 large carrots, julienned

5-7 stalks celery, julienned
½ cup Parmesan cheese, grated

In large saucepan, heat bouillon to boiling. Add vegetables. Cover and cook over medium-low heat to desired tenderness, approximately 15 minutes. Remove vegetables from liquid with slotted spoon and place in serving dish. Sprinkle with grated cheese and serve immediately. (Note: Parsnips may also be used with or in place of carrots.)

Serves 6-8

Brussels Sprouts à L'Orange

16 Brussels sprouts, halved
3 tablespoons butter or margarine
1 tablespoon sesame seeds
3 tablespoons honey

⅛ teaspoon ground cloves
1 can (11-ounce) mandarin oranges,
  drained

Cook Brussels sprouts to desired tenderness. Melt butter in frying pan and sauté sesame seeds. Stir in honey and cloves. Combine mixture with Brussels sprouts. Add oranges, toss gently, and serve.

Serves 4

Hummus

1 tablespoon sunflower oil	2 tablespoons tamari or soy sauce
1½ cups onion, finely chopped	½ cup lemon juice
¾ cup carrots, finely diced	1 teaspoon ground cumin
5 cloves garlic, minced	2 tablespoons fresh parsley, minced
2 cans (15-ounce) garbanzo beans	¼ teaspoon cayenne pepper
1 cup tahini	½ teaspoon salt

Heat oil in 10-inch frying pan. Add onion, carrots and garlic. Sauté until browned and tender. Rinse garbanzo beans and mash well. Add remaining ingredients and vegetables, mixing thoroughly. Chill before serving. May be served with pita bread wedges, if desired.

Serves 4-6

Red Bean Toss

1 can (15 or 16-ounce) red or kidney beans, drained	½ teaspoon chili powder
1 cup celery, thinly sliced	½ teaspoon Worcestershire sauce
⅓ cup sweet pickles, chopped	2-3 drops red pepper sauce
¼ cup onion, finely chopped	½ cup mayonnaise
1 cup sharp Cheddar cheese, diced	1 cup corn chips, coarsely crushed
½ teaspoon salt	Green pepper rings, for garnish

Combine beans, celery, pickles, onion and cheese in bowl. In another bowl, blend salt, chili powder, Worcestershire sauce and red pepper sauce with mayonnaise. Add to bean mixture and toss lightly. Spoon mixture into 1-quart shallow baking dish. Sprinkle with corn chips and bake uncovered at 450° for 15 minutes. Garnish with pepper rings and serve immediately.

Serves 4-6

Triple Bean Bake

1 cup dry black beans
1 cup dry Great Northern beans
1 cup dry red kidney beans
3 bay leaves
2 quarts water
16 ounces whole tomatoes, with liquid
1 medium onion, chopped
1 medium green pepper, chopped

1 cup brewed coffee or water
⅔ cup ketchup
½ cup dark molasses
⅓ cup brown sugar, packed
2 teaspoons mustard seed
1 tablespoon Worcestershire sauce
1 teaspoon salt (optional)

Soak and drain beans to point of cooking (*see sidebar*). Place beans in Dutch oven
or roasting pan. Add bay leaves and water. Heat to boiling over high heat. Bake
covered at 350° for 1 hour. Remove pan from oven and stir in remaining
ingredients. Bake uncovered, stirring occasionally, 2 hours longer or until beans
are tender and mixture thickens. Discard bay leaves and serve.

Serves 10

Apple Bean Bake

3 cups tart apples, cubed
½ cup brown sugar, packed
¼ cup white sugar
1 teaspoon cinnamon
½ cup ketchup

1 tablespoon molasses
1 teaspoon salt
1 pound Great Northern beans, prepared
Bacon bits (optional)

In saucepan, cook apples with sugars, stirring until sugars are melted. Stir in
cinnamon, ketchup, molasses, and salt. Add beans and mix well. Pour mixture
into 2-quart casserole and bake uncovered at 400° for approximately 60 minutes.
Sprinkle with bacon bits, if desired.

Serves 6-8

Prepare dried beans
for cooking by
rinsing and sorting
beans. Soak
overnight in three
times as much cold
water as beans, or
place beans and
water in saucepan
and boil for two
minutes. Let sit for
one hour. For both
methods, cook beans
over medium heat
until just tender, and
drain. Use in any
recipe requiring
prepared beans.

Navy beans first
became a cash crop in
Orleans County,
New York, in the
1830s. It was after
the Civil War that
they became popular,
and soon New York
State was producing
two million bushels
per year for national
distribution.

Sweet Potatoes with Fruit & Nuts

2 pounds sweet potatoes, canned or fresh
  (cooked and peeled), cut lengthwise
1 cup brown sugar, packed
1½ tablespoons cornstarch
⅛ teaspoon cinnamon

1 teaspoon orange zest, shredded
1 can (16-ounce) apricots, with syrup
2 tablespoons butter
½ cup pecan halves

Place potatoes in greased casserole dish large enough to hold them. In saucepan, combine brown sugar, cornstarch, cinnamon and orange zest. Drain apricots, pouring 1 cup of the syrup into saucepan. Cook over medium heat until mixture boils, stirring constantly. Boil for 2 minutes, then add apricots, butter and pecans. Stir gently to coat fruit and pour over potatoes. Bake uncovered at 375° for 25 minutes. (Note: If apricot syrup does not measure 1 cup, add water or orange juice.)

Serves 6-8

Make Ahead Potatoes

10 medium potatoes, peeled and quartered
½ cup butter or margarine
1 teaspoon salt
1 cup scalded milk
¼ teaspoon pepper

4 ounces cream cheese with chives and
  onion
Bread crumbs
Parmesan cheese, to taste
Pats of butter

In large saucepan, cover potatoes with water. Cook over medium high heat until tender. Drain off water and coarsely mash potatoes. Add next 5 ingredients and beat with electric mixer until fluffy. Transfer potatoes to greased 1-quart casserole dish and top with bread crumbs, cheese and a few pats of butter. Refrigerate for several hours or overnight. Before baking, bring dish to room temperature. Bake at 350° for 25 minutes, or until heated through.

Serves 8-10

Oven Roasted Potatoes - Four Variations

Buttery Wedges

8 baking potatoes, scrubbed
¼-½ cup butter, melted

Salt and pepper, to taste

Curried Wedges

8 baking potatoes, scrubbed
¼-½ cup butter, melted

½-1 teaspoon curry powder
½ teaspoon seasoned salt

Zesty Wedges

8 baking potatoes, scrubbed
¼ cup olive oil
4 tablespoons dried minced onions

Garlic salt, to taste
Chili powder, to taste (optional)
Black pepper, to taste (optional)

Crusty Wedges

8 baking potatoes, scrubbed
¼-½ cup butter, melted

1 cup (or more) fine bread crumbs

For all variations, preheat oven to 425°. Cut potatoes in half lengthwise. With cut side down, cut each half on the diagonal into four thick sticks. Rinse and dry to remove excess starch. Place in large bowl and toss with desired ingredients. Lay potatoes in single layer in large baking pan with sides. Roast for approximately 45 minutes, turning potatoes for even browning.

Serves 8

Potatoes in Wine

4 medium potatoes, peeled
4 small onions, peeled
2 tablespoons margarine, melted
2 tablespoons flour
1 cup chicken broth

½ cup water
½ cup dry vermouth or chablis
Salt and pepper, to taste
½ teaspoon rosemary leaves, crushed

Quarter potatoes and onions, set aside. Pour margarine into 2-quart dish, then add remaining ingredients, stirring until sauce is smooth. Add potatoes and onions. Bake at 350° for 60 minutes. (Note: Can also be prepared in microwave oven. Cover dish with waxed paper and cook on high power for 22 minutes, stirring twice.)

Serves 4

· P A S T A & G R A I N S ·

By the middle of the 1800s,

New York State was growing 70% of the nation's barley supply.   Slowly the state's barley production center moved west to Genesee Country.   Barley producers had a ready market in Rochester, which had a thriving brewing industry.   By the 1880s, Rochester was considered one of the leading beer-producing cities in the nation, with companies like Bartholomay, Rochester, Genesee and Miller.   Today the Genesee Brewing Company is America's largest regional brewery, and is the seventh-largest brewery in the country.

Genesee Country is also the heart of the buckwheat-growing area of New York State.   Native to China, buckwheat was introduced to America by the Dutch, who planted it in eastern New York State. Buckwheat is really a fruit, but after drying it is milled into flour and used to make griddle cakes and buckwheat noodles, or soba.   Buckwheat groats, or kasha, are roasted and used as a cereal or a side dish.   Another popular product from buckwheat is a rich, flavorful honey. Today, Penn Yan, New York, is the home of the National Buckwheat Institute.

P A S T A & G R A I N S

Pumpkin Tortellini

This recipe was contributed by photographer John Griebsch.

Tortellini

3 tablespoons butter
1 cup shallots, minced
3 cloves garlic, minced
1 teaspoon sage
½ teaspoon salt
1 cup pumpkin, solid pack

¼ teaspoon lemon zest
⅓ cup Parmesan cheese, freshly grated
1 pound fresh pasta dough, cut into 2-inch circles
Flour or fine corn meal

Sauce

1 tablespoon olive oil
1 tablespoon butter
½ pound fresh mushrooms, quartered
1 yellow pepper, diced
1 bunch broccoli, stems julienned and florets separated

2½ cups chicken broth
½ pound plum tomatoes, seeded and diced
½ cup pumpkin, solid pack
Parmesan cheese

Melt butter in saucepan. Cook shallots and garlic until softened. Add sage, salt, pumpkin, lemon zest and Parmesan cheese. Mix well and remove from heat. Place 1 teaspoon of filling on the bottom half of each pasta circle. Fold circle in half, pressing edges together. Curve edges toward you, seam side out, to form a ring. Press overlapping points of original circle firmly together. Place finished tortellini on a wax paper-lined cookie sheet dusted with either flour or fine corn meal. Cover loosely until ready to cook. In large skillet, combine olive oil and butter. Add mushrooms, pepper and broccoli, and cook until vegetables are just tender. Add chicken broth, tomatoes and pumpkin, simmering gently for 5 minutes. Cook tortellini in boiling salted water for 2-3 minutes, or until al dente. Drain tortellini, place in bowls and ladle sauce around them. Serve with Parmesan cheese at table. (Note: Won ton skins may be substituted for pasta dough.)

Serves 4-6

Sesame Noodles

6 tablespoons peanut butter
½ cup rice vinegar
1 tablespoon brown sugar, packed
¼ cup vegetable oil
3 cloves garlic, minced
6 tablespoons soy sauce

1 tablespoon hot sesame oil
2 tablespoons fresh ginger, minced (optional)
1 pound noodles or spaghetti-type pasta, cooked

Combine first eight ingredients, mixing well. Stir in noodles or pasta and serve at room temperature. (Note: May also be tossed with a mixture of chopped blanched green beans, scallions, poached chicken and toasted almonds.)

Serves 5-6

Pasta Limonetta

1 large yellow onion, minced
3 large cloves garlic, mashed
4 tablespoons butter or olive oil
2 cups water
2 tablespoons flour
2 cups chicken stock
1 teaspoon lemon zest, grated
Juice of one lemon
¾ teaspoon sugar
¼ teaspoon turmeric or saffron

½ teaspoon salt
4 tablespoons heavy cream or Crème Fraîche (see p. 138)
4 tablespoons fresh tarragon or parsley, chopped
¼-½ teaspoon red pepper flakes, or to taste
1 pound linguine or non-tubular pasta, cooked
½ cup Parmesan cheese, freshly grated

Combine onion, garlic, butter and water in 3-quart saucepan. Boil until water has almost evaporated. Whisk in flour, chicken stock, lemon zest, lemon juice, sugar, turmeric or saffron, and salt. Cook until mixture reaches consistency of heavy cream. Add cream, tarragon or parsley, and red pepper flakes. Toss with pasta and Parmesan cheese and serve.

Serves 6

Festive Pesto Pasta

The thin peel of the bell pepper will come off easily if the pepper is roasted over a gas flame or under the broiler and the skin is allowed to blister and char. Place pepper in a paper bag, close top, and let pepper sit for 10-20 minutes. Skin should then peel off. Discard interior membrane and seeds.

1 pound fresh asparagus, washed and cut into 1½-inch pieces
½ pound fresh green beans, washed and cut into 1½-inch pieces
1 pound fettucine
1 tablespoon butter

2 large red or yellow bell peppers, peeled and sliced into strips
¾ cup frozen peas, thawed
1½ cups Reduced Fat Pesto Sauce
¾ cup milk
2 tablespoons fresh lemon juice

Bring large pot of salted water to a boil. Cook asparagus and beans until crisp but tender, approximately 5 minutes. Remove from water with strainer and set aside. Add fettucine to boiling water and cook until al dente. Melt butter in large skillet. Add asparagus, beans, peppers, and peas. Heat through. Drain pasta and add to vegetables in skillet. Add pesto sauce, milk and lemon juice. Stir over low heat until pasta is coated with sauce. Serve immediately. (Note: Broccoli may be substituted for the asparagus.)

Serves 6

Reduced Fat Pesto Sauce with Pasta

Caspar Pfaudler developed the vacuum process for making beer in Rochester in 1884.

1 cup fresh basil leaves, packed
2 large cloves garlic
1 tablespoon olive oil
½ cup pine nuts or chopped almonds
½ cup chicken broth
½ cup Parmesan cheese, freshly grated

2 tablespoons Romano cheese, freshly grated
Salt and pepper, to taste
1 pound pasta (linguine, fettucine, angel hair, tortellini)
2 tablespoons milk

Put basil leaves, garlic and olive oil in food processor or blender and purée. Add pine nuts and process until nuts are coarsely chopped. While motor is running, pour in chicken broth and blend. Stop motor. Add cheeses, salt and pepper and process briefly until just combined. Cook and drain pasta, reserving 2 tablespoons water. Toss pasta with pesto sauce, milk and reserved pasta water. Serve hot. (Note: This sauce may be stored in the refrigerator for several weeks or frozen. Return to room temperature before using.)

Serves 4

Homemade Italian Egg Pasta

2 cups flour
⅓ cup Romano cheese, freshly grated
Dash of salt

2 eggs
⅓ cup water
1 tablespoon olive oil

Combine dry ingredients in medium bowl. Make large "well" in center. Add remaining ingredients to "well" and lightly beat eggs with fork. Gradually add in surrounding flour mixture and stir to form a ball of dough. Turn onto floured surface and knead for 8-10 minutes, until dough is stiff and no longer sticky, adding more flour if necessary. Let dough rest by setting under inverted bowl for 30 minutes. Divide into 2 equal portions, and replace unused portion under bowl. Roll each portion through a pasta machine several times to achieve desired thinness. Flour dough as needed. Cut into desired shape and dry for 1 hour before cooking. When cooking, always keep water boiling rapidly to prevent sticking. Cooking time for spaghetti is 2 minutes, fettucine 2½ minutes, and ravioli 6-7 minutes. (Note: If doubling recipe, use 3 eggs, not 4. Dough may be rolled by hand, on floured board, to a thickness of no more than ⅛-inch.)

Makes 1 pound of pasta

Penne Pasta & Cheese

1 onion, finely chopped
Olive oil
3 cloves garlic, finely chopped
½ pound ham, chopped
½ pound escarole, coarsely chopped
1 cup fresh parsley, chopped
1 pound penne pasta, cooked al dente
1 can (28-ounce) tomatoes, drained and
  coarsely chopped

½ cup red peppers, roasted and chopped
1½ pounds sharp Cheddar cheese, finely
  chopped
1 quart milk
½ teaspoon salt
½-1 teaspoon pepper
½ cup Parmesan cheese, grated

In frying pan, sauté onion in olive oil until soft. Add garlic, ham, escarole and parsley and sauté until slightly limp. In large casserole dish, toss onion mixture with next four ingredients. In large pan, heat milk, salt and pepper to boiling. Pour milk over pasta mixture and sprinkle with Parmesan cheese. Bake at 350° for 30-45 minutes.

Serves 8

Pasta with Camembert & Scallops

1 pound sea scallops
1 cup water
2 cups broccoli florets
2 cups celery, sliced
1 red pepper, sliced
8 ounces fettucine
2 tablespoons butter
2 cups fresh mushrooms, sliced

1 clove garlic, minced
1½ cups light or heavy cream
4 ounces Camembert cheese, rind removed
4 ounces Parmesan cheese, freshly grated
1 teaspoon salt
Pinch of nutmeg
½ cup walnuts, chopped and toasted
Black pepper, coarsely ground, to taste

Poach scallops in water in large saucepan or skillet for approximately 3 minutes (do not overcook). Drain, return scallops to pan and set aside. In another large saucepan, blanch broccoli, celery, and red pepper by covering with boiling water for 5 minutes. Drain vegetables and let stand in colander. Cook fettucine according to package directions. While pasta is cooking, melt butter in large skillet and add mushrooms and garlic, sautéing for 2 minutes. Add mixture to scallops and set aside. In same skillet, add cream, Camembert cheese, half of the Parmesan cheese, salt and nutmeg. Simmer until cheeses have melted, about 5 minutes. Drain fettucine and transfer to large bowl. Add vegetables, scallop mixture, walnuts and cheese sauce, mixing well. Top with remaining Parmesan cheese and pepper. Serve immediately.

Serves 4-6

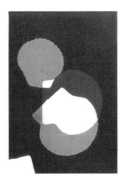

Plum Spicy Szechuan Noodles

12 ounces buckwheat soba noodles
⅓ cup favorite picante sauce
⅓ cup bottled plum sauce
⅓ cup chunky peanut butter
½ tablespoon ginger root, finely minced

2 cups lettuce, shredded
2 carrots, finely shredded
3 scallions, thinly sliced
½ cucumber, peeled and shredded

This is a prize-winning recipe from the National Buckwheat Institute.

Cook noodles according to package directions. Rinse under cold water and drain. In small pan, combine picante sauce, plum sauce, peanut butter and ginger. Bring to a boil over medium heat, stirring constantly. Reduce heat and simmer for 5 minutes, until well blended. Toss noodles with sauce. Arrange lettuce on large serving platter and top with noodles. Garnish with carrots, scallions and cucumber.

Serves 6

Succulent Shrimp & Pasta

1 pound tri-colored spiral pasta
½ cup butter
1½ pounds extra large shrimp, peeled and
  deveined
Salt and pepper, to taste
2 tablespoons olive oil
2 tablespoons butter

¾ pound fresh mushrooms, quartered
2 cloves garlic, minced
14 ounces artichoke hearts, quartered
1½ teaspoons thyme
⅓ cup fresh parsley, chopped
3 tablespoons capers
12-16 cherry tomatoes

Cook pasta according to package directions until al dente. While pasta is cooking, heat butter in wok. Sauté shrimp, salt and pepper over very high heat for 2-3 minutes, until shrimp turns pink. Transfer to oven-safe dish and keep warm. Heat olive oil and additional butter in wok. Sauté mushrooms and garlic over high heat for 2 minutes. Add artichoke hearts and thyme and sauté for 1½-2 minutes, then add parsley and capers and cook 30 seconds longer. Add warm shrimp, with cooking juices, and cherry tomatoes. Stir to blend ingredients. Drain pasta and pour into large bowl. Pour shrimp mixture over pasta and serve.

Serves 6-8

Linguine with Spinach & Shrimp

2 cups chicken broth
1 teaspoon crushed red pepper flakes
½ teaspoon garlic powder
3 tablespoons olive oil
2 cloves garlic, minced
1 red pepper, sliced into strips
1 green pepper, sliced into strips
½ pound mushrooms, sliced

1 pound shrimp, peeled and deveined
3 scallions, chopped
1 pound linguine
3 cups spinach, washed and torn into
    pieces
Fresh parsley, snipped
Romano cheese, grated

In medium saucepan, heat chicken broth, red pepper flakes and garlic powder to boiling. Reduce heat and simmer for 5 minutes. Keep warm. Heat olive oil in large skillet or Dutch oven. Add garlic, red and green peppers, mushrooms, and shrimp. Sauté until shrimp is pink. Add scallions and continue cooking until vegetables are tender. Cook linguine according to package directions until al dente. Spoon shrimp mixture over pasta on serving platter. Stir spinach into hot broth for a few seconds, until barely wilted. Remove spinach from liquid and place on top of shrimp. Sprinkle with parsley and cheese, and serve with broth. (Note: For variation, reduce amount of shrimp to ½ pound and add ½ pound cooked, cubed chicken.)

Serves 4-6

Linguine Estivo (Summertime Pasta)

6 ripe home-grown tomatoes, peeled and
    diced (see p. 26)
1 clove garlic, minced
10-12 fresh basil leaves, minced
Sprig of parsley, minced

4 tablespoons olive oil
Splash of wine vinegar
Salt and pepper, to taste
1 pound linguine
Romano cheese, grated

Combine all ingredients except linguine and cheese. Warm mixture briefly to blend flavors. Cook linguine according to package directions until al dente, then top with tomato mixture and sprinkle with cheese.

Serves 4-6

In 1888, Rochester had eleven beer companies and two ale breweries in operation. Brewing had become a major Rochester industry.

Linguine with Clam & Vegetable Sauce

4 tablespoons olive oil
3 large stalks celery, chopped
2-3 cloves garlic, pressed
1½ teaspoons oregano
½ pound fresh mushrooms, sliced
14 ounces artichoke hearts, drained and chopped
¼ cup white wine or dry vermouth
Salt and pepper, to taste
2 cans (6½-ounce) chopped clams, with liquid
1 large tomato, chopped into large pieces
3 tablespoons fresh parsley, chopped
1¼ pounds linguine, cooked
Parmesan cheese, freshly grated

Heat oil. Sauté celery, garlic and oregano for 2-3 minutes. Add mushrooms and sauté for 2-3 minutes. Add artichokes, wine, salt and pepper and heat for 1 minute. Reduce heat, add clams, and cook slowly for 5 minutes. Do not allow liquid to boil. Add tomato and parsley to clam sauce, stirring gently. Pour mixture over linguine and serve with Parmesan cheese.

Serves 6

Spinach Fettucine Con Pignoli

2 teaspoons olive oil
2-3 bell peppers, cut into ½-inch strips
1 onion, sliced
1 clove garlic, minced
½ cup water
28 ounces plum tomatoes, crushed
½ cup milk
1 sprig fresh basil, or pinch of dried
1 pound spinach fettucine
2 cups fresh spinach, trimmed and packed
1 cup pine nuts or chopped almonds
Parmesan cheese, to taste
Red pepper flakes, to taste

Preheat oven to 400°. In baking dish, combine oil and peppers and roast for 20 minutes. Stir in onion, garlic and water and bake 25 minutes longer. Transfer mixture to skillet, add tomatoes, and cook over medium heat for 2 minutes. Add a small amount of tomato mixture to milk and pour into skillet. Add basil and boil mixture until it thickens. Cook fettucine according to package directions. Just before draining pasta, add spinach to water. Drain. Top with tomato sauce and nuts. Serve with Parmesan cheese and red pepper flakes.

Serves 6

Pierogi

Dough
6 cups flour
3 egg whites

2 tablespoons margarine
1-2 cups water

Filling
3 egg yolks
1¾ pounds farmer's cheese
4 tablespoons margarine
2 teaspoons salt, or to taste

1 onion, diced and sautéed until tender
    (optional)
10 ounces frozen chopped spinach, thawed
    and squeezed dry (optional)
Margarine, for frying

Mix together first three ingredients with enough water to make a smooth dough.
Roll out dough on lightly floured surface to ¼-inch thickness. Cut into 2-inch
circles. In large bowl, mix together next six ingredients. Place 1 teaspoon of filling
on each circle and pinch edges to seal. Let dry for 5-10 minutes. Boil pierogi for
5-10 minutes in salted water, being careful not to place too many in pot at once.
Remove from water, drain and place in frying pan with margarine. Fry until
golden in color and serve.

Makes 45-50

Golden Lasagna

3 tablespoons butter
¼ pound fresh mushrooms, sliced or
    8-ounce can, drained
½ cup onions, chopped
1 can (10¾-ounce) cream of chicken soup
⅓ cup milk
6 lasagna noodles, cooked

24 ounces ricotta cheese
2 cups Cheddar cheese, shredded
4 cups chicken, cooked and cubed
½ cup vegetable of choice, chopped and
    cooked
½ cup Parmesan cheese, grated

Melt butter in medium frying pan and sauté mushrooms and onions. Mix in
chicken soup and milk. Place 3 lasagna noodles in greased 13x9-inch pan. Layer
with half of the ricotta cheese, half of the Cheddar cheese, half of the chicken, and
all of the vegetable. Cover with half of the soup mixture. Layer remaining
noodles, ricotta and Cheddar cheeses, chicken and soup. Sprinkle with Parmesan
cheese and bake at 350° for 45 minutes. Let stand for 10 minutes before serving.

Serves 6-8

Italian Crêpes

1 cup flour
4 eggs
1 cup water
1 teaspoon salt
Margarine, for cooking

24 ounces ricotta cheese
2 eggs, beaten
½ cup ham, chopped
Favorite tomato sauce
½ cup Parmesan cheese, grated

Mix together flour, eggs, water and salt until smooth. Melt small amount of margarine in 5-inch diameter frying pan. Spoon in enough batter to cover bottom of pan. Swirl quickly and return excess batter to bowl, working quickly before batter sets. Cook on one side only and place on tray with waxed paper between layers. Set aside. Mix together ricotta cheese, eggs, and ham. Place large spoonful of mixture on each crêpe, and roll up. Spoon tomato sauce into bottom of 13x9-inch baking dish. Place crêpes, seam side down, in single layer in baking dish and cover with more tomato sauce. Sprinkle with Parmesan cheese and bake at 325° for 20-25 minutes. (Note: Unfilled crêpes may be stored tightly covered in refrigerator for one day before use, or frozen in plastic bag or container.)

Serves 6

"The Reason I Married Him" Pasta

½ cup butter or olive oil
1 small onion, chopped
2 cloves garlic, chopped
4 ounces fresh mushrooms, sliced

½ cup white wine
9 ounces angel hair pasta
Parmesan cheese, grated, to taste

Heat butter or oil in small frying pan. Add onion and sauté until translucent. Add garlic and mushrooms and continue cooking until onion is slightly browned. Add wine and simmer, uncovered, for 5 minutes. Cook pasta according to package directions. Drain. Place pasta in serving dish and top with sauce. Sprinkle liberally with Parmesan cheese and mix well. Serve immediately.

Serves 2-4

Torta Italiano

Blue mould, new fields planted in the West, and Prohibition brought an end to most of Rochester's breweries by the 1920s.

1 pound ground Italian sausage
½ cup onion, chopped
½ cup celery, diced
1 cup mushrooms, sliced
16 ounces stewed tomatoes
8 ounces tomato sauce
1 tablespoon fresh basil, chopped
½ teaspoon garlic salt

¼ cup water
6 ounces spaghetti
2 tablespoons margarine, room temperature
⅓ cup Parmesan cheese, grated
2 eggs, beaten
1 cup ricotta cheese
½ cup mozzarella cheese, shredded

Sauté first four ingredients. Drain well. Stir in tomatoes, tomato sauce, basil, garlic salt, and water. Cook over medium heat for about 20 minutes, until thickened. Meanwhile, cook and drain spaghetti. Stir margarine, Parmesan cheese and eggs into spaghetti and press into 10-inch pie plate to form crust. Spread ricotta cheese over spaghetti and fill with tomato mixture. Bake uncovered at 350° for 20-25 minutes. Sprinkle with mozzarella cheese and bake 5 minutes longer. Serve immediately.

Serves 6

Lentil Spaghetti

2 teaspoons olive oil
1 medium onion, finely chopped
1 large clove garlic, minced
2 stalks celery, chopped
1 cup favorite tomato sauce
½ cup lentils
1 teaspoon basil

½ teaspoon oregano
½ teaspoon thyme
½ teaspoon salt
1 teaspoon red pepper sauce (optional)
2 cups water
1 pound spaghetti, cooked
Parmesan cheese

Heat oil. Sauté onions, garlic and celery. Add tomato sauce, lentils, basil, oregano, thyme, salt, red pepper sauce (if using), and water. Simmer for 45-60 minutes. (Note: If lentils are cooked ahead of time, cooking time may be reduced.) Serve over hot spaghetti and sprinkle with Parmesan cheese.

Serves 6

Roasted Red Pepper Couscous with Capocollo

Olive oil, for sautéing
1 onion, finely chopped
4 cloves garlic, finely chopped
1 cup red peppers, roasted, peeled and
   chopped
1 cup fresh parsley, chopped

½ teaspoon red pepper flakes
2 cups chicken broth
1 cup couscous
¼ pound capocollo, finely chopped
Salt and pepper, to taste

Heat olive oil in large pan and sauté onions until tender. Add garlic, red peppers, parsley and red pepper flakes, mixing together. Stir in chicken broth and couscous. Cover pan, remove from heat, and let stand for 5 minutes. When couscous is done, stir in capocollo, salt and pepper. Serve immediately.

Serves 4

Roasted peppers are available in jars at most supermarkets.

Eggplant with Bulgur

1 large eggplant, peeled and cut into
   1-inch cubes
1 cup onion, chopped
2 cloves garlic, minced
⅛-¼ cup olive oil
1 cup bulgur

2½ cups vegetable juice
½ cup almonds, slivered or sliced
1½ teaspoons oregano
¼ cup fresh parsley, chopped
Salt and pepper, to taste

Cook eggplant in boiling water for 3 minutes. Drain and set aside. In large pot or 2-quart oven-proof casserole dish, sauté onion and garlic in olive oil until onion is translucent. Add eggplant and remaining ingredients and simmer for approximately 5 minutes. (If using pot, transfer mixture to casserole dish.) Cover dish and bake at 350° for 30 minutes. Serve hot or cold.

Serves 4 as entree, 8-10 as sidedish

Bulgur can be found in supermarkets, health food stores and Middle Eastern markets. Whole wheat kernels are steamed, dried and crushed to produce bulgur, which is the principal ingredient in tabbouleh, a popular Middle Eastern salad.

Moghul Rice

1⅓ cups water
½ cup long-grain rice
1 teaspoon chicken bouillon granules
1 teaspoon dried minced onion
⅛ teaspoon dried minced garlic
¼ teaspoon curry powder

½ teaspoon salt
Pinch of parsley flakes
1½ tablespoons margarine
2 dried apricots, minced
¼ cup yellow raisins
¼ cup toasted almonds, slivered

Bring water to a boil in 2-quart saucepan. Reduce heat and stir in rice, bouillon, onion, garlic, curry, salt, parsley and margarine. Cover tightly and simmer for 20 minutes. Remove from heat. Add apricots and raisins. Let stand, covered, until all water is absorbed, about 5 minutes. Sprinkle with almonds just before serving.

Serves 4

Lemon Dill Rice

1 cup long-grain rice
3 tablespoons olive oil
1 cup celery, finely diced
1 cup onion, finely diced
1 large clove garlic, minced
1¾ cups chicken broth

2 tablespoons lemon juice
2 tablespoons unsalted butter
¼ cup fresh dill, or 2 teaspoons dried
1 tablespoon sugar
Salt and pepper, to taste
Lemon slices and fresh dill, for garnish

In 3-quart saucepan, cook rice in oil over moderate heat until rice is golden, approximately 5 minutes. Add celery, onion, and garlic and cook until slightly softened, about 3 minutes. Add remaining ingredients. Bring to a boil, cover pan, and reduce heat to low, cooking until rice is tender and liquid is absorbed, approximately 20 minutes longer. Garnish with lemon slices and sprigs of fresh dill.

Serves 6

Spring Vegetable Risotto

3 tablespoons butter
3 tablespoons olive oil
½ cup scallions, white part only, chopped
2 stalks celery, coarsely chopped
½ cup fresh parsley, coarsely chopped
2 cups rice (preferably arborio)
4 cups chicken broth

¾ pound asparagus, trimmed and cut into
   1-inch lengths
¾ cup fresh peas, shelled
½ teaspoon pepper
¼ cup scallions, green part only, minced
Parmesan cheese

Combine butter and oil in 14x11-inch glass dish. Cover and place in microwave oven, cooking on high power for 3 minutes. Add white scallions, celery, parsley and rice, stirring to coat. Cook uncovered for 4 minutes on high power. Stir in broth and cook uncovered for 12 minutes. Stir in asparagus and peas and cook uncovered for another 12 minutes. Remove dish from microwave oven. Stir in pepper and green scallions. Cover loosely and allow to sit for 8-10 minutes. Serve with Parmesan cheese at table.

Serves 6

Risotto, a classic Italian rice dish, is usually made with arborio rice, but will work with long and short-grain rice as well. The rice should be creamy, while still being "al dente", or having an inner bite.

Herb & Barley Casserole

1½ cups barley
½ cup margarine
3 cups water
1 envelope onion soup mix

½ teaspoon marjoram
½ teaspoon basil
½ teaspoon rosemary
¾ cup pine nuts or chopped almonds

In frying pan, brown barley in margarine for approximately 20 minutes. Stir in remaining ingredients, then place in 2-quart casserole dish. Cover and bake at 300° for 60 minutes.

Serves 6-8

Hiram G. Hotchkiss manufactured pearl barley at his Crystal Palace Mills in Lyons, New York.

contributed to the sweet side of life. In 1912, Robert Douglas of Fairport, New York, developed the process to extract and concentrate pectin from apples. Pectin assures the gelling of syrups to a smooth semi-solid consistency. His product, Certo, was distributed commercially to manufacturers of jellies, jams, confections and pharmaceuticals. In 1921, Certo became available for home use.

One of Douglas' customers was probably Frank O'Connor, who opened the first Fanny Farmer Candy Shop on Main Street in Rochester in 1919. O'Connor named his shop after Fannie Merritt Farmer, who brought quality to cooking and cookbooks by advocating precise measurement in food preparation. O'Connor brought quality to the candy industry by using only the freshest and best chocolates. In addition, in order to supply the freshest candy, he insisted that all stores be located no more than 200 miles from a Fanny Farmer production "studio".

▪ D E S S E R T S & F R U I T S ▪

Almond Butter Crunch

1¼ cups sugar
⅓ cup light corn syrup
⅓ cup water
½ cup butter
½ cup margarine
½ teaspoon salt

¼ teaspoon baking soda
¾ cup almonds, coarsely chopped
4 ounces dark sweet chocolate
2 ounces unsweetened chocolate
1 teaspoon vegetable oil
¾ cup almonds, finely chopped

In medium saucepan, combine sugar, corn syrup and water. Bring to a boil over moderate heat. Reduce heat, cover and simmer for 2 minutes. Add butter and margarine, stirring until melted. Bring to a boil over moderate heat and cook, stirring occasionally, until mixture turns a dark caramel color. While candy is cooking, butter a baking sheet and metal spatula. Remove candy mixture from heat and stir in salt, baking soda and coarsely chopped almonds. Pour mixture onto prepared baking sheet, spreading to ¼-inch thickness with spatula. Let cool. Melt chocolate with oil in double boiler. Pour chocolate over candy, spreading evenly. Cover with finely chopped almonds, pressing them into the chocolate. Refrigerate until ready to serve. Cut or break into small pieces.

Serves 20

Frank O'Connor was also the owner of Laura Secord Candy Shops in Canada.

Frozen Yogurt Crunch

⅔ cup peanut butter chips
12 ounces milk chocolate candy

6 cups favorite crispy cereal (rice or multi-grain)
1 gallon vanilla frozen yogurt

Melt peanut butter chips and chocolate in large pan, then add cereal. Spread on ungreased cookie sheet and let cool. Break into small pieces. Soften frozen yogurt and fold in all but one cup of the chocolate pieces. Spoon into 10-inch springform pan and level top. Decorate top with remaining chocolate pieces, then freeze. Allow to stand at room temperature for 10 minutes before slicing.

Serves 12-16

Chocolate Striped Ice Box Cake

1 pint heavy cream
Chocolate syrup, to taste

2½-3 packets graham crackers

In large bowl, whip heavy cream until firm. While whipping, slowly pour chocolate syrup into cream until desired color is reached. Frost tops of whole graham crackers, one at a time, and put 4 or 5 together to make a stack. On rectangular serving plate, stand stacks on edge to make one log, approximately 12 inches long. Frost entire cake with remaining whipped cream and drizzle with chocolate syrup. Refrigerate for at least 8 hours. To serve, slice diagonally at 45° angle.

Serves 12

Fresh Fruit Kuchen

Crust
1½ cups flour
1 tablespoon sugar
½ teaspoon salt

¼ teaspoon baking powder
6 tablespoons butter or margarine

Filling
Apples or peaches, peeled and cut into
    ½-inch slices
½ cup sugar
½ teaspoon cinnamon

¼ teaspoon nutmeg
1 egg
1 cup heavy cream or half-and-half

Preheat oven to 400°. Lightly grease a 9-inch round cake pan. To make crust, combine dry ingredients and cut in butter with pastry blender or fork until crumbly. Press firmly against bottom and sides of prepared pan. Arrange single layer of apple or peach slices on top of crust. Mix sugar, cinnamon and nutmeg and sprinkle over fruit. Bake for 15 minutes. Beat together egg and cream and pour over fruit. Return pan to oven and bake 25-30 minutes longer, until custard is set. Remove from oven and let stand for 10 minutes before serving.

Serves 6-8

Mixed Fruit Crisp

1 cup fresh raspberries
1 cup sweet cherries, pitted
2 large peaches, sliced
1 cup sugar

¾ cup flour
1 teaspoon cinnamon
6 tablespoons cold butter
¼ cup oatmeal

Preheat oven to 400°. Generously grease a 9-inch square baking dish. In large bowl, mix together fruits and toss with ½ cup of the sugar. Pour into prepared dish and set aside. In another bowl, stir together the remaining sugar, flour and cinnamon. Cut in butter until mixture resembles coarse meal. Stir in oatmeal. Spread mixture over fruit and bake for 30 minutes, until topping is golden. (Note: Any fresh or frozen fruit may be used in this recipe.)

Serves 6-8

The first cultivated black raspberry, known as the Doolittle, was raised in the Finger Lakes area.

Caramel Pear Pudding Cake

1 cup flour
⅓ cup white sugar
1½ teaspoons baking powder
½ teaspoon cinnamon
¼ teaspoon salt
Dash of ground cloves
½ cup milk

4 ripe medium pears, peeled and cut into
    ½-inch pieces, or 1 can (16-ounce)
    drained and chopped
½ cup pecans, chopped
⅔ cup brown sugar, packed
¼ cup butter or margarine, room
    temperature
¾ cup boiling water
Ice cream or whipped topping

Preheat oven to 375°. In large mixing bowl, stir together flour, white sugar, baking powder, cinnamon, salt and cloves. Add milk and beat until smooth. Stir in pears and pecans. Turn into an ungreased 2-quart casserole. In another bowl, combine brown sugar, butter and water. Mix well and pour evenly over batter. Bake for 45 minutes. Serve with ice cream or whipped topping.

Serves 8

Blueberry Pudding~Richardson's Canal House

6 cups blueberries, fresh or frozen
½ cup honey
1 egg, beaten
1 tablespoon cornstarch
1½ cups flour
½ cup sugar

2 teaspoons baking powder
Pinch of salt
½ cup milk
½ cup unsalted butter, melted
1 egg, beaten
Ice cream or whipped cream

Preheat oven to 375°. Grease an 8-inch square pan. If using frozen blueberries, thaw and drain them. Mix first four ingredients in large bowl. Pour into prepared pan. In medium bowl, combine flour, sugar, baking powder and salt. Set aside. In smaller bowl, combine milk, butter and egg. Add to dry ingredients and mix until just combined. Spoon over blueberry mixture, spreading to edges. Bake for 45 minutes, or until toothpick inserted near center comes out clean. Serve warm with ice cream or whipped cream.

Serves 6

Southwest Bread Pudding

Syrup
¼ cup margarine
1½ cups brown sugar, packed
2 cups water

1 stick cinnamon
1 clove

Pudding
8 slices toast or stale bread
1 cup raisins
1 cup apples, diced (optional)

½ cup pine nuts or chopped pecans
1 cup favorite cheese, grated

Preheat oven to 350°. Grease a 13x9-inch casserole dish. Combine first five ingredients in saucepan and cook over medium heat until light syrup is formed. In casserole dish, layer pudding ingredients, in order given, until all ingredients are used. Remove cinnamon and clove from syrup and pour syrup over pudding. Bake for 30 minutes. Serve warm or cold.

Serves 10-12

Rum Rice Pudding

2 quarts milk
1 cup sugar
½ cup butter
1 cup long-grain rice

1 cup raisins
¼ cup rum
Cinnamon, for garnish

In large saucepan, heat milk, sugar and butter to boiling. Reduce heat to low, add rice, and cook for 45 minutes. Watch carefully, stirring occasionally to prevent scorching. Add raisins and cook for 10 minutes longer. Stir in rum, cooking for an additional 5 minutes. Pour into serving dish and sprinkle with cinnamon.

Serves 8

Lemon Delight

1 cup flour
½ cup margarine, room temperature
½ cup pecans, chopped
2 packages (3-ounce) lemon pudding and
   pie filling

½ cup powdered sugar
8 ounces cream cheese, room temperature
12 ounces frozen whipped topping, thawed

Preheat oven to 375°. Combine first three ingredients in bowl, mixing well. Press into 13x9-inch baking dish and bake for 15 minutes. Remove pan from oven and allow crust to cool. Prepare lemon pudding according to package directions and set aside. In another bowl, combine powdered sugar, cream cheese and 1 cup of the whipped topping, mixing well. Spread mixture on top of the cooled crust. Pour lemon pudding over cream cheese layer and let cool for approximately 30 minutes. Refrigerate until pudding has completely set. Serve with a dollop of whipped topping on each piece.

Serves 12-15

Baked Apple Pudding

1 cup sugar
¼ cup butter or margarine, room
   temperature
1 egg, beaten
1 cup flour
1 teaspoon baking soda

1 teaspoon cinnamon
1 teaspoon nutmeg
3 medium apples, finely chopped
½ cup nuts, chopped
Apple Pudding Sauce

Preheat oven to 350°. In large bowl, cream sugar and butter. Stir in egg. Add remaining ingredients, except Apple Pudding Sauce, and mix well. Pour batter into an 8-inch square pan. Bake for approximately 35 minutes. Top with Apple Pudding Sauce.

Serves 8-10

Honey Almond Pears

3 fresh pears
Lemon juice
⅓ cup sugar
2 tablespoons honey

2 tablespoons butter or margarine
1 tablespoon milk
⅔ cup unblanched almonds, slivered
Ice cream or whipped cream

Preheat oven to 350°. Peel, core and halve pears. Coat with lemon juice and place round side up in large baking dish. Set aside. Combine sugar, honey, butter and milk in small saucepan. Simmer until mixture begins to thicken, stirring to prevent burning. Stir in almonds. Pour syrup over pears and bake for 45 minutes or until pears are tender. Serve hot or cold with ice cream or whipped cream.

Serves 6

Apple Pudding Sauce
_____

½ cup butter or
margarine

½ cup heavy cream or
evaporated milk

½ teaspoon vanilla
extract

½ cup brown sugar,
packed

½ cup white sugar

Combine ingredients
in saucepan and
bring to a boil. Cook
for 5 minutes,
stirring occasionally.
Serve warm over
pudding.

The Ida Red apple
was developed at the
nation's first
Agricultural
Experiment Station
located in Geneva,
New York. It is one
of the varieties that
contribute to the
apple's ranking as the
#2 fresh fruit snack,
second only to
bananas.

Fruit-N-Cream

1 can (20-ounce) pineapple chunks,
   drained
1 can (16-ounce) peach slices, drained
1 can (11-ounce) mandarin oranges,
   drained
1 package (3-ounce) instant French vanilla
   pudding

1½ cups milk
3 ounces frozen orange juice concentrate,
   thawed
¾ cup sour cream or plain yogurt
3 medium bananas, sliced

In large bowl, mix together pineapple, peaches, and oranges. In medium bowl,
mix dry pudding, milk and orange juice concentrate. Blend in sour cream or
yogurt. Fold mixture into fruit and chill well. Just before serving, fold in sliced
bananas.

Serves 12-15

Frozen Macaroon Soufflé

1 quart vanilla ice cream
12 almond macaroons, crumbled
8 teaspoons orange-flavored brandy

1 cup heavy cream, whipped
Raspberry Sauce

Soften ice cream. Stir macaroons and brandy into ice cream, then fold in whipped
cream. Spoon into 6-cup metal mold. Cover with plastic wrap and freeze. When
ready to serve, unmold by running a knife around edge, then dipping mold quickly
in hot water. Serve with Raspberry Sauce.

Serves 12

Raspberry Sauce

2 packages
(10-ounce) frozen
raspberries, thawed

5 tablespoons sugar

8 teaspoons orange-
flavored brandy

Simmer raspberries
with sugar until soft.
Strain raspberries to
remove seeds, stir in
brandy and mix well.
Drizzle over soufflé.

Fruit Sorbet

1 pound frozen fruit (strawberries, melon,
 blueberries, peaches, pears)
⅓-½ cup superfine granulated sugar

2 teaspoons fresh lemon juice
1 cup plain yogurt or buttermilk

Chop frozen fruit in food processor until fine. Add remaining ingredients and
blend. Serve immediately. (Note:Yogurt gives tangier taste, while buttermilk gives
richer taste. Do not prepare ahead, since texture will not be right.)

Serves 4-6

Chocolate Snowball

8 ounces German sweet chocolate, broken
 into pieces
2 teaspoons instant coffee granules
1 cup sugar
½ cup boiling water
1 cup unsalted butter, cut into pieces,
 room temperature

4 eggs
1 tablespoon cognac or vanilla extract
1 cup heavy cream
2 tablespoons sugar
2 tablespoons cognac or favorite flavoring
Grated chocolate, for garnish

Preheat oven to 350°. Line a 5-cup mold or soufflé dish with a double thickness of
foil. Combine chocolate, coffee granules and sugar in food processor and process
until chocolate is finely chopped. With machine running, add boiling water and
continue to process until chocolate has melted. Add butter, blending completely.
Add eggs and cognac or vanilla and process for 10 seconds. Pour mixture into
prepared mold. Bake for 45 minutes, or until a thick crust has formed on top.
(The mixture will recede as it cools.) Wrap tightly and refrigerate. When ready to
serve, whip cream with sugar and desired flavoring. Invert mold and remove foil
from chocolate ball. Frost with whipped cream and sprinkle with grated
chocolate.

Serves 8-12

CAKES

developed in England in 1835. The first commercial baking powder appeared around 1850. In 1852, D. B. DeLand and Company was founded in Fairport, New York, and by 1870 was the largest producer of baking powder in the country.

Baking powder is a mixture of acid, alkali and starch that produces carbon dioxide gas in batters and doughs, and helps them to rise. Before its development, cooks had to rely on laborious and unreliable methods to produce lightness in baked goods. Cooks used "pearl ash", purified potash and bicarbonate of soda, along with acids, to cause rising. Cream of tartar was a favorite acid to use, as well as liquids such as sour milk, vinegar and fruit juice. Both bicarbonate of soda and cream of tartar had to be pounded into powder before use, and then had to be sifted many times to be sure that no solid pieces remained. The correct proportions were also very important, or the baker would produce discolored baked goods with a disagreeable odor and flavor.

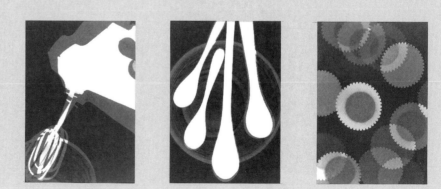

C A K E S

Aruba Chocolate Cake

This recipe was contributed by photographer Judy Sánchez.

2 eggs
3 cups flour
1 cup baking cocoa
2 cups sugar
2 teaspoons baking soda

2 teaspoons vanilla extract
1 teaspoon salt
1 cup vegetable oil
1 cup sour milk
1 cup hot water

Preheat oven to 350°. Grease and flour a large bundt or tube pan. Place all ingredients, except hot water, in large mixing bowl. Stir ingredients until blended, then add hot water. Beat for 1 minute with electric mixer at high speed. Pour batter into prepared pan and bake for 60-70 minutes, or until toothpick inserted near center comes out clean. If desired, dust with powdered sugar and serve with whipped cream or ice cream.

Serves 10-12

Making Sour Milk

Add 2 tablespoons lemon juice or vinegar to 1 cup milk and mix well.

Chocolate Angel Food Cake

¼ cup + 1 tablespoon baking cocoa
¼ cup boiling water
2 teaspoons vanilla extract
¾ cup sugar
1 cup cake flour, sifted

¼ teaspoon salt
16 egg whites
2 teaspoons cream of tartar
1 cup sugar

One of the oldest methods of lightening cakes consisted of entrapping air in the batter. Angel food cake is a good example. Vigorous beating of the eggs traps air and produces a high, light cake.

Preheat oven to 350°. Combine cocoa and water in medium bowl and stir until very smooth. Stir in vanilla. In another medium bowl, combine sugar, flour and salt, blending well. In large bowl, beat egg whites until frothy. Add cream of tartar and beat until soft peaks form. Gradually add sugar, beating until stiff peaks form. Remove 1 cup of beaten egg whites and stir into cocoa mixture. Sprinkle flour mixture over remaining egg whites, ¼ cup at a time, folding in quickly and gently. Fold cocoa mixture into batter until uniformly mixed. Pour into 10-inch tube pan. (Run a small spatula through batter to prevent air pockets.) Bake for 40 minutes. Remove pan from oven and invert over neck of soda or wine bottle to cool.

Serves 10

Coffee & Cream Cake

1 package devil's food cake mix
4 eggs
3 ounces instant chocolate pudding
¾ cup vegetable oil
¾ cup coffee-flavored liqueur or
 crème de cacao

1 pint sour cream
1 cup chocolate chips
1 cup pecans, chopped (optional)
Chocolate Glaze

Preheat oven to 350°. Grease and flour a bundt pan. In large bowl, beat together cake mix and eggs. Add pudding, oil, liqueur and sour cream, mixing well. Fold in chocolate chips and pecans (if using). Pour batter into prepared pan and bake for 60 minutes, or until done. Drizzle with Chocolate Glaze, or dust cake with powdered sugar.

Serves 10-12

Chocolate Glaze

1 cup powdered sugar

1 teaspoon baking cocoa

4-6 teaspoons coffee-flavored liqueur, milk or water

Combine ingredients, using enough liquid so that mixture will drizzle.

Citrus Sponge Cake

9 eggs, separated
1½ cups sugar
½ cup flour

¼ cup cornstarch
Juice and zest of one lemon (or orange)
½ teaspoon vanilla extract

Preheat oven to 350°. Beat egg whites until frothy. Gradually add sugar and continue beating until stiff peaks form. Sift flour and cornstarch, and fold into above mixture. Set batter aside. Beat egg yolks, then add lemon juice, zest, and vanilla. Fold mixture into batter. Pour into large, ungreased tube pan. Bake for 50-60 minutes. Remove pan from oven and invert over neck of soda or wine bottle to cool.

Serves 8-10

Devilishly Rich Chocolate Cake

Cake

⅔ cup unsalted butter, room temperature	1¼ teaspoons baking soda
2 cups sugar	¼ teaspoon baking powder
3 eggs	1½ cups milk
2 cups flour	1 teaspoon vanilla extract
¾ cup baking cocoa	¼ cup chocolate-mint liqueur

Fudge Filling

⅔ cup sugar	1 tablespoon light corn syrup
½ cup heavy cream	2 tablespoons unsalted butter
2½ ounces unsweetened chocolate	3 tablespoons chocolate chips

Chocolate Cream

2½ cups heavy cream	7 tablespoons powdered sugar
3½ tablespoons baking cocoa	

Chocolate Syrup

2 tablespoons baking cocoa	1 tablespoon sugar
2 tablespoons light corn syrup	2 tablespoons water

Preheat oven to 350°. Line two 9-inch round cake pans with waxed paper, then grease and flour them. In mixing bowl, beat butter and sugar until light and fluffy. Beat in eggs, one at a time, until blended. Set aside. In another bowl, combine flour, cocoa, baking soda and baking powder. Add to the egg mixture in thirds, alternating with milk, mixing only until blended. Stir in vanilla and liqueur. Pour batter into prepared pans. Bake for 40-45 minutes, until cakes are springy to touch. Let cool for 5 minutes. Remove cakes from pans and cool completely on wire rack.

To make fudge filling, combine sugar, cream, chocolate and corn syrup in small heavy saucepan. Bring to a simmer over moderate heat, stirring frequently. Reduce heat to low and cook for 10 minutes, or until mixture thickens. Remove from heat, dot top with butter and let cool to room temperature, about 15 minutes. When cool, stir in the butter until the filling is smooth and creamy. To begin assembling cake, place one of the cooled layers onto a serving plate and cover top with all of the fudge filling. Sprinkle evenly with chocolate chips and set aside.

To make chocolate cream, beat heavy cream and cocoa until soft peaks form. Gradually add powdered sugar and continue to beat until stiff. To finish assembling cake, spread ½ cup of the chocolate cream on top of the layer with filling and chocolate chips. Top with second cake layer. Cover top and sides of cake with half of the remaining chocolate cream. Use rest of cream in pastry bag to decorate the cake as desired. Refrigerate for up to 3 hours. Shortly before serving, combine chocolate syrup ingredients in small saucepan. Bring to simmer over low heat and cook, stirring constantly, for 2 minutes. Transfer syrup to small bowl and cool to room temperature, stirring once or twice, to prevent skin from forming. Drizzle syrup over top of cake in lacy design and serve.

Serves 10-12

Chocolate Cupcake Surprises

Batter

1½ cups flour
1 cup sugar
¼ cup baking cocoa
1 teaspoon baking soda
½ teaspoon salt

1 cup water
⅓ cup vegetable oil
1 tablespoon vinegar
1 teaspoon vanilla extract

Filling

8 ounces cream cheese, room temperature
1 egg
⅓ cup sugar
⅛ teaspoon salt

1 cup chocolate chips
Sugar, for garnish
Chopped almonds, for garnish

Preheat oven to 350°. Grease muffin tins or line with paper cups. Combine first five batter ingredients in large mixing bowl. Add remaining batter ingredients, mixing until blended. Fill prepared muffin tins ⅓ full. In another bowl, beat together cream cheese, egg, sugar, and salt. Stir in chocolate chips. Place one heaping tablespoon of filling mixture onto batter in each muffin tin. Sprinkle with additional sugar and almonds. Bake for 30 minutes.

Makes 2 dozen

Hazelnut Cheesecake ~ Richardson's Canal House

Crust
1½ cups graham cracker crumbs
¼ cup sugar

¼ cup butter, melted

Filling
27 ounces cream cheese, room temperature
1 cup sugar
1 cup toasted hazelnuts, ground
4 eggs, room temperature
1 egg yolk, room temperature
½ teaspoon fresh lemon juice

½ teaspoon vanilla extract
¼ teaspoon almond extract
Pinch of salt
2 tablespoons plus 1 teaspoon cornstarch
1 cup half-and-half

Preheat oven to 350°. Grease a 10-inch cheesecake pan. Mix graham cracker crumbs, sugar and butter in medium bowl. Press into bottom and sides of prepared pan. Bake until golden brown, 10-12 minutes. Cool to room temperature on wire rack. Using electric mixer, beat cream cheese and sugar in large bowl until smooth and light. Mix in nuts, eggs, yolk, lemon juice, vanilla, almond extract and salt. Combine cornstarch and half-and-half and add to cake mixture. Pour into crust. Place cheesecake pan in large roasting pan. Add enough boiling water to roasting pan to come halfway up sides of cake pan. Bake until cheesecake is light brown and pulls away from sides of pan, about 1 hour. Cool cheesecake completely on wire rack. Cover and refrigerate at least 4 hours or overnight. Let stand at room temperature for 20 minutes before serving.

Serves 10-12

Grand Cheesecake ~ Pamela's Pastry Kitchen

Crust

½ cup butter

¼ cup sugar

1 egg

1½ cups flour

Batter

24 ounces cream cheese, room temperature

1¼ cups sugar

5 eggs

2 cups sour cream

Zest of one orange

¼ cup orange-flavored liqueur

1 teaspoon orange flavoring

Preheat oven to 400°. Grease bottom and sides of a 9-inch springform pan. Combine butter and sugar in food processor. Pulse until mixture holds together. Add egg and pulse until blended. Add flour and pulse again. Remove sides of springform pan and set aside. Pat half of the crust mixture onto the bottom of the springform pan and bake for 6 minutes. Remove pan from oven, allow crust to cool, then attach sides to pan. Pat remaining pastry up the sides of the pan. In large bowl, beat cream cheese and sugar until smooth. Add eggs, one at a time, stirring well after each addition. Blend in remaining ingredients. Pour batter into crust and bake at 425° for 10 minutes. Reduce oven temperature to 225°. Bake for 45 minutes, or until center jiggles slightly. Turn off heat and allow cake to remain in closed oven for an additional 2 hours. Remove pan from oven and cool on wire rack. Cover and refrigerate for several hours or overnight.

Serves 10-12

Grasshopper Cheesecake

1½ cups chocolate wafer crumbs (about 26)
¼ cup margarine, melted
24 ounces cream cheese, room temperature
1 cup sugar
5 eggs

1 tablespoon flour
⅓ cup green crème de menthe
3 tablespoons white crème de cacao
4 ounces semisweet chocolate
½ cup sour cream, room temperature

Preheat oven to 350°. Combine chocolate wafer crumbs and margarine and press in bottom of 9-inch springform pan. Beat cream cheese until light and fluffy. Add sugar gradually, then add eggs one at a time, beating well after each addition. Add flour, mixing thoroughly. Stir in crème de menthe and crème de cacao, then pour batter into crust. Bake for 55-60 minutes. Cool thoroughly. Melt chocolate in top of double boiler, and let cool. Stir in sour cream and spread mixture over top of cheesecake. Chill.

Serves 12-16

Walnut Mocha Roll

Mocha Cream

4 teaspoons Swiss mocha instant coffee, or to taste

2 tablespoons hot water

⅓-½ cup powdered sugar

2 pints heavy cream, whipped

Dissolve coffee in hot water. Add powdered sugar and whipped cream and beat together until stiff peaks form.

4 eggs
¾ cup sugar
1 teaspoon vanilla extract
1 cup walnuts, finely minced

½ cup fine bread crumbs
Powdered sugar
Mocha Cream

Preheat oven to 350°. Grease and flour a 10½x16-inch jelly roll pan. Beat eggs and sugar until thick and fluffy, about 10 minutes. Add vanilla, and fold in walnuts and bread crumbs. Pour into prepared pan. Bake for 18-20 minutes or until edges are golden. Immediately loosen edges with spatula or knife. Invert cake over brown paper which has been coated with powdered sugar. Carefully roll the cake with the paper, and place on wire rack to cool. When cool, unwrap slowly and spread with mocha cream, then re-roll, removing paper carefully. Place on plate with seam side down and sprinkle with powdered sugar.

Serves 8

Pumpkin Pie Cake

Cake

1 package yellow cake mix
½ cup margarine, melted
1 egg, beaten
29 ounces pumpkin, solid pack
3 eggs
½ cup brown sugar, packed

¼ cup white sugar
⅔ cup milk
1½ teaspoons cinnamon
¼ teaspoon nutmeg
⅛ teaspoon ground cloves

Topping

½ cup white sugar
1 cup yellow cake mix

1 cup pecans, chopped
¼ cup margarine

Preheat oven to 350°. Grease and flour a 13x9-inch pan. Set aside one cup of the cake mix, and put remainder in mixing bowl. Add margarine and beaten egg, mixing thoroughly. Press mixture into prepared pan and set aside. In another mixing bowl, combine pumpkin, eggs, sugars, milk and spices. Beat well and spread over cake mixture. Set aside. Combine topping ingredients and mix until crumbly. Sprinkle over top of cake. Bake for 50-55 minutes.

Serves 12

Orange Crunch Cake

Crunch Layer

1 cup graham cracker crumbs
½ cup brown sugar, packed

½ cup walnuts, chopped
½ cup margarine or butter, melted

Cake

1 package yellow cake mix
½ cup water
½ cup orange juice

⅓ cup vegetable oil
3 eggs
2 tablespoons orange zest, grated

Frosting

16 ounces vanilla frosting
1 cup frozen whipped topping, thawed
3 tablespoons orange zest, grated
1 teaspoon lemon zest, grated

1 can (11-ounce) mandarin oranges, drained
Mint leaves, for garnish (optional)

Preheat oven to 350°. Grease and flour two 8 or 9-inch round cake pans. In small bowl, combine ingredients for crunch layer and mix until crumbly. Press half of crunch mixture into each prepared pan. In large bowl, blend cake ingredients with electric mixer at low speed until moistened, then beat for 2 minutes at highest speed. Pour half of cake batter evenly over crunch layer in each pan. Bake for 30-35 minutes, or until toothpick inserted near center comes out clean. Cool in pans for 10 minutes, then remove from pans and cool completely on wire rack. In small bowl, beat vanilla frosting until fluffy, add whipped topping, and continue beating until mixture is light and fluffy. Add orange and lemon zests. To assemble, place one layer, crunch side up, on serving plate. Spread with ¼ of frosting. Top with remaining layer, also crunch side up. Spread top and sides of cake with remaining frosting and arrange orange sections on top. Garnish with mint leaves, if desired, and store in refrigerator.

Serves 16

Orange Carrot Cake

Cake

3 cups flour
2 cups sugar
1 cup coconut
2½ teaspoons baking soda
1 teaspoon salt
2 teaspoons cinnamon
2 cups carrot, shredded

1 cup margarine, melted and cooled
2 teaspoons vanilla extract
1 teaspoon orange zest, grated
3 eggs
1 can (11-ounce) mandarin oranges, with juice

Frosting

3 cups powdered sugar
8 ounces cream cheese, room temperature
2 tablespoons margarine, melted

1 teaspoon vanilla extract
½ cup walnuts, finely chopped

Preheat oven to 350°. Grease a 13x9-inch pan. Combine all cake ingredients in large bowl. Blend with electric mixer at low speed until moistened, then beat for 2 minutes at highest speed. Pour batter into prepared pan. Bake for 45-55 minutes, or until toothpick inserted near center comes out clean. Transfer pan to wire rack and let cool completely. Combine all frosting ingredients, except nuts, in large bowl and beat until smooth. Spread over cake and sprinkle with nuts. Refrigerate cake until ready to serve.

Serves 16-20

DeLand, Florida, is also the home of Stetson University, Florida's oldest private university. It was originally DeLand Academy, founded by Henry DeLand.

Whole Wheat Applesauce Cake

½ cup vegetable oil
¾ cup brown sugar, packed
1 cup applesauce
1 teaspoon baking soda
1 teaspoon cinnamon
1 cup whole wheat flour

½ cup unbleached flour
1 cup walnuts, chopped
1-1½ teaspoons plain yogurt
Powdered sugar
Walnut halves, for garnish

Preheat oven to 375°. Grease and flour an 8-inch round or square pan. In large bowl, combine oil and brown sugar. Add next six ingredients, blending well after each addition. Pour batter into prepared pan and bake for 30 minutes. Let cake cool in pan for 10 minutes, then remove from pan and allow to cool completely. In small bowl, mix yogurt with enough powdered sugar to form thick glaze. Spread over top of cake and decorate with walnut halves.

Serves 6-8

Delicious Apple Cake

¾ cup shortening
1½ cups white sugar
2 eggs
2½ cups flour
1 teaspoon baking soda
¾ teaspoon cinnamon
¾ cup warm coffee

2 cups Golden Delicious, Greening,
   Cortland or Ida Red apples, peeled
   and diced
½ cup walnuts, chopped
⅓ cup brown sugar, packed
½ teaspoon cinnamon

Preheat oven to 350°. Grease and flour a 13x9-inch pan. In large bowl, cream shortening until light, gradually beating in sugar. Add eggs, one at a time, beating well after each addition. In another bowl, combine flour, baking soda and cinnamon. Add to shortening mixture, alternating with coffee. Fold in apples and walnuts. Pour batter into prepared pan. Mix together brown sugar and cinnamon and sprinkle over top. Bake for 45 minutes. Cool cake in pan on wire rack. Serve with whipped cream.

Serves 12-15

Banana Cake with Butter Cream Frosting

½ cup margarine, room temperature
1 cup sugar
1 egg
2 ripe bananas, mashed
1½ cups flour

1 teaspoon baking soda
1 teaspoon salt
¼ cup sour milk (see p. 200)
1 teaspoon vanilla extract
Butter Cream Frosting

Preheat oven to 350°. Grease two 8-inch layer pans. Cream margarine and sugar, then add egg and mix well. Add bananas. In separate bowl, combine flour, baking soda and salt. Blend into margarine mixture, alternating with milk. Stir in vanilla and pour into prepared pans. Bake for 25-30 minutes. Allow to cool, then frost top and middle layers with Butter Cream Frosting.

Serves 10-12

Tropical Cake

1½ cups vegetable oil
2 cups sugar
3 eggs
8 ounces crushed pineapple, with juice
1½ teaspoons vanilla extract
1 teaspoon baking soda

1 teaspoon cinnamon
½ teaspoon salt
3 cups flour
2 cups bananas, diced
1½ cups nuts, chopped

Preheat oven to 350°. Grease and flour a 10-inch tube pan. In large bowl, combine oil and sugar, then beat in eggs. Add pineapple and vanilla, mix well and set aside. Combine dry ingredients and add to batter. Stir in bananas and nuts, blending completely. Pour batter into prepared pan and bake for 70 minutes. Cool for 15 minutes, then remove from pan. (Note: Cake will be crusty on top.)

Serves 8-10

Butter Cream
Frosting

¼ cup butter or
margarine

2 cups powdered
sugar

1 teaspoon vanilla
extract

2 tablespoons milk

Cream margarine
and sugar. Add
vanilla and milk,
beating until frosting
is smooth.

Easy Pineapple Cake

Cake

2 cups flour
1½ cups sugar
2 teaspoons baking soda

1 can (20-ounce) crushed pineapple,
    with juice
2 eggs

Frosting

½ cup butter, room temperature
8 ounces cream cheese, room temperature

1½ cups powdered sugar
2 teaspoons vanilla extract

Preheat oven to 350°. Grease and flour a 13x9-inch pan. In large bowl, combine all cake ingredients, mixing well by hand. Pour batter into prepared pan and bake for 30-35 minutes. Remove from oven and let cool. Cream butter and cream cheese. Stir in powdered sugar and vanilla and spread over cooled cake. Refrigerate until ready to serve.

Serves 16-20

California Cake

15 ounces dark raisins
2 cups boiling water
2 teaspoons baking soda
3 tablespoons margarine, room
    temperature

1 cup sugar
2 eggs
2 cups flour
12 ounces chocolate chips
1 cup walnuts, chopped

In large bowl, mix raisins, water and baking soda. Let sit overnight. Preheat oven to 350°. Grease and flour a 13x9-inch pan. In another bowl, cream margarine and sugar. Beat in eggs, then add flour and undrained raisin mixture. Pour batter into prepared pan. Top with chocolate chips, pushing them into the batter. Sprinkle walnuts on top and bake for 45-50 minutes. Let cool in pan before cutting.

Serves 10-12

Holiday Fruit Loaf

2 cups walnuts
2 cups pecans
1¾ cups Brazil nuts
16 ounces pitted dates, halved
1 pound dried apricots, halved
½ pound pitted prunes, halved
½ pound dried figs
⅓ cup raisins
⅓ cup golden raisins

1 cup maraschino cherries, drained
1½ cups unbleached flour
1 teaspoon baking powder
1 teaspoon salt
6 eggs
1 cup sugar
2 teaspoons vanilla extract
¾ cup brandy

Preheat oven to 300°. Grease bottom and sides of four 9x5-inch loaf pans. Line with waxed paper which has been greased. In large bowl, combine nuts and fruits. In smaller bowl, combine flour, baking powder and salt. Sift mixture over nuts and fruits. Toss lightly until well coated. In medium bowl, beat eggs, sugar and vanilla until light and fluffy. Pour over nuts and fruits. Stir gently to combine. Fill prepared pans, pressing cake mixture firmly so its shape will hold after baking. Bake for 60-90 minutes, or until toothpick inserted near center comes out clean. Place pans on wire rack. Spoon ¼ cup of the brandy over loaves. Let stand for 1 hour. Invert pans and peel off paper. Turn loaves right side up and let cool completely on wire rack. Place rack in shallow pan. Spoon remaining brandy over loaves. To store, wrap loaves in cheesecloth which has been soaked in brandy. Wrap in heavy-duty foil or store in tightly covered container. (Note: If fruits brown too quickly during baking, cover pan with buttered foil.)

Makes 4 loaves

Double-acting baking powder releases carbon dioxide gases at room temperature and again when baked.

Before double-acting baking powder, cooks had to be very fast in getting their batters into the oven. Some of the leavening agents produced gas so quickly that the baked good had fallen before it went into the oven.

· PIES & PASTRIES ·

nursery in the Rochester area was started in 1833, and in less than twenty years over half of the nurserymen in New York State lived in the Rochester area. By 1856, this region was the world's center for fruit trees. The nursery that stood apart from the more than 150 others was that of George Ellwanger and Patrick Barry.

Opened in 1840 on eight acres of land on Mt. Hope Avenue, the nursery grew to 650 acres before it closed in 1916. For a time, it was the leading wholesale and retail nursery in the country. Ellwanger and Barry knew the West would need tree stocks, and the Lake Ontario climate gave their trees the hardiness they needed to survive in the West. Their nursery based its success on supplying the finest plants, correctly labeled and carefully shipped. Ellwanger and Barry's shipping expertise enabled them to fill orders for Japan, India, Australia and the Dutch East Indies.

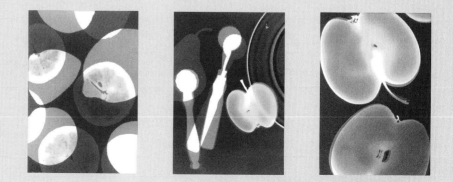

PIES & PASTRIES

Deluxe Lemonade Pie

½ cup margarine
1¾ cups graham cracker crumbs
6 ounces frozen lemonade concentrate

14 ounces sweetened condensed milk
12 ounces frozen whipped topping, thawed
Graham cracker crumbs, for garnish

Melt margarine and blend with graham cracker crumbs. Line bottom and sides of 9-inch pie plate. Whip lemonade and milk in blender or with wire whisk until smooth. Fold in whipped topping and pour filling into pie crust. Sprinkle with graham cracker crumbs. Refrigerate for 2-3 hours or overnight. (Note: Limeade or orange juice concentrate may be substituted for lemonade.)

Serves 8-10

Mt. Hope Nursery included six acres of greenhouses where Ellwanger and Barry raised lemon and orange trees.

Mt. Hope Nursery sent rare trees to the Japanese Royal Gardens in Tokyo.

Strawberry Banana Pie

Crust
½ cup margarine, room temperature
¼ cup sugar
1 egg yolk

½ teaspoon vanilla extract
1¼ cups flour

Filling
3 cups bananas, sliced
1 pint strawberries, washed and quartered
1½ cups cold water

¾ cup sugar
2 tablespoons cornstarch
3 ounces strawberry-flavored gelatin

Whipped topping, for garnish

Preheat oven to 325°. Lightly grease a 10-inch pie plate. Cream margarine and sugar in medium bowl. Stir in egg yolk, vanilla and flour, mixing well. Press mixture into prepared pie plate and bake for 20 minutes. Cool thoroughly. Arrange bananas and strawberries on crust. Combine water, sugar and cornstarch in saucepan. Cook over medium heat, stirring until mixture comes to a boil. Reduce heat to low and continue to cook for another 2 minutes. Add gelatin, stirring until dissolved. Carefully spoon gelatin mixture over fruit. Refrigerate until set and serve with whipped topping. (Note: This recipe may be doubled and made in a jelly roll pan. Also, recipe may be varied by using other fruits and gelatin flavors.)

Serves 8

Peanut Patch Pie ~ The Daisy Flour Mill

Crust
1 cup graham cracker crumbs
¼ cup sugar

¼ cup butter or margarine, room
   temperature

Filling
8 ounces cream cheese, room temperature
1 cup creamy peanut butter
1 cup powdered sugar
2 tablespoons clarified butter (see p. 133)

½ cup heavy cream
⅛ cup powdered sugar
1 tablespoon vanilla extract

Topping
6 ounces semisweet chocolate

½ cup heavy cream

Grease a 9-inch pie pan. Combine crust ingredients and mix until crumbly. Press mixture evenly into prepared pan and chill for one hour, or until firm. Whip together cream cheese and peanut butter. Add powdered sugar and butter and whip until fluffy. Set aside. Combine heavy cream, powdered sugar and vanilla and whip. Fold into peanut butter mixture. Spoon filling into chilled graham cracker crust. Refrigerate until firm. Melt chocolate and stir in heavy cream. Spread evenly over top of pie and refrigerate until firm.

Serves 8

Coconut Candy Bar Pie

1⅓ cups grated coconut
2 tablespoons butter or margarine, melted
1 teaspoon instant coffee granules
2 tablespoons water

1 candy bar (7½-ounce), milk chocolate
   with almonds, broken
4 cups frozen whipped topping, thawed

Preheat oven to 325°. Combine coconut and butter and press into an 8-inch pie plate. Bake for 10 minutes, or until coconut is golden. Cool thoroughly. In small saucepan, dissolve coffee granules in water, then add candy bar. Stir mixture over low heat until chocolate melts, then let cool. Fold in whipped topping and pile mixture into coconut crust. Chill in freezer for several hours or overnight. (Note: Filling will not freeze solid.)

Serves 8

Pumpkin Ice Cream Pie

1 quart vanilla ice cream, slightly softened
1 pie crust (9-inch), baked
1 cup cooked pumpkin
¾ cup brown sugar, packed
½ teaspoon salt
¼ teaspoon ginger
¼ teaspoon nutmeg
¼ teaspoon cinnamon

1 cup heavy cream
½ cup brown sugar, packed
¼ cup dark corn syrup
¼ cup hot water
½ teaspoon vanilla extract
Toasted almonds, slivered
Whipped cream, for garnish (optional)

Spread softened ice cream in pie crust. Place in freezer until ice cream has hardened. Combine pumpkin, sugar, salt and spices in large bowl. In smaller bowl, whip cream until stiff and fold into pumpkin mixture. Spoon mixture over ice cream. Return to freezer until ready to serve. In medium saucepan, combine sugar, corn syrup and water. Bring to a boil over medium heat and cook until thick and syrupy. Remove from heat, let cool, and stir in vanilla. Just before serving pie, drizzle with syrup and sprinkle with almonds. Garnish with whipped cream, if desired.

Serves 8

Easy-As-Pie Crust

¾ cup shortening
¼ cup boiling water
1 tablespoon milk

1 teaspoon salt
2 cups flour

In medium bowl, whip shortening, water, milk and salt with an electric mixer until soft peaks are formed. Blend flour into shortening mixture with pastry blender. Form dough into two balls. Place first ball of dough between two sheets of waxed paper and roll out to desired thickness. Roll out second crust in same manner. Bake at 350° for 8-10 minutes or fill and bake according to pie recipe directions. (Note: Do not add any more flour. If pastry tears, patch together and continue forming crust.)

Makes two 9-inch pie crusts

Chocolate Ecstasy Pie

1 cup evaporated milk
1 cup water
2 ounces unsweetened chocolate, chopped
  in half or quarters
1 cup sugar
⅓ cup flour

¼ teaspoon salt
3 egg yolks, slightly beaten
2 tablespoons butter or margarine
1 teaspoon vanilla extract
1 pie crust (8-inch), baked

Mix together milk and water in medium saucepan. Add chocolate pieces and melt over medium heat, stirring occasionally to keep chocolate from sticking to pan. Remove from heat. In small bowl combine sugar, flour and salt. Add to saucepan, and cook for about 2 minutes over medium heat, stirring occasionally. When mixture starts to bubble, remove from heat. Stir a small amount of chocolate mixture into beaten egg yolks, then add to saucepan. Continue to stir constantly, cooking mixture for another 2 minutes over medium heat. Remove from heat and add butter and vanilla. Cover with waxed paper or plastic to prevent skin from forming, and let cool to room temperature. Pour into baked pie crust and refrigerate, if desired.

Serves 6-8

Almond Fudge Pie

½ cup flour
¾ cup sugar
1 cup miniature chocolate chips
½ cup margarine, melted

1 cup almonds, chopped
2 eggs, beaten
½ teaspoon almond extract
1 pie crust (9-inch), unbaked

Preheat oven to 350°. In large bowl, mix together flour and sugar. Add remaining ingredients, mixing well. Pour into pie crust and bake for 45 minutes.

Serves 6-8

Pear Pie

Ellwanger and Barry were especially known for their development of 118 varieties of pear trees. Samples of all varieties were sent to the 1900 Paris Exhibition.

1 cup flour
½ cup brown sugar, packed
½ cup margarine, room temperature
¼ teaspoon cinnamon
¼ teaspoon nutmeg
½ cup pecans, chopped
2 cans (8-ounce) pear halves, drained and
    liquid reserved

¼ cup white sugar
2 tablespoons cornstarch
⅛ teaspoon salt
¼ teaspoon nutmeg
2 tablespoons butter
1 tablespoon lemon zest, grated
1 tablespoon lemon juice
1 pie crust (9-inch), unbaked

Preheat oven to 400°. Combine first six ingredients in large bowl and blend until coarse crumbs are formed. Set aside. Combine liquid from pears, white sugar, cornstarch, salt and nutmeg in saucepan and cook over medium heat until mixture is clear and has thickened. Remove from heat and stir in butter, lemon zest and lemon juice. Cut pear halves in half lengthwise and arrange in pie crust. Heat in oven for 2 minutes. Remove from oven, cover with hot syrup and top with crumb mixture. Return to oven and bake for 25 minutes.

Serves 6-8

Sugar Free Apple Pie

The Ellwanger and Barry Nursery introduced the dwarf fruit tree to the United States.

6-8 apples, peeled, cored and sliced
½ cup apple juice concentrate, thawed
Juice of ½ lemon
1 tablespoon cinnamon, divided

¼-½ teaspoon nutmeg
7 tablespoons flour
2 pie crusts (9-inch), unbaked

In large bowl, combine apples with apple juice, lemon juice, ¾ tablespoon of the cinnamon and nutmeg. Mix well to coat apples. Add flour, one tablespoon at a time, until juice forms a thin paste. Pour mixture into bottom pie crust and sprinkle with remaining cinnamon. Top with second crust, flute edges and pierce top of crust. Bake at 375° for 1 hour.

Serves 6

Summertime Fruit Pizza

Crust

2¾ cups flour

1 teaspoon baking powder

½ teaspoon salt

¾ cup butter or margarine, room
    temperature

1 cup sugar

2 eggs

1 teaspoon vanilla extract

Filling

8 ounces cream cheese, room temperature

¼ cup powdered sugar

½ teaspoon vanilla extract

Fresh fruit (strawberries, bananas, grapes,
    raspberries, blueberries, etc.), sliced

Glaze

½ cup orange juice

2 tablespoons water

2 teaspoons cornstarch

6 tablespoons powdered sugar

In medium bowl, combine flour, baking powder and salt, set aside. In large bowl, cream butter and sugar until smooth, then add eggs and vanilla, beating until mixture is light and fluffy. Blend in dry ingredients. Chill for one hour or until firm. Preheat oven to 375°. Lightly grease a 12-inch pizza pan. Roll dough into circle and put into pan. Bake for 10-12 minutes. Let cool. Combine cream cheese, powdered sugar and vanilla and spread on cookie crust. Top with favorite fruit arranged in a single layer. In small saucepan, combine glaze ingredients and bring to a boil, stirring constantly. Remove from heat, let cool slightly, and spoon over fruit. Allow glaze to set before serving.

Serves 8-10

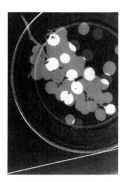

Raspberry Bavarian Pie

Pastry

⅓ cup butter, room temperature
2½ teaspoons sugar
⅓ teaspoon salt

1 egg yolk
1 cup flour
⅓ cup almonds, finely chopped

Filling

10 ounces frozen raspberries, partially
    thawed and drained
2 egg whites
1 cup sugar
1 tablespoon lemon juice

¼ teaspoon vanilla extract
¼ teaspoon almond extract
⅛ teaspoon salt
1 cup heavy cream

Preheat oven to 400°. Grease a 10-inch pie pan. Cream butter, sugar and salt until fluffy. Add egg yolk and beat thoroughly. Mix in flour and almonds, then press into prepared pie pan. Bake for 12 minutes. Let cool. In large bowl, combine all filling ingredients except heavy cream. Beat with electric mixer until mixture thickens and expands in volume, approximately 8-10 minutes. In another bowl, whip cream and fold into raspberry mixture. Pour into pastry and freeze for 6-8 hours.

Serves 8-10

Bakewell Tart

1 pie crust (9 or 10-inch), unbaked
¾-1 cup raspberry preserves
⅓ cup sugar
3 eggs, separated
¾ cup almonds, ground

½ cup dry bread crumbs
½ cup unsalted butter, melted
2 teaspoons almond extract
Whipped cream, for garnish (optional)

Preheat oven to 425°. Roll out crust and fit into a 9 or 10-inch tart or springform pan. Spread ½ cup of the preserves over crust. In medium bowl, mix sugar and egg yolks until blended. Stir in almonds, bread crumbs, butter and almond extract. In small bowl, beat egg whites with electric mixer until stiff peaks form. Fold gently into filling. Pour into pan, spreading filling to edges (jam should be covered). Bake for 10 minutes. Lower oven temperature to 350° and bake 15 minutes longer, or until golden on top. Let cool in pan and spread with remaining preserves. Garnish with whipped cream, if desired. (Note: If using pan with removable bottom/sides, remove tart from pan after cooling for 20 minutes.)

Serves 10-12

The Bakewell Tart originated in Bakewell, Derbyshire, England and is also called Bakewell Pudding. Any other red-colored jam can be used to make the tart.

Sawdust Pie

1 cup sugar
1½ cups graham cracker crumbs
1½ cups pecan pieces

1½ cups flaked coconut
7 egg whites
1 pie crust (9-inch), unbaked

Preheat oven to 325°. Combine sugar, graham cracker crumbs, pecans, and coconut, mixing well. Stir in egg whites and pour into pie crust. Bake for 25-30 minutes, until pie is glossy and set. Let cool and serve with vanilla ice cream, if desired.

Serves 8

Hazelnut Cups

1 cup milk
⅓ cup sugar
1½ tablespoons cornstarch
1 egg yolk, beaten
½ cup chocolate chips
1 tablespoon hazelnut liqueur
1 tablespoon butter, room temperature

½ teaspoon vanilla extract
½ cup heavy cream
⅓-½ cup powdered sugar
1 teaspoon almond extract
¼ cup roasted hazelnuts, grated
2 packages small phyllo cups
Grated chocolate bar, for garnish

In microwave-safe bowl, combine milk, sugar and cornstarch. Cook on high power for 2 minutes, stir mixture, then cook for an additional 2 minutes. Add 3 tablespoons of the milk mixture to the egg yolk, stirring in one tablespoon at a time. Add egg mixture, chocolate chips and hazelnut liqueur to milk mixture. Cook on high power for 1 minute, then stir. Add butter and vanilla and allow pudding to cool. Whip heavy cream with powdered sugar and almond extract. Add hazelnuts. Fill each phyllo cup with 1 tablespoon of the pudding mixture and top with 1 tablespoon of the whipped cream. Sprinkle with chocolate.

Makes 30 cups

Blender Pecan Pies

3 eggs
½ cup heavy cream
2 tablespoons sherry or bourbon
½ cup dark corn syrup
⅛ teaspoon salt

1 cup sugar
1 teaspoon vanilla extract
2 tablespoons butter
1½ cups pecans, chopped
2 pie crusts (8-inch), unbaked

Preheat oven to 400°. Combine eggs, cream, sherry or bourbon, corn syrup, salt, sugar, vanilla and butter in blender container. Blend for 10 seconds or until well mixed. Stir in pecans and pour into pie crusts. Bake for 30-35 minutes.

Makes two 8-inch pies

Pecan Tarts

Crust
1 cup unsalted butter, room temperature
6 ounces cream cheese, room temperature

2 cups flour

Filling
2 eggs
1¾ cups brown sugar, packed
2 tablespoons butter, melted

1 teaspoon vanilla extract
½ cup pecans, ground
Pinch of salt

Cream together butter and cream cheese until smooth. Add flour, mixing well.
Form dough into 48 balls. Flatten each ball in palm of hand to form small circle.
Press circle of dough into bottom and sides of miniature muffin tins. Preheat oven
to 350°. Beat eggs, then add remaining ingredients, mixing well. Pour filling to a
level just below the top of each tart. Bake for 30 minutes.

Makes 48 tarts

Puff Pastry Fingers

1 package (17¼-ounce) frozen puff pastry
¾-1 cup apricot, strawberry or other fruit
  preserves, or orange marmalade

½ cup almonds, slivered or sliced
Powdered sugar, for garnish

Defrost pastry according to package directions. Roll out dough to ⅛-inch thick
and cut into 3x1½-inch strips. (Do not cut strips too narrow or they will fall over
while baking.) Place on ungreased cookie sheet. Bake at 425° on upper rack of
oven for approximately 7 minutes, or until the pastry is golden and able to retain
its shape. Remove from oven and spread each strip with preserves or marmalade.
Return to oven and cook for an additional 5 minutes. Remove from oven and
allow to cool slightly. Quickly remove pastry from cookie sheet and arrange
almonds on top. When completely cool, dust with powdered sugar.

Makes 40-50

Before the Erie Canal
opened, it took over
two weeks to ship
goods to New York
City at $400 per ton.
After the canal's
opening in 1825, the
trip took 5-8 days
and the cost plunged
to $10 per ton.

COOKIES & BARS

of Lyons, New York, started a business that would eventually carry the catchy name of "The H. G. Hotchkiss International Prize Medal Essential Oil Company". Essential oils are thought to hold the essence of odor and flavor of a plant, and have been sought after since the time of ancient Persia. Hotchkiss decided to specialize in peppermint oil, although his company did produce other products. He found that he had to send his oil to Europe to earn any recognition for its quality and acceptance here at home.

Hotchkiss's company lived up to its name, winning seventeen first-place medals at international expositions over the years. And Hotchkiss himself can be called the "father of the essential oil industry in America". Late in the 1800s, his company led the world in peppermint oil production. The United States is today the world's largest producer of peppermint oil used in candy, dentifrices, ointments and pharmaceuticals.

COOKIES & BARS

Grandma's Tea Cookies

This recipe was submitted by photographer Andy Olenick.

3 eggs, beaten
1½ cups sugar
1 cup shortening
1 teaspoon vanilla extract

¼ cup buttermilk
½ teaspoon baking soda
3-4 cups flour

Preheat oven to 375°. Grease a cookie sheet. Blend eggs, sugar and shortening in large bowl. Stir in vanilla, buttermilk and baking soda. Add flour, one cup at a time, until dough becomes stiff. Place on floured surface and roll out to ⅛-inch thickness. Cut dough with cookie cutters and place on prepared cookie sheet. Bake for 8-10 minutes, or until edges turn light brown. Remove from cookie sheet and let cool on wire rack.

Makes 3-4 dozen

Peppermint Meringues

Mint is the most widely used of the aromatic herbs.

Because of Hotchkiss's success, in 1876 peppermint was the major crop grown in Wayne County, New York.

2 egg whites, room temperature
⅛ teaspoon salt
⅛ teaspoon cream of tartar

½ cup sugar
12 peppermint candies or 2 canes, crushed (preferably green and red)

Place one oven rack in middle of oven and second rack directly above. Preheat oven to 225°. Line 2 cookie sheets with foil. In large bowl, beat egg whites with electric mixer until foamy. Add salt and cream of tartar. Beat until soft peaks form when beaters are lifted. Beat in sugar, 1 tablespoon at a time. Continue to beat for 5-6 minutes, until mixture is very stiff, smooth and glossy. Gently spoon meringue into gallon-sized, zipper-type, plastic food storage bag. Snip off one corner to make a 1-inch opening. Holding bag upright, squeeze mounds 1½-inches in diameter and 1½-inches high onto prepared cookie sheets, placing them close together but not touching. Lightly sprinkle with crushed candy. Bake for 1½ hours. (Meringues should look dry and white, not browned.) Turn off oven. Keep oven door slightly ajar and let meringues cool in oven until crisp and dry. Loosen from foil with metal spatula. Store loosely covered in a cool, dry place for up to 2 months. (Note: These cookies should not be made on a rainy or humid day.)

Makes 4 dozen

Mint Cookie Bars

Bar

2 ounces unsweetened chocolate
½ cup margarine
2 eggs, beaten
1 cup sugar

½ teaspoon peppermint extract
½ cup flour
½ cup walnuts, chopped

Frosting

2 tablespoons margarine, room
  temperature
1 tablespoon milk

1 cup powdered sugar
1 teaspoon peppermint extract

Topping

½ ounce unsweetened chocolate

1½ teaspoons margarine

Preheat oven to 350°. Grease and flour an 8-inch square pan. Melt chocolate and margarine in saucepan over low heat. Add remaining bar ingredients, mixing well. Spread into prepared pan and bake for 25 minutes. Let cool in pan. Combine frosting ingredients, stirring well. Spread on cooled bars. Melt topping ingredients and pour over frosting. Pull spatula or knife through topping to create a marbled effect. Let set before cutting.

Makes 16-24 bars

Double-Frosted Bourbon Brownies

¾ cup flour
¼ teaspoon baking soda
¼ teaspoon salt
½ cup sugar
⅓ cup shortening
2 tablespoons water
6 ounces chocolate chips

1 teaspoon vanilla extract
2 eggs
1½ cups nuts, chopped
4 tablespoons bourbon
White Frosting
Chocolate Glaze

Preheat oven to 325°. Grease a 9-inch square pan. Combine flour, baking soda and salt, set aside. In medium pan, combine sugar, shortening and water and bring to a boil, stirring constantly. Remove from heat and stir in chocolate chips and vanilla. Beat in eggs, one at a time, then add flour mixture and nuts. Spread in prepared pan and bake for 25-30 minutes. Sprinkle with bourbon and let cool. Top with White Frosting and Chocolate Glaze. Chill before cutting.

Makes 1-2 dozen

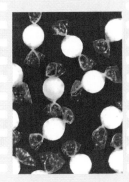

Black peppermint yields more oil than white peppermint, and is the type grown in America.

White Frosting

½ cup butter, room temperature

1 teaspoon vanilla extract

2 cups powdered sugar

Mix together until smooth. Spread over cooled brownies.

Chocolate Glaze

6 ounces chocolate chips

1 tablespoon shortening

Melt chocolate chips and shortening. While still hot, drizzle over White Frosting.

Grand Slam Brownies

Brownies

4 ounces unsweetened chocolate, chopped

6 tablespoons unsalted butter, cut into
  pieces

½ cup flour

⅛ teaspoon baking powder

¼ teaspoon salt

½ teaspoon instant coffee granules

2 teaspoons water

2 eggs, room temperature

1½ cups sugar

½ cup walnut pieces, toasted

⅓ cup chocolate-covered raisins (optional)

Topping

4½ ounces semisweet chocolate, chopped

8 ounces cream cheese, room temperature

¼ cup sugar

1 egg, room temperature

Preheat oven to 325°. Grease and flour a 9-inch square baking dish. Melt unsweetened chocolate and butter in small saucepan over very low heat, stirring until smooth. Let cool. Combine flour, baking powder and salt in small bowl. In large bowl, combine coffee granules and water, stirring to dissolve. Add eggs and sugar, beating with electric mixer until mixture is pale yellow and slowly dissolving ribbon forms when beaters are lifted. Fold in melted chocolate, then dry ingredients. Stir in walnuts and raisins (if using). Spread batter in prepared dish. Bake for approximately 38 minutes, or until top is dry and cracked and toothpick inserted near center comes out with some wet batter on it. Remove dish from oven and place on wire rack. Gently press down any raised edges of brownies. Leave oven on. For topping, melt chocolate in top of double boiler over simmering water, stirring until smooth. Set aside. Blend cream cheese and sugar until smooth. Add warm chocolate and blend well. Add egg and blend until just combined. Pour topping over hot brownies. Return dish to oven and bake for approximately 10 minutes, or until topping moves slightly in center when shaken. Transfer pan to wire rack. When completely cool, cover dish with foil and refrigerate overnight. Cut into small squares to serve.

Makes 2 dozen

Cheesecake Mud Bars

Bar
½ cup + 1 tablespoon butter or margarine
3 tablespoons baking cocoa
1 cup sugar
1 cup flour

¾ cup pecans, chopped
1 teaspoon baking powder
1 teaspoon vanilla extract
2 eggs

Filling
8 ounces cream cheese, room temperature
½ cup sugar
2 tablespoons flour
¼ cup butter, room temperature

1 egg, slightly beaten
½ teaspoon vanilla extract
6 ounces chocolate chips

Toppings
Pecan Icing

2 cups miniature marshmallows

Pecan Icing

¼ cup butter or margarine

2 tablespoons baking cocoa

3 tablespoons milk

2 cups powdered sugar

½ teaspoon vanilla extract

1 cup pecans, chopped

Combine ingredients and bring to a boil, while stirring. Allow to cool slightly and thicken. Pour over bars.

Preheat oven to 350°. Grease and flour a 13x9-inch pan. Melt butter in saucepan over low heat, then add cocoa. Add remaining bar ingredients and mix well. Spread in prepared pan. Next, combine all filling ingredients except chocolate chips. Beat until fluffy, and spread over bar mixture. Sprinkle chocolate chips over entire mixture and bake for 25-35 minutes, until knife inserted near center comes out clean. During last half of baking time, prepare icing. Turn off oven. Sprinkle marshmallows over bars, and let pan sit in turned-off oven until marshmallows are melted, about 5 minutes. Pour icing over bars, let cool and refrigerate.

Makes 4-5 dozen small bars

Chocolate Revel Bars

Bars
1 cup butter, room temperature
2 cups brown sugar, packed
2 eggs
2 teaspoons vanilla extract

2½ cups flour
1 teaspoon baking soda
1 teaspoon salt
3 cups quick oats

Filling
2 cups chocolate chips
2 tablespoons butter
14 ounces sweetened condensed milk

½ teaspoon salt
2 teaspoons vanilla extract
1 cup walnuts, chopped (optional)

Preheat oven to 350°. Beat together butter, brown sugar, eggs and vanilla. Stir in flour, baking soda, salt and oats. Pat two-thirds of the dough mixture into a 13x9-inch pan and set aside. Melt chocolate chips and butter with milk and salt on stovetop or in microwave oven (on low power for 2 minutes), then stir in vanilla and walnuts (if using). Spread filling mixture over bars, then dot with remaining bar mixture. Bake for 25-30 minutes. Cool completely before cutting.

Makes 30-40 bars

Decadent Chocolate Cookies

12 ounces chocolate chips
2 tablespoons butter
14 ounces sweetened condensed milk

1 cup flour
1 teaspoon vanilla extract
Pinch of salt

Preheat oven to 350°. Grease a cookie sheet. In top of double boiler, heat chocolate chips, butter and milk, stirring to combine. Add flour, vanilla and salt and mix well. Remove from heat. (Mixture will be consistency of fudge.) Drop by rounded teaspoonfuls onto cookie sheet. Bake for 8-11 minutes, then remove from baking sheet to cool.

Makes 2-3 dozen

White Chocolate Brownies

½ cup unsalted butter
8 ounces white chocolate chips or bar,
    coarsely chopped
2 eggs
Pinch of salt

½ cup sugar
½ teaspoon vanilla extract
½ teaspoon salt
1 cup flour
1¼ cups semisweet chocolate chips

Preheat oven to 350°. Lightly grease an 8-inch square pan. Melt butter in small saucepan over low heat. Remove pan from heat and add 4 ounces of the white chocolate. Do not stir. In large bowl, beat eggs and salt with electric mixer until frothy. Gradually add sugar and beat until pale yellow and slowly dissolving ribbon forms when beater is lifted. Add white chocolate mixture, vanilla, salt and flour, mixing until just combined. Stir in semisweet chocolate chips and remaining white chocolate. Spoon mixture into prepared pan, smoothing top with spatula. Bake for about 30 minutes, or until knife inserted near center comes out clean. Cover with foil if batter browns too quickly. Cool in pan before cutting. (Note: If desired, decrease semisweet chocolate chips to ⅔ cup and add ⅓ cup chopped nuts.)

Makes 16 brownies

Soft Surprises

1½ cups sugar
1 cup shortening
2 eggs
1 teaspoon vanilla extract
4 cups flour
1 teaspoon baking soda

2 teaspoons baking powder
1 teaspoon salt
1 cup milk
2 cups chocolate chips
1 cup raisins
1 cup walnuts, chopped

Preheat oven to 375°. Grease a cookie sheet. Cream sugar and shortening. Beat in eggs, then add vanilla. In separate bowl, mix together flour, baking soda, baking powder, and salt. Add dry ingredients to sugar mixture, alternating with milk. Fold in chocolate chips, raisins, and walnuts. Drop by rounded teaspoonfuls onto cookie sheet and bake for 12-14 minutes. Remove from baking sheet to cool.

Makes 4-6 dozen

Chocolate Pepper Cookies

Cookie

5 cups flour	1 teaspoon cinnamon
1 teaspoon baking powder	½ teaspoon nutmeg
1 teaspoon baking soda	½ cup baking cocoa
1 cup vegetable oil	1 teaspoon salt
1¼ cups sugar	Zest of one orange, grated
2 eggs	Zest of one lemon, grated
1 cup milk	2 cups walnuts or pecans, chopped
½-1 teaspoon pepper	

Frosting

1 cup powdered sugar	Juice of one lemon, strained

Preheat oven to 375°. In large bowl, combine all cookie ingredients, mixing well. Drop by rounded teaspoonfuls onto cookie sheet. Bake for 8-10 minutes. Let cool. Combine frosting ingredients in small bowl. Dip cooled cookies into frosting and place on waxed paper until set.

Makes 4-5 dozen

Chinese Marble Cookies

1 cup shortening	½ teaspoon salt
1 cup sugar	½ teaspoon cream of tartar
1 egg	1 teaspoon vanilla extract
2 cups flour	1 ounce unsweetened chocolate, melted

Preheat oven to 400°. Beat shortening, sugar and egg until light and fluffy. Add flour, salt and cream of tartar, blending well. Stir in vanilla. Slowly add chocolate, but do not stir. Shape dough into walnut-sized balls and place on ungreased cookie sheet. Flatten dough with bottom of glass coated with sugar. Bake for 8-10 minutes.

Makes 2 dozen

Checkerboard Cookies

1 cup butter, room temperature
½ cup sugar
2½ cups flour

2 tablespoons baking cocoa
1½ teaspoons vanilla extract

Cream butter and sugar in large bowl. Add flour, stirring until smooth. Divide dough into two portions. Add cocoa to one of the portions, blending until cocoa is evenly mixed into dough. Add vanilla to the other portion and blend in well. Divide each portion of dough into two pieces. Roll each piece by hand into a long strand. Place one chocolate and one vanilla strand next to each other. Top with remaining two strands, alternating colors so that checkerboard pattern is formed. Press together tightly. Wrap dough in waxed paper and refrigerate. Preheat oven to 350°. Grease a cookie sheet. Cut dough with sharp knife into ¼-inch slices. Place on prepared cookie sheet and bake for 8-10 minutes. (Note: For larger cookies, put 4 cookie slices together before baking. To make spiral cookies, roll out each portion of dough, place one on top of the other, and roll up together before slicing. Another variation is to wrap the rolled-out chocolate dough around log of white dough before slicing.)

Makes 5-6 dozen

Glazed Coffee Squares

½ cup margarine
1 cup brown sugar, packed
1 egg
1½ cups flour
½ teaspoon baking powder
½ teaspoon baking soda

½ teaspoon salt
½ teaspoon cinnamon
½ cup raisins
½ cup nuts, chopped
½ cup strong hot coffee
Vanilla Glaze

Preheat oven to 350°. Grease and flour a 13x9-inch pan. Cream margarine and brown sugar. Mix in remaining ingredients, except Vanilla Glaze. Pour batter into prepared pan and bake for 15-20 minutes. Spread glaze over hot bars and cut into 2-inch squares.

Makes 2 dozen

Vanilla Glaze

½ cup powdered sugar

2 teaspoons margarine, melted

¼ teaspoon vanilla extract

Hot water, as needed

Mix together sugar, margarine and vanilla. Add water by drops to make a thin glaze. Spread over hot bars.

Buttercup Squares

Pastry

1 cup flour
3 tablespoons powdered sugar

½ cup margarine or butter, room
   temperature

Filling

1 cup sugar
¼ cup flour
½ teaspoon baking powder
¼ teaspoon salt
2 eggs, slightly beaten
1 teaspoon milk

½ teaspoon almond extract
½ cup coconut, flaked
¾ cup walnuts, finely chopped
½ cup maraschino cherries, cut into
   quarters

Preheat oven to 350°. Grease an 8-or 9-inch square pan. Combine pastry
ingredients and press into prepared pan. Bake for 15 minutes, or until edges are
light golden brown. Combine filling ingredients, mixing well, and pour over
baked pastry. Return pan to oven and bake 30-40 minutes longer, until a
toothpick inserted near center comes out clean. Cool pan on wire rack, then cut
into squares.

Makes 16-20

Biscotti

"Biscotti" is the
Italian word for rusk,
a plain or sweet
bread that is baked,
sliced and rebaked
until crisp and dry.

½ cup butter, room temperature
1 cup sugar
4 eggs
2 egg yolks
1½ cups flour

¾ cup filberts, chopped
½ cup candied cherries, chopped
2 cups flour
4 teaspoons baking powder
1 teaspoon salt

Preheat oven to 350°. Grease a cookie sheet. Cream butter and sugar in large
bowl. Add eggs, egg yolks and flour, mixing with electric mixer until blended.
Add remaining ingredients and mix by hand. Divide dough evenly into 6 parts
and, with moistened hands, shape each part into a log 2 inches wide x ½-inch
thick. Place on prepared cookie sheet and bake for 30 minutes, or until golden.
Let logs cool for 10 minutes, then remove from cookie sheet and cut into ½-inch
slices. Lay slices flat on cookie sheet and bake for an additional 10 minutes.

Makes 3 dozen

Pumpkin Face Cookies

Cookies

¾ cup shortening, room temperature
½ cup brown sugar, packed
1 egg
¼ cup molasses

1 cup quick rolled oats
2 cups flour
½ teaspoon baking soda
½ teaspoon salt

Pumpkin Filling

½ cup canned pumpkin, solid pack
½ cup sugar
½ teaspoon cinnamon

½ teaspoon ginger
¼ teaspoon nutmeg

In medium bowl, cream shortening and sugar. Beat in egg and molasses. Place oats in food processor and process until finely chopped. In large bowl, mix oats, flour, baking soda and salt. Stir in shortening mixture, cover and chill for 1 hour. Combine filling ingredients in saucepan. Cook over moderate heat, stirring frequently, until mixture bubbles. Remove from heat and let cool. Preheat oven to 375°. Turn dough onto floured surface and roll to ⅛-inch thickness. Cut into thirty-six 3-inch circles. Place half of the circles on ungreased cookie sheets. Place one teaspoon of filling on each circle. Cut pumpkin faces in remaining circles and place on top of filling. Seal edges. Cut out stems from dough scraps and press onto cookies. Bake for 12 minutes. (Note: May leave top cookie whole to make filled pumpkin cookies.)

Makes 18

Nature Cookies

½ cup margarine, room temperature
⅓ cup honey
½ cup brown sugar, packed
½ cup peanut butter
1 teaspoon vanilla extract
1 egg
1 banana, mashed
¾ cup whole wheat flour

¼ cup wheat germ
1 cup oatmeal
½ teaspoon baking soda
½ teaspoon baking powder
½ teaspoon salt
1 cup sunflower seeds
1 cup sesame seeds
1 cup golden raisins

Preheat oven to 375°. Grease a cookie sheet. Cream margarine, honey and brown sugar. Add peanut butter, vanilla, egg and banana, mixing well. Blend in dry ingredients, then stir in sunflower seeds, sesame seeds and raisins. Drop by rounded teaspoonfuls onto prepared cookie sheet, and bake for 15 minutes.

Makes 3 dozen

Old-Fashioned Farm Cookies

4 cups flour
1½ teaspoons salt
1 tablespoon baking soda
4 cups quick oats
1¼ cups sugar
1½ teaspoons ginger
1 cup vegetable oil

1 cup molasses
2 eggs, beaten
2 tablespoons hot water
1½ cups raisins
1 cup walnuts, ground
Water
Sugar

Preheat oven to 375°. Lightly grease cookie sheets. In large bowl, mix together flour, salt and baking soda. Add remaining ingredients, making sure that dough is well blended. (Note: If cookie dough is too soft, add an additional ¼ cup flour.) Place dough on floured surface and roll out to ¼-inch thickness. Cut out cookies with large biscuit cutter. Brush tops with water and sprinkle lightly with sugar. Place on prepared cookie sheets and bake for 8-10 minutes.

Makes 2-3 dozen

Raisin Sugar Cookies

3 cups raisins
1¼ cups water
1 cup butter, room temperature
1 cup margarine, room temperature
3 cups sugar
4 eggs

2 teaspoons vanilla extract
6 cups flour
2 teaspoons baking soda
½ teaspoon salt
Sugar, for topping

Place raisins and water in saucepan and simmer until water is almost evaporated. Drain and let cool. Cream butter, margarine and sugar in large bowl. Stir in eggs, mixing well. Add vanilla. In another bowl, combine flour, baking soda and salt. Add to butter mixture. Stir in raisins and refrigerate for 30 minutes. Preheat oven to 350°. Grease cookie sheets. Shape dough into walnut-sized balls. Roll in sugar and place on cookie sheets. Bake for 10-12 minutes. Remove cookies from cookie sheet and cool on wire rack.

Makes 5-6 dozen

In the late 1800s, Rochester was the center of the nation's evaporated and dried fruit industry. Over 15,000 evaporators were in operation, and companies like Michael Doyle & Company were suppliers to all major foreign markets.

Apricot Oatmeal Bars

3 cups dried apricots
3 cups water
½ cup sugar
2 cups flour
1¾ cups rolled oats

1 cup brown sugar, packed
¾ cup butter, melted
¼ cup wheat germ
1 teaspoon baking soda
1 teaspoon vanilla extract

Combine apricots, water and sugar in medium saucepan over medium-high heat. Stir until sugar dissolves, about 5 minutes. Reduce heat and simmer until most of the water is absorbed, about 15-20 minutes. Remove from heat and mash apricots. Preheat oven to 350°. Grease a 13x9-inch baking pan. Combine remaining ingredients in large bowl and mix well. Press half of crumb mixture into bottom of prepared pan, then spread with apricot mixture. Top with remaining crumb mixture, pressing down lightly to flatten. Bake until lightly browned, 30-35 minutes. Cool in pan and cut into bars.

Makes 2 dozen

Raspberry Almond Cookies

½ cup butter or margarine, room
   temperature
⅓ cup sugar
½ teaspoon vanilla extract
¼ teaspoon salt

1 egg, separated
1 cup flour
¾ cup blanched almonds, finely chopped
3 tablespoons raspberry jam

In medium bowl, cream butter and sugar. Add vanilla, salt and egg yolk, beating until light and fluffy. Stir in flour and blend well. Cover and chill for 30 minutes, or until firm enough to handle. Preheat oven to 300°. Divide dough into three pieces. On lightly floured surface, shape first piece of dough into a 1-inch thick log. Cut into ¾-inch thick slices, then roll each slice into a ball. Repeat entire process with remaining dough. In small bowl, slightly beat egg white. Dip each ball into egg white, roll in almonds, and place one inch apart on ungreased cookie sheet. With floured index finger, make deep indentation in center of each cookie and fill with ¼ teaspoon jam. Bake for 20 minutes or until golden. Let cool on wire rack.

Makes 3 dozen

Meringue Cookies

2 egg whites
⅔ cup sugar

6 ounces chocolate chips
Pinch of salt (optional)

Preheat oven to 350°. In medium bowl, beat egg whites with electric mixer until stiff peaks form. Gradually add sugar while continuing to beat. Stir in chocolate chips and salt (if using). Drop by rounded teaspoonfuls onto ungreased cookie sheet, making sure that batter forms a peak. Place in oven, then immediately turn oven off. Leave cookies in unopened oven for at least 2 hours.

Makes 2 dozen

Orange Cookies

2½ cups cake flour
½ teaspoon salt
½ teaspoon baking soda
½ cup shortening
1 cup sugar

2 eggs
1 tablespoon orange zest, grated
½ cup orange juice
½ cup filberts or walnuts, chopped

Preheat oven to 400°. Grease cookie sheets. In small bowl, combine flour, salt
and baking soda. In large bowl, mix together shortening, sugar, eggs and orange
zest until creamy. Stir in flour mixture, alternating with orange juice. Mix in
nuts. Drop by rounded teaspoonfuls approximately 2 inches apart on prepared
cookie sheets. Bake for 8-10 minutes. (Note: Flaked coconut may be substituted
for the nuts.)

Makes 4 dozen

Apple Cookies

1⅓ cups brown sugar, packed
½ cup shortening
⅓ cup milk
1 egg, beaten
2 cups flour
1 teaspoon baking soda

1 teaspoon cinnamon
½ teaspoon nutmeg
⅛ teaspoon ground cloves
1 cup apples, peeled and chopped
1 cup nuts, chopped
1 cup raisins

Preheat oven to 350°. Grease a cookie sheet. In large bowl, cream brown sugar
and shortening. Stir in milk and egg, and set aside. In another bowl, combine
flour, baking soda, cinnamon, nutmeg, and cloves. Add to creamed mixture, then
add apples, nuts and raisins. Drop by rounded teaspoonfuls onto cookie sheet and
bake for 8-10 minutes. Cool and frost with powdered sugar glaze, if desired.
(Note: 1 cup chopped candied fruit may be substituted for apples.)

Makes 3-4 dozen

NOT JUST FOR KIDS

baby needed a special soup. Clapp, experimenting in his Rochester kitchen, developed the first commercial line of baby food. Clapp's Baby Food was distributed through drug stores before being moved onto grocery shelves across the nation. When Gerber Products Company opened a plant in 1949, Rochester became one of the largest producers of baby foods.

Another food, loved "not just by kids", was started in LeRoy, New York. A concentrated gelatin substance was patented in 1845, but did not catch on until Orator Francis Woodward started to produce his product, named Jell-O. Woodward had little success initially and almost sold the rights to the product for $35, but at the turn of the century, Jell-O's sales started to increase, and by 1906 had reached $1 million. One reason for Jell-O's success was its ease of use. Previously, cooks needed to boil animal horns or hooves, seaweed or other products to obtain gelatin for making fancy molded dishes.

Gelatin is also used in the production of marshmallows, which were originally made using a root extract of marsh-growing mallow plants. They were formed by hand until William Demoreth, a candy worker in Rochester, invented a machine to form them.

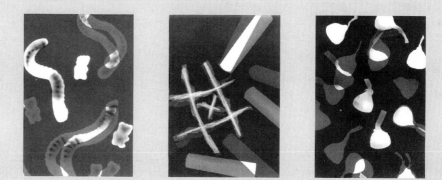

NOT JUST FOR KIDS

Island Gelatin Mold

6 ounces lime-flavored gelatin
2 tablespoons sugar
1¼ teaspoons salt
3 cups boiling water

2 cups evaporated milk
1 cup sour cream
1 teaspoon vanilla extract
8 ounces crushed pineapple, drained

In large bowl, dissolve gelatin, sugar and salt in boiling water. Stir in evaporated milk, sour cream and vanilla. Chill for 1½ hours. Beat gelatin mixture until smooth and stir in crushed pineapple. Pour mixture into 8-cup mold and chill until firm.

Serves 10-12

S'More Brownies

Crust
6 whole graham crackers, broken into small
    pieces
3 tablespoons sugar

3 tablespoons unsalted butter, room
    temperature, cut into pieces

Brownies
8 ounces milk chocolate, chopped
6 tablespoons unsalted butter, cut into
    pieces
¼ cup flour
⅛ teaspoon salt

2 eggs, room temperature
¼ cup + 1½ teaspoons sugar
4 ounces milk chocolate, chopped
25 large marshmallows, halved
1 ounce milk chocolate, grated

Preheat oven to 325°. Grease a 9-inch square pan. In food processor or blender, blend graham crackers, sugar and butter until moist crumbs form. Press crumbs evenly into bottom of prepared pan and bake for 7 minutes, or until golden. Remove from oven and let cool on rack. Melt milk chocolate and butter in saucepan over very low heat, stirring until smooth. Allow mixture to cool to room temperature. In small bowl, combine flour and salt, and set aside. In medium bowl, whisk eggs and sugar until well-blended. Stir in melted chocolate mixture, then gently fold in dry ingredients. Mix in chopped chocolate. Spread batter over crust and bake for 23 minutes, or until a toothpick inserted near center comes out clean. Place marshmallows on top of hot brownies, spacing them evenly. Cover tightly with foil and let stand for 15 minutes. Uncover pan. Using wet fingertips, press marshmallows together to fill any uncovered spaces. Sprinkle with grated chocolate and let cool completely on rack. Cut into squares.

Makes 2 dozen

Part of the success of Jell-O was due to advertising. L. Frank Baum, author of the *Wizard of Oz* series of books, wrote children's books sponsored by Jell-O. Also, prominent artists such as Maxfield Parrish, Rose O'Neil, and Norman Rockwell had their artwork featured in advertisements for Jell-O.

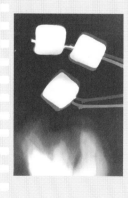

Dirt Pudding

1 package (24-ounce) chocolate sandwich
  cookies
8 ounces cream cheese, room temperature
1 cup powdered sugar
¼ cup margarine, room temperature
3½ cups milk

6 ounces vanilla instant pudding
12 ounces frozen whipped topping, thawed
Silk flowers
Gummie worms
Chocolate chips

Crush cookies and set aside. In large bowl, mix together cream cheese, powdered
sugar and margarine. Set aside. In another bowl, combine milk, pudding and
whipped topping. Add to cream cheese mixture and blend well. Pour into clean
8-inch plant pot (without holes). Cover with crushed cookies. "Plant" silk
flowers, gummie worms and chocolate chips (as stones) in pot, and refrigerate until
cool. Use clean trowel to serve.

Serves 10-12

Wrestling Treats

Bars
1 cup water
4 tablespoons baking cocoa
1 cup butter
2 eggs, beaten

2 cups sugar
2 cups flour
½ teaspoon baking soda
½ cup sour cream

Frosting
½ cup butter
4 tablespoons baking cocoa
6-7 tablespoons milk
1 pound powdered sugar

1 teaspoon vanilla extract
6 ounces miniature chocolate chips
  (optional)

Preheat oven to 400°. Combine water, cocoa and butter in saucepan and cook
over medium heat until cocoa and butter have melted. Let cool. Stir in eggs,
sugar and flour. In small bowl, blend baking soda into sour cream, then add to
chocolate mixture. Pour into 13x9-inch pan and bake for 20 minutes, or until a
toothpick inserted near center comes out clean. While batter is baking, combine
butter, cocoa and milk in saucepan and heat to boiling. Let boil for one minute.
Reduce heat and add powdered sugar and vanilla, stirring mixture until smooth.
Remove bars from oven, frost immediately, and sprinkle with chocolate chips, if
desired.

Makes 3-4 dozen

Chocolate No-Bake Cookies

¼ cup baking cocoa
½ cup butter
½ cup milk
2 cups sugar

½ cup peanut butter
1 teaspoon vanilla extract
3 cups quick oats

Cover two cookie sheets with waxed paper and set aside. In saucepan, combine cocoa, butter, milk and sugar and bring to a boil. Let boil for 1-2 minutes, then remove from burner and add peanut butter and vanilla. Put oats into large bowl, then pour chocolate mixture over them and mix quickly. Drop by rounded teaspoonfuls onto prepared cookie sheets. Let cool before serving. (Note: For variation, increase cocoa to ½ cup, eliminate peanut butter, and add ½ cup chopped nuts.)

Makes 3-4 dozen

Peanut Butter & Jelly Pie

1 pie crust (9-inch), chocolate or graham cracker
¼ cup raspberry jam
8 ounces cream cheese, room temperature
1 cup chunky peanut butter
1 cup powdered sugar

1 teaspoon vanilla extract
12 ounces frozen whipped topping, thawed or 2 cups heavy cream, whipped
½ cup chocolate chips
1 tablespoon peanut butter

Spread pie crust with jam, set aside. In large bowl, beat cream cheese and peanut butter until smooth, then add powdered sugar and vanilla, beating after each addition. Fold whipped topping or cream into mixture and place in crust. Melt chocolate chips, add peanut butter, and stir until smooth. Drizzle sparingly over pie and refrigerate. (Note: This pie is very rich, so small pieces should be served.)

Serves 8-10

Peanut Butter Apple Crisp

4 large apples, cored, peeled and sliced
½ cup white sugar
⅔ cup brown sugar, packed
½ cup flour
1 cup quick rolled oats

⅔ teaspoon cinnamon
½ teaspoon salt
6 tablespoons butter or margarine, chilled
6 tablespoons peanut butter, smooth or
  chunky

Preheat oven to 350°. Grease a 13x9-inch baking dish. Mix together apples and
white sugar in large bowl. Spread mixture evenly in bottom of prepared baking
dish. In another bowl, combine brown sugar, flour, oats, cinnamon and salt. Cut
in butter and peanut butter until crumbly mixture forms. Sprinkle over apples and
bake for 40-50 minutes, until apples are tender. Serve warm or cold. (Note:
McIntosh, Granny Smith, Yellow Delicious or Empire apples are great to use in
this recipe.)

Serves 10

Peanut Chow Mein Noodle Cookies

12 ounces butterscotch chips
12 ounces chocolate chips

14 ounces cocktail peanuts, salted or
  unsalted
9-11 ounces chow mein noodles

In large saucepan, melt butterscotch and chocolate chips over low heat, stirring
occasionally. Add peanuts and noodles, stirring to coat. Drop by rounded
teaspoonfuls onto waxed paper. Let set until cool, then refrigerate.

Makes 4 dozen

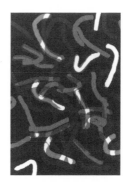

Peanut Butter Sticks

1 loaf sandwich bread, crusts removed
1⅓ cups creamy peanut butter

½ cup honey
4-5 cups corn flake cereal, crushed

Preheat oven to 200°. Cut each slice of bread lengthwise into 4-5 pieces. Place on baking sheet and dry in oven for approximately 1-1½ hours. Mix together peanut butter and honey. Heat on stove in double boiler over low heat until blended. (This can also be heated in a microwave oven, on low, for 1-2 minutes.) Place sticks of dried bread into mixture and stir carefully until covered. Remove from mixture with slotted spoon, drain and toss in corn flake cereal. Place on waxed paper-covered cookie sheet until cool.

Makes 60-75 sticks

Peanut Butter Sundae Sauce

1 cup brown sugar, packed
⅓ cup milk
¼ cup light corn syrup

1 tablespoon butter
¼ cup creamy peanut butter (not natural)

Combine all ingredients, except peanut butter, in saucepan. Cook over low heat until sugar dissolves. Remove from heat and add peanut butter. Return pan to low heat and cook until sauce becomes smooth.

Makes approximately 1¾ cups

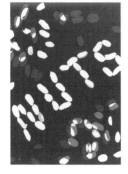

Dutch Diamonds

1 cup unsalted butter, room temperature
1 cup sugar
2 cups flour
1 egg, separated

1 teaspoon vanilla extract
½-¾ cup walnuts, finely chopped or
    almonds, slivered

Preheat oven to 275°. Grease a cookie sheet with sides. Cream butter and sugar.
Lightly beat in flour, egg yolk and vanilla. Using your hands, spread dough over
cookie sheet to thickness of ¼-inch. Set aside. In small bowl, slightly beat egg
white. Again using your hands, spread egg white over cookie dough. Sprinkle
nuts over dough and bake for 60-75 minutes, or until golden. Remove from oven
and immediately cut into 1½x2-inch diamond-shaped bars. Remove from cookie
sheet and allow to cool on rack. (Note: These cookies improve with age when
stored in airtight container.)

Makes 50 cookies

Fig Bar Fool-'Ems

2 packages (12-ounce) fig bar cookies
24 ounces chocolate chips

1 cup walnuts, chopped

Cut fig bars lengthwise into thirds. Melt chocolate chips on stove in double boiler
over hot (not boiling) water. Using toothpick, dip fig bar pieces into melted
chocolate, then into nuts. Place on tray covered with waxed paper and refrigerate.

Makes 90 pieces

In the later part of
the 19th century,
"-ine" was a popular
ending for new
medical products
(Vaseline), and
"-o" was used for
new food products
(Jell-O).

Sweet & Chewy Squares

1 pound oat square cereal
2 cups dried apricots, chopped
2 cups almonds, slivered

2 teaspoons cinnamon
¼ cup margarine or butter
¾ cup maple syrup

Grease a 17x12-inch or larger pan. In large bowl, combine cereal, apricots, almonds and cinnamon. Melt margarine in small saucepan. Add syrup and bring to a boil. Cook for 3-4 minutes over medium-high heat, stirring constantly. Immediately pour syrup mixture over cereal mixture, stirring until well-coated. Spread mixture evenly on prepared pan. Bake at 350° for 15 minutes. When mixture has cooled, break apart into smaller pieces. (Note: Chopped pecans or walnuts may be substituted for almonds.)

Serves 15-20

Rolled Cream Cheese Logs

8 ounces cream cheese, room temperature
1 egg
½ cup sugar
15 slices white bread, crusts removed

½ cup butter, melted
½ cup powdered sugar
1 tablespoon cinnamon

Preheat oven to 350°. Lightly grease a cookie sheet. Blend cream cheese, egg and sugar. Set aside. Roll each slice of bread flat, then cut each slice in half lengthwise. Spread cream cheese mixture onto each half-slice. Roll into log, making sure that seam is sealed. Dip each log into melted butter, then into a mixture of powdered sugar and cinnamon. Place logs, seam side down, onto prepared cookie sheet and bake for 12 minutes.

Makes 30 logs

Razzleberry Punch

12 ounces frozen cranberry juice
  concentrate, thawed
12 ounces frozen raspberry-cranberry juice
  concentrate, thawed

48 ounces lemon-lime soda
24 ounces club soda
10 ounces frozen raspberries

Combine all ingredients in large punch bowl, mixing well.

Makes 3 quarts

Non-Edible Cinnamon Ornaments

1 cup cinnamon
1 cup applesauce

5 tablespoons white glue

Combine all ingredients and stir until mixture forms a dough. Knead dough
slightly and turn onto a cinnamon-dusted cutting board. Roll out to ¼ - ⅜-inch
thickness and cut with your favorite cookie cutters. Poke holes for hanging, using
a toothpick or straw. Place on waxed paper to air dry for a day. When top of
ornament is dry, turn over and place on wire rack. Allow to dry for 1-2 days
longer. When completely dry, decorate with acrylic paints, if desired.

Makes 2-3 dozen 2-inch ornaments

Sidewalk Chalk

1 cup plaster of Paris
½ cup less 1 tablespoon cool water
3 tablespoons liquid tempera paint

2 tablespoons white glue
8-10 paper cups (3-ounce)

In 2-cup measuring cup, mix first four ingredients until well blended. Pour into
paper cups and let set and dry overnight. Peel off cups before using.

Makes 8-10 pieces

ABOUT THE ARTISTS

Friends of Strong Memorial Hospital wishes to thank the following individuals for their generous donations of time and talent.

Robert P. Barker *(Poultry)*

In 1985, Robert Barker founded Robert Barker Photography in Rochester, where he specializes in location photography. Mr. Barker studied photo illustration at Brooks Institute.

Wayne Calabrese *(Eggs & Brunch)*

Wayne Calabrese opened CR2 Studios Inc. in 1986, and specializes in concept, people and location photography. He takes great pride in working with his clients to determine the best possible visual solution for their projects. Mr. Calabrese has served many Fortune 500 clients.

Walter Colley *(Soups & Stews)*

Walter Colley specializes in studio still-life and product photography. He joined Kamper Sprouse Colley as senior photographer in 1992, and is active in the local chapter of the American Society of Media Photographers. Mr. Colley earned his bachelor's degree in commercial photography from Rochester Institute of Technology's School of Photographic Arts and Sciences.

Kathy D'Amanda *(Cookbook Designer)*

Kathy D'Amanda received her bachelor's degree from Boston University's School for the Arts and has owned her own business, D'A Design, since 1985. She specializes in corporate communication and has developed a special interest in not-for-profit organizations. Ms. D'Amanda's fondness for cooking was a real "plus" in working on *Delicious Developments*.

John Griebsch *(Pasta & Grains)*

John Griebsch, a commercial photographer in Rochester, has spent years developing and refining his love of food and his tastes. He enjoys the challenges of illustrating ideas photographically. He has been involved in numerous advertising and public information endeavors for major companies in both the United States and Europe. Mr. Griebsch also does aerial photography in what he calls "an on-going quest for truth and beauty".

Mary Hazelwood *(Seafood, artist)*

Mary Hazelwood is a fourth-year student at Rochester Institute of Technology, working toward her Bachelor of Fine Arts degree. Because of her interest in motion and perception, she is considering continuing her education toward a master's degree in computer animation.

George Kamper *(Appetizers)*

George Kamper, of Kamper Sprouse Colley, is a commercial photographic illustrator. More than a still-life photographer, he uses his creativity to be a problem-solver for his clients, which include all of the major advertising firms in Rochester. Mr. Kamper is a graduate of Rochester Institute of Technology.

Roxanne Malone *(Salads)*

According to Roxanne Malone, "Food and art can be complementary to each other, resonating a song of love between eye and mouth. Cooking is a creative act of love and enjoyment...it is both aesthetically and practically pleasing." Ms. Malone received her Master of Fine Arts degree from the University of Arizona, and has studied abroad in France and England. She has taught at Rochester Institute of Technology, and at near-by Cornell University. Her work is in major international collections, both public and private.

Andy Olenick *(Cookies & Bars)*

Andy Olenick received his degree in fine arts from Rochester Institute of Technology, and started Fotowerks Limited after several years as a freelance corporate/industrial photographer. He is active in the local chapter of the American Society of Media Photographers. Mr. Olenick is also a corporate sponsor with the Rochester Landmark Society, and is the photographer of the new book, *200 Years of Rochester's Architecture & Gardens*.

Woody Packard *(Meats)*

Woody Packard has made his living doing product and still life photography since starting his Rochester studio in 1981. He enjoys the challenge of making complicated things look simple and common objects look special. Of his work he says, "I'm good at pushing little things around until they look right. I'm patient, and I love the details."

Judy Sánchez *(Cakes)*

Judy Sánchez is involved in various aspects of commercial photography, ranging from large-format portraiture and architecture to small and medium-format editorial assignments. Her award-winning work has been exhibited in Europe, Japan, Iran, and the United States. Ms. Sánchez received her Bachelor of Fine Arts degree in photographic illustration from Rochester Institute of Technology's School of Photographic Arts and Sciences. She currently teaches advertising photography there.

James M. Via *(Seafood, photographer)*

James Via's studio, JMV Photographic Services, specializes in photographing works of art for museums and artists. The heart of Via's personal work has been large-format studies of architectural ruins in Europe and America. Mr. Via has a master's degree in photography and painting from Illinois State University. He has done post-graduate work at Visual Studies Workshop in Rochester, where he now teaches.

Leslie Wilson Wu *(Cover, illustrator)*

Leslie Wu is a painter and illustrator, whose illustrations can be seen on book jackets and in publications for large corporate clients. Her work appears in corporate and private collections in both the United States and Japan. Ms. Wu received her Bachelor of Fine Arts degree from Rochester Institute of Technology.

Ron Wu *(Cover, photographer)*

Ron Wu is a commercial assignment photographer based in Rochester. His photography is used primarily in advertising, corporate reports and catalogs. Mr. Wu's work is included in the permanent collection of the George Eastman House International Museum of Photography and Film, Rochester, New York.

Friends of Strong Memorial Hospital gratefully acknowledges the staff of the George Eastman House International Museum of Photography and Film for their assistance with the research for historical photographs. The following photographers are represented in the book:

John G. Capstaff (1879-1959) *(Vegetables)*

Born in England, John Capstaff came to Rochester in 1913. Working in the Research Laboratories at Eastman Kodak Company, he accepted the challenge of developing a commercially acceptable color process.

Victor Keppler (1904-1987) *(Breads & Muffins ; Pies & Pastries)*

Victor Keppler was a master of the eloquent, attention-grabbing advertising image. His work was especially notable for its use of vibrant color, which he was among the first to use commercially. Mr. Keppler also founded the Famous Photographers' School in Westport, Connecticut.

Arthur Rothstein (1915-1985) *(Not Just For Kids)*

Arthur Rothstein was employed as a photographer for the Farm Security Administration from 1935 to 1940, and later worked for *Look* magazine. His photographs are poignant documents of rural and small-town America emerging from the Depression.

The photograms appearing throughout the book were created by Kathy D'Amanda and Ron Wu.

RECIPE CONTRIBUTORS

Deborah Rubin Ades
Karen Ager
Freyda E. Albin
Janet M. Albright
Violet C. Allen
Mona Alongi
Janet M. Altimonda
Adela Amador
Diane Amann
Patricia Ames
Rose Amico
Bonnie E. Anderson
Elizabeth H. Anderson
Rose Mary Anderson
Linda Andrews
Karen Marie Bader
Judith Gedney Baggs
Andrea Bailey
Roberta F. Baker
Sugi Balconi
Lynn Baldwin
Patricia Balena
Nancy Bales
Katy Barber
Roberta K. Barber
Sandra Barden
Robert P. Barker
Christine Anne Bastian
Joanne Bates
Cindy J. Baxter
Elizabeth Baxter
Marge Bayer
Carolyn Bayne
Kim M. Bednarcyk
Carole A. Bell
C. Allyn Bender
Deanne Bender
Susan Kim Bennett
Gretchen K. Berger
Fran Brach Bergstrom
Edith Hecht Bernstein
Sherry Best
Heather S. Bickel
Susan B. Bickel
Christopher J. Bigelow, M.D.
Angela Binotto
Michelle Binotto
Elaine Birnbaum
Pearl Gabriel Bloom
Sue Boerschlein
Mary Rice Bonfiglio
Janet F. Bopp
Jean Austin Boyce
Mary Jo Brach
Nancy L. Brandston

Cheryl Breitenbuecher
Kathleen Quinlan Brideau
Leo P. Brideau
Ann Marie T. Brooks
Barbara Lorraine Brown
Sue Witken Brown
Mary Lou Bryant
Jessie Amidon Bucchin
Timothy William Buck
Jan L. Bullington
Joyce Bulsiewicz
Sally A. Burtis
Robert Bush
Vinnie Bush
Laura L. Butler
Wayne Calabrese
Mel Callan
Jamie Calway
Frances Cammarata
Rose H. Cammarata
Ann Cammerata
Adeline B. Campanaro
Sarah S. Campbell
Joan Case
Ann E. Casey
Aida Esther Casiano-Colon
Debbie Kay Caskey
Cara M. Cassata
Cathy Chapman, M.D.
Rosanne Chauncey
Eleanor Cherin
Janet W. Chisholm
Sharon Fralonardo Chiumento
Joan K. Chodosh
Lenora A. Ciccone
Cheryl I. Cicero
Tony J. Cicero
Flora R. Cilento
Erma Clark
Dorothy King Cleary
Janet Cleary
George H. Clement
Mary R. Clement
Lawrence Cohen
Walter Colley
Mary Frances D. Collins
Louise Coluccelli
Marie Inez Coluccelli
Janice M. Comstra
Joanne N. Conlon
Riki Connaughton
Nancy M. Connolly
Mary K. Cooper
Elizabeth A. Corrigan
Dawn Costello

Elaine K. Costello
Linda Costich
Mary S. Cott
Nicki Cottle
Minata 'Mimi' Coulibaly
Mary Anne Courtney
Jo Craytor
Louise S. Criticos
Ellen H. Croog
Karen Ann Crotinger
A. Elizabeth Crozier
Elizabeth Anne Culhane
Matilda R. Cuomo
Sarah K. Curtis
Judith Marie Cushman
Katherine M. D'Agostino
Kathryn L. D'Amanda
Elizabeth Ann D'Angelo
Linda Wells Davey
Norma A. Davidson
Linda Marie Davies
Richard Joseph DeFranco
Susan M. Degler
Nancy L. Dehmler
Cindy Demitry
Figgy Demorest
Judith Anne Dennis
Phyllis E. Dennis
Thomas H. Dennison
Jeanne N. Dent
Marcia DeWandler
Scema Dhaliwahl
Gloria S. DiAngelo
Doramae C. Dickson
Pamela Cronin DiMuzio
Lorrie D. Divers
Michelle Donovan
Martha R. Dorn
Christine M. Downs
Jacquelyn G. Doyle
Karen Driscoll
Mary Parsons DuBois
Mae C. Dummer
Josi A. Eckert
Sandra Jean Eich
Abby Emanuele
Laurie Walsh Ernest
Marjorie Ewell
Martha E. Fabian
Kelly Fallon
Cynthia Anne Falkoff
Victor Favasuli
Nancy Feehan
Debbie Beck Feinberg
Lynne Feldman

John J. Felzer
Anita Ferguson
Mary Jo Ferr
Priscilla M. Field
Mark Alan Finke
Peter Albert Finke
Richard Finkelstein
John I. Fish III
Betty Fleischacker
Lynda Lee Fleming
Barbara Lyons Florack
Carol J. Flynn
Katherine McMahon Flynn
Dan Foley
Patricia Foley
Tracy Ann Fontaine-Matteson
Denise B. Forster
Sylvia Forster
Pamela Fose
William Y. Fowlkes
Fran Nadine Fox
Jan Frankel
Marilyn S. Frappolli
James Frederiksen
Kathy M. Frost
Laurel K. Gabel
Billie Gaenzle
Dobby Gallagher
Marikaye Gargione
The Gateway
Carol Gayeski
Charles Joseph Geilfuss, M.D.
Joseph G. Gentile
Nancy George
Mary Louise Gerek
Nancy Germond
Dawn M. Gerstner
Sally W. Gillan
Dorothy C. Gleason
Joyce Ann Gollel
Nancy Gong
Ruth B. Goodell
Deborah J. Gorochow
Douglas W. Gorsline
Patricia W. Gorsline
Mary Graham
Howard C. Green
Frances N. Greene
John Griebsch
Sue Grinnell
Elizabeth H. Grip
Joan Gruendike
Paula Halewski
Kay Hallagan
Marlene A. Hamilton

G. Hanfling
Kathleen Louise Hanson
Dottie S. Hargrove
Bob Harr
Mary Willson Harrigan
Judy B. Harrington
Jackie K. Harris
Nettie Hartigan
Louise B. Haskins
Allyson Ann Haymes
Mary Hazelwood
Diane E. Healy
Lianne K. Heath
Erna L. Hennick
Sonia M. Herz
Bettie A. Hinkley
Joan Hoeffel
Suzanne Illene Hoffman
Helen Hogan
Mark Hopkins
Tala Hopkins
Debbie Howe
Joy Howe
Carole Huber
Amy R. Hughes
Ann Hughes
Charles V. Husted
Angela Iacchetta
Rene M. Iacona
Gail Laura Ingersoll
Sharon Insero
Carol Irwin
Sharri K. Jackson
Walter Jahnke
Joanne W. Jay
Carol J. Johnson
Ionie A. Johnson
Jean Johnson
JoAnn M. Johnson
Diane S. Jones
Mary A. Jones
Patricia K. Judd
Dorothy Kaiser
George Kamper
Deb Karlin
Melanie Mary Kates
Brenda G. Kavanaugh
Patricia E. Kavanaugh
Wendy Keck
Sharon L. Kendall
Pamela B. Kimmet
Jeanne Kirby
Jane Kitchen
Betty Kittrell
Heidi Melinda Knickerbocker

Karen Rose Knickerbocker
Gloria K. Korth
Jean W. Kraley
Judi Krause
Beth A. Krueger
Debbie J. Kruse
Rose Kull
Mary Ellen Kunz
Wilma Kuzmuk
Tricia Labuzetta
Ardis L. Langenhan
Barbara P. LaRue
Beth Whitley LaVigne
Yvette Foon-Yee Law
Grace Lee
Pat Lehman
Ann Lenane
Pierrette M. Lepel
Mary LeRoy
Sonia K. Liberatore
Lois Vollmer Likly
Patricia Hryzak Lind
Arne Lindquist
Peggy E. Linton
Linda E. Lipani
Ronald S. Litman
Karen B. Livent
Deborah Ann Locke
Linda M. Logan
Susan Lubin
Sandrea Louise Lukasiak
Cheryl Michele MacCracken
Steven Mackey
Suzy Magill
Roxanne Malone
Maria A. Marconi
Addie Massau
Margaret Mathes
Regina Maxwell
Charlotte A. McCabe
Karen McCready
Priscilla F. McDaniel
Leslie McDaniel, M.D.
Sandra McDonald, M.D.
Diana McGonegal
Irma Meier
Shirley Mendola
Carolyn Merriam
Myrtle A. Merritt
Theresa M. Messenger
Donna Lynn Metelsky
Jane I. Metras
Beverly A. Miceli
Francisco E. Mijares
Jody Leigh Mikasen

Ellen F. Miles
Ann P. Miller
Judy Mincher
Shama Mohammed
Kathleen Montesano
Sally S. Moore
Shirley Mitchell Moore
Kathleen E. Morris
Luba K. Morsch
Gail Mowrer
Ann G. Muhs
Marty Mullane
Donna Lynn Murano
Rita J. Murphy
Pat Nadel
Michael Nenno
James R. Newell
Lucille S. Newell
Beulah Newton
Lisa Norsen
Catherine C. Norton
Michael B. Norton
Anne L. Nowack
Dennis O'Brien
Mary Ann O'Brien
Christina Oddleifson
William Rajendra Ogle, M.D.
Andy Olenick
John L. Olivier
Claire Olson
Jeanette S. Olson
Nancy W. Olson
Ellen Osadciw
Woody Packard
Stephanie Liniger Page
Eileen T. Palmer
Alison Palphreyman
Pamela's Pastry Kitchen
Renè Denise Panosian
Tina Paris
Park Ave. Pub
Ruth Elizabeth Parratt
Diane Davies Parrinello
Ann B. Partridge
Vicki Pasternak
Cheryl Peacock-Clarke
Nancy Pedersen
Lori Jeanne Peloquin, Ph.D.
Marge Peterson
Hilda Petralia
Joan Pettis
Lynne M. Phelps
Maime T. Piazza
Marigrace Piazza
JoAnn E. Pierson

Robert Q. Pollard, Jr.
Susan J. Powell
Penny Powers
Michele A. Prame
Karen C. Pryor
Suzanne E. Puleo
Donna R. Quinzi
Susan Radke
Barbara Rapin
Cheryl A. Reagan
Janet S. Reed
Mary Remenicky
Susan H. Richane
Nancy Ricotta
Penny Riedel
Sue Riolo
Susan J. Roberts-Davis
Sally W. Rogers
Clare Rotenberg
Alice K. Rubenstein
Midge Ruffner
Ann Rugelis
Dolores Rupert
Ruth B. Sachs
Judy Sánchez
Leslie Miller Sax
Kathleen A. Saxby
Gene Scherline, M.D.
Marcia Schirazi
Lynn Schran
Dianne Schubert
Sylvia Theresa Schwartzman
Harriet Seigel
Catharine Serr
Christine Diane Sevilla
Kathryn A. Shacur
Kathleen Coluccelli Sheets
Mary E. Sheldon
Nancy Shepard
Nancy Shields
Sharon Marie Sibble
Jack L. Simmonds
Patricia Louise Simmons
Christina Skeels
Carol Zink Skotnicki
Jane M. Smith
Karen Ann Smith
M. Eileen Smith
Therese Smudzin
Society of Rochester Landmark
  Restaurants:
    The Clark House
    The Crystal Barn
    The Daisy Flour Mill
    Edwards

    Richardson's Canal House
    The Rio
    The Spring House
Trude K. Sparks
Elizabeth Kearney Spreng
Meredith L. Spuck
Carol Ann Stafford
Jean N. Stanley
Julie Starowicz
Judy A. Sterry
Jay Stetzer
Chris Stevens
Mary L. Stiker
Sylvia Stiller
Kathryn Stimson
Barbara Ann Stirrat
Joanne Niles Stoller
Michele Stratton
Strong Cardiac Care Staff
Marcianne Suda
Sheryl M. Sugrue
Julie A. Sullivan
Jane T. Summers
Robin Summers
Joan Swanson
Patricia R. Sweeney
Kimberly S. Talbert
Esther Tanzman
Atilla Terzioglu
Margaret L. Thirtle
Mona Thomas
Peggy Holden Thompson
Helene M. Thompson-Scott
Jean Tieppo
David Tinnes
Mary Ann Toler
Susan Trenkner
Phyllis Trickey
Corky Tryon
Susan R. Turiano
Loel C. Turpin
Deborah Tuttle
Pamela A. Urban
Kelly Valerio
Marion Valerio
Kathryn Valerioti
Jan Van Ess
Paula VanRyne
Lynne Ville
Eileen R. Volk
Wanda R. Voorheis
William A. Voter
Barbara Wager
Rebecca Lynn Wagner
Sharon S. Wallach

Mary Ellen Webb
Janie H. Webster
Betsy Webster
Carol B. Weed
Amy Weisbach
Elise Weisbach
Kathy Doane Weiss
Jane Ann Welch
Karen Ann Weldon
Ann Weller
Lucy S. Welsh
Dianne F. Westbrook
Betsey Wheeler
Estelle S. White
Jean G. Whitney
Margery Wilkie
Candace Williams
Marion G. Wilmot
Rosemary Gottry Wilson
Jill A. Winchester
Jennifer Winfield
Lil Winfield
MaryAnne Winfield
Megan Winfield
Marion Irene Winkler
Joan F. Witiak
Clare T. Wolcott
Heidi M. Wollschleger
Joy A. Woodley
Gretchen Wright
June T. Wright
Leslie Wilson Wu
Ron Wu
Nancy S. Wurtz
Susan Davis Yanchisin
Tina York
Lynn A. Zampano
Stacy Zamudio
Rosemary Ziemba
Suzanne T. Zigrossi
Margaret Zimmerman
Mae R. Zink

We wish to thank the many contributors, testers, and tasters, as well as those who assisted us in our historical research. Without them, Delicious Developments would not have become a reality.

INDEX

Recipes in italics appear in sidebars.

Recipes in italics appear in sidebars.

Recipes in italics appear in sidebars.

Recipes in italics appear in sidebars.

Recipes in italics appear in sidebars.

Recipes in italics appear in sidebars.

Recipes in italics appear in sidebars.